D0609607

Controversial Issues
in Policing

Controversial Issues in Policing

Edited by

James D. Sewell

Series Editor

Steven A. Egger

University of Illinois at Springfield

ALLYN AND BACON

Boston • London • Toronto • Sydney • Tokyo • Singapore

Editor-in-Chief, Social Sciences: Karen Hanson
Series Editorial Assistant: Heather Ahlstrom
Marketing Manager: Brooke Stoner
Sr. Editorial Production Administrator: Susan McIntyre
Editorial Production Service: Ruttle, Shaw & Wetherill, Inc.
Manufacturing Buyer: Dave Repetto
Cover Administrator: Jenny Hart
Electronic Composition: Omegatype Typography, Inc.

Copyright © 1999 by Allyn and Bacon
A Viacom Company
160 Gould Street
Needham Heights, MA 02494
Internet: www.abacon.com

All rights reserved. No part of the material protected by this copyright notice may be reproduced or utilized in any form or by any means, electronic or mechanical, including photocopying, recording, or by any information storage and retrieval system, without written permission from the copyright owner.

Library of Congress Cataloging-in-Publication Data
Controversial issues in policing / edited by James D. Sewell.
    p. cm.
   Includes bibliographical references (p.).
   ISBN 0-205-27209-6
   1. Police–United States.   2. Police administration–United
States.   3. Law enforcement–United States.   I. Sewell, James D.
(James Daniel).
   HV8141.C625 1999
   363.2'0973–dc21   98-39662
                                      CIP

Printed in the United States of America
10 9 8 7 6 5 4 3 2 1   04 03 02 01 00 99 98

Credits
Pages 106–107: Excerpts from *On the dotted line: Police executive contracts* by S. F. Greenberg. Washington, DC: Police Executive Research Forum. Reprinted with permission. Police Executive Research Forum copyright © 1992.

Page 109: Excerpt from "Chief's policy thrust into debate" by T. Roche in the *St. Petersburg Times,* October 31, 1996. Copyright © St. Petersburg Times 1996. Reprinted with permission.

Page 109: Excerpt from "Help Stephens succeed," an editorial in the *St. Petersburg Times,* October 31, 1996. Copyright © St. Petersburg Times 1996. Reprinted with permission.

Page 110: Excerpt from "Boulder leadership missing in action" by Chuck Green in the *Denver Post,* May 30, 1997. Reprinted with permission of The Denver Post.

Dedicated to:
A. J. and T. J.
Ally, Kate, Vincent, Maggie, and Leah
Della, Dave, Ken, and Will
Brian and Austin
The Future Generation is not a controversial issue.
JDS

Dedicated to:
A. J. and T. J.
Ally, Kate, Vincent, Maggie, and Leah
Della, Dave, Ken, and Will
Brian and Austin
The Future Generation is not a controversial issue.
JDS

Contents

I. Controversial Issues: The Police and Our Legal Framework

II. Controversial Issues: Police Personnel Practices

III. Controversial Issues: The Police Organization

IV. Controversial Issues: Policing Our Communities

Preface

Never when controversy avoided the subjects which are large and important enough to kindle enthusiasm, was the mind of a people stirred up from its foundations, and the impulse given which raised even persons of the most ordinary intellect to something of the dignity of thinking beings.

John Stuart Mill
On Liberty

Few areas in a free society are as subject to controversy and debate as those relating to criminal justice. In few areas are the "battle lines," especially those between liberal and conservative thought, so clearly drawn and *not* subject to civil dialogue between opposing points of view. Yet critical discourse is the best method we as a democracy have found to assure the safety of our citizens collectively while protecting our rights individually.

Consequently, *Controversial Issues in Policing* is part of the Allyn and Bacon series examining some of the most important issues faced by our society and the components of our criminal justice system. In each, we have used a similar format: a question that will generate debate is posed, and separate authors explore the "yes" or "no" sides of that issue. As part of this exchange, each author also directly responds to the specifics of his or her colleague's position. We believe that such an approach allows a comprehensive discussion and fosters a more complete understanding of some of the most contentious topics in criminal justice.

Controversial Issues in Policing submits fifteen topics to this debate process. These particular subjects are the product of the "brainpower" of a number of individuals occupying both academic and professional positions in policing.

Members of the Police Executive Research Forum, especially Darrel Stephens, Dr. Gerald Williams, and Eduardo Gonzales, played a key role in identifying the most controversial and critical issues facing contemporary policing.

And our authors? They are a wide variety of individuals with differing backgrounds, experiences and perspectives on policing and its role in our society. They represent the legal and academic communities, the law enforcement profession, and yes, one is even a Pulitzer Prize–winning reporter! Yet they share a common denominator: an enlightened, comprehensive understanding of the criminal justice system combined with the ability to clearly articulate their point of view.

At the outset we gave the authors a pithy challenge: enthusiastically argue your position in a manner that captures the readers' interest and forces them to critically examine their beliefs about contemporary policing. Do the authors all agree with the position they took on any debate? No, but they recognize the need to be able to analyze and objectively debate both sides of any controversial issue. Intellectual growth and, in our democracy, good law enforcement policy demand a complete, objective, and extensive discourse about the issues we hold most dear and which challenge most the balance of individual rights and collective well-being. The authors' efforts in this work are crafted to push the boundaries of our own thoughts, theories, and philosophies to ensure the most effective, most innovative, and best use of our policing resources.

Have the authors succeeded? I think so, and I believe the reader will agree. For this I owe the authors a debt of gratitude. I am proud of their contributions and their willingness to labor so hard to meet the intellectual requirements of our profession. I appreciate their friendship and admire the leadership role they play in their communities and in our criminal justice profession.

Introduction

The history of policing is one of controversy. From its rocky and oftentimes unpopular formal beginnings in nineteenth-century England to its use as an arm of political machines and government control in twentieth-century America, law enforcement organizations, policies, and practices have often been the subject of debate and dispute. As America faces the twenty-first century, policing as a series of controversial issues has not changed.

Yet American policing and the society it protects *have* changed, and it is the breadth and depth of change that fosters the most significant discussion and dialogue. On the positive side, American law enforcement, as the most visible symbol of our democracy, is generally held in high regard by the American public. Police agencies are, by their very nature, far more involved in the daily lives of citizens and their communities. Consequently, they are not as tainted by the stigma of an uncaring, distant, uninvolved bureaucracy as other units of government frequently are.

On the negative side, American policing has had more than its share of egregious practices that have harmed specific individuals or disenfranchised large groups of citizens. One has only to examine local police activities during the Civil Rights movement or Vietnam War era; federal investigative activities targeting dissidents or antigovernment activities; illegal searches of homes and seizures of vehicles; or highly publicized incidents such as Rodney King to recognize the depth of our problems.

All of this is occurring within a context of tremendous change within American society. The civil rights movement of the 1960s and the subsequent women's movement, along with significant demographic changes, have dramatically affected the workforce from which policing draws its membership and the society it protects. American political institutions are in the midst of upheaval, in terms of their roles, their demographic and political composition, and their very political dynamics. Public expectations about the involvement of government in an individual's life and the American sense and definition of community have undergone major change. Within the workforce, both police and civilian, the job and life expectations of workers and their relationship with their employers are dramatically different from a generation ago.

At the same time, fear of crime permeates American communities. Citizens publicly decry "crime in the streets" and, especially in urban areas, isolate themselves in home fortresses. They demand that the police "do something" and express the need for a strong police presence and aggressive police practices.

Is it any wonder that American policing is at the forefront of both change and controversy?

A number of areas are at the forefront of both controversy and change, the focus of this book. From a legal perspective, statutory and case law applied by and to American law enforcement continues to undergo significant ebb and flow. The United States Supreme Court and lesser appellate bodies continue to fine tune Constitutional protections afforded American citizens, particularly through the use of the Exclusionary Rule. Legislative bodies—at all levels—seek new and better ways of controlling criminal behavior and the potential for misconduct.

Concurrently, the police organization is undergoing major transition. Agencies are closely examining the ways they are structured, seeking to assure efficient response to community needs, effective management of often scarce resources, and thorough communication of an agency's values to all of its employees. Academicians in particular are looking at the traditionally accepted police subculture and questioning its very existence; their results will have dramatic impact on training, on organizational structure, and on the very self-concept of police officers.

As part of this self-analysis, the American police organization is critically examining its own personnel practices in light of a changing society and dramatically different and differing social expectations of law enforcement. Diversity of the police workforce, the educational level of police officers, minimum physical requirements, the structure of the police job itself, and job protection of employees are all under intense review. Today, even law enforcement officers are attempting to ensure that their jobs are adequately protected from unwarranted governmental intrusion . . . by their own agency administrators.

American law enforcement also is examining how it relates to the community. Incidents such as Rodney King have forced us to reevaluate the cold professional officer removed from his community in light of the need for an officer who can more clearly understand issues and independently solve problems. Concurrently, community policing as a concept has forced policing and its community to assess their relationship, to assure active participation of citizens in the policing process, and to provide for law enforcement practices "in the sunshine," subject to media and public scrutiny.

Futurists tell us that change is not without its cost. Yet, ensuring timely and appropriate change of social institutions, such as policing, or society itself requires fervent discourse on and enlightened debate of those issues about which there is controversy.

So . . . let the debates begin.

The Changing Fourth Amendment: An Inevitable Evolution or an Unfortunate Devolution?

EDITOR'S NOTE: The United States Constitution was developed as a blueprint for government action and balance, and the Bill of Rights as a document ensuring the protection of citizens. Over the last 200 years, additional amendments and court decisions have served to refine both documents and ensure that they met the changing needs of society and its citizenry. In no area of criminal law has the change been as pronounced as the Fourth Amendment, protecting citizens against unreasonable searches and seizure. Amplified by the Exclusionary Rule as it became applied to first federal, then state and local, law enforcement, the Fourth Amendment is a critical component of our criminal justice system. Yet, a real dilemma exists: Have these changes through the years been a natural evolution or have our individual rights and protections, in fact, been eroded?

Professor Mark R. Brown is Professor of Law at the Stetson University College of Law. He holds a B.S. from the University of Dayton; a J.D. from the University of Louisville; and an LL.M. from the University of Illinois. Professor Brown's teaching interests include Constitutional Law, Administrative Law, Criminal Law and Procedure, and Critical Legal Studies. Before coming to Stetson, Professor Brown clerked for the Honorable Harry W. Wellford of the United States Court of Appeals for the Sixth Circuit. Professor Brown has also taught at the University of Illinois College of Law (1991–92) and served as Judicial Fellow in the Supreme Court of the United States (1993–94). He graduated valedictorian from the University of Louisville School of Law, where he served on the Law Review's editorial board.

Paula C. Coffman received a B.A. in Sociology from the University of Florida in 1980 and a J.D. from the University of Florida College of Law in 1983. Ms. Coffman served as Assistant Attorney General with the Florida Department of Legal Affairs, Criminal Appeals Division, from 1985 to 1989. She has been Assistant State Attorney with the Ninth Judicial Circuit of Florida, specializing in criminal appeals and postconviction remedies since 1989. She and her husband and their two sons reside in Orlando, Florida.

AN INEVITABLE EVOLUTION

PAULA C. COFFMAN

Practically everyone has heard of the Exclusionary Rule. Regarded by many of the participants in the American criminal justice system as an offensive "legal technicality," the Exclusionary Rule bars the admission of evidence at trial if that evidence is deemed to have been obtained in violation of a defendant's constitutional rights.

Its critics contend that the Exclusionary Rule impedes law enforcement and permits criminals to escape punishment by operation of the law. They also argue that it does not accomplish its primary objective, the deterrence of misconduct by law enforcement. This view is shared by a growing number of scholars, legislators, prosecutors, and judges who support its restriction or total elimination. To no one's surprise, criminal defendants and their legal representatives are conspicuously absent from this consensus.

Regardless of one's view of the Exclusionary Rule, one might reasonably wonder how it came to be in the first place. Just whose idea was it, anyway, to punish perceived wrongdoing by law enforcement by bestowing a windfall on the criminals they are trying to catch? As Justice (then Judge) Benjamin Cardozo once put it, "There has been no blinking the consequences. The criminal is to go free because the constable has blundered."

An examination of the historical development of the Exclusionary Rule is helpful in understanding our current predicament. Realizing how we wound up where we are also may provide clues to where we are headed in the current debate over the future of the Exclusionary Rule.

Origin of the Right

Our United States Constitution is "the Supreme Law of the Land." The authority for its supremacy above all other laws is the Constitution itself, as expressly provided in Article VI, section 2, of that document. The origin of our protection against unreasonable searches and seizures is found in the Fourth Amendment to the United States Constitution. Grounded in English and colonial history and ratified on December 15, 1791, the Fourth Amendment holds that

> The right of the people to be secure in their persons, houses, papers, and effects, against unreasonable searches and seizures, shall not be violated, and no Warrants shall issue, but upon probable cause, supported by Oath or affirmation, and particularly describing the place to be searched, and the persons or things to be seized.

The impetus for the inclusion of the Fourth Amendment in our Bill of Rights was the virtually unlimited authority of British soldiers to search American colonists, as well as their homes and offices, before the Revolution. At that time, "general warrants" that did not specify the persons to be searched were issued by the British Crown without probable cause. These documents were valid for the life of the monarch. Another version of the general warrant, the "writ of assistance," was used by customs inspectors to search for contraband among political dissidents.

The concepts embodied in the Fourth Amendment emerged from the colonial experience with general warrants and writs of assistance as tools of censorship and tyranny. The recognition of a presumptive right of privacy against government intrusion represented a complete repudiation of traditional English law. Thus, the Fourth Amendment fairly revolutionized the law of search and seizure.

Interpretation of the Right

The framers of the Bill of Rights intended reasonable searches and seizures to be permissible. This is undoubtedly the case, because only those searches and seizures deemed to be "unreasonable" are prohibited under the Constitution. However, what is "unreasonable" is left undefined. Even more significantly, the Constitution provides no specific remedy for a perceived violation of the prohibition against "unreasonable" searches and seizures.

So, what does the Fourth Amendment mean? The simplest answer, but one that is nevertheless always correct, is that the Fourth Amendment means whatever judges say it means. Under the Tenth Amendment to the United States Constitution

> The powers not delegated to the United States by the Constitution, nor prohibited by it to the States, are reserved to the States respectively, or to the people.

Clearly, the judiciary is one of the three branches of government established by the Constitution against which the constraints of the Bill of Rights operate. However, amidst this separation of powers, the courts have a distinct advantage.

In 1803, while our new nation was still in its infancy, the United States Supreme Court seized the opportunity in *Marbury v. Madison* (1803) to establish itself as the final arbiter in matters of constitutional interpretation. It is the function of the judiciary, and most particularly the United States Supreme Court, to interpret what the Constitution means.

A more specific answer to our question is possible, but the details depend on when the question is asked, for the Court's interpretation of the Fourth Amendment has changed significantly over time. In this regard, it has been observed that

> in no other western society has the regulation of police and prosecutorial officials, as well as the functioning of the courts, been understood in comparable degree to be a function of judges. In no other nation has so large and intricate a corpus of constitutional doctrine emerged relating to the functioning of criminal justice as that created or influenced by the Supreme Court of the United States. (Francis A. Allen—*The Judicial Quest for Penal Justice: The Warren Court and the Criminal Cases,* 1975 U.Ill.L.F. 518, 525–42).

After more than two hundred years and countless decisions, the meaning of that single fifty-four-word sentence is still in flux.

Expansion of the Right

For nearly a century after its ratification, the Fourth Amendment had almost no impact on the development of American criminal jurisprudence. However, in 1886, the United States Supreme Court first justified the exclusion of evidence from a judicial proceeding on constitutional grounds. In *Boyd v. United States* (1886) the unsuccessful defendant in a forfeiture proceeding claimed that company invoices used to establish his violation of the federal import and revenue laws had been seized in violation of his constitutional rights under the Fourth (search and seizure) and Fifth (self-incrimination) Amendments.

Finding no substantial difference between compelling an individual to become a witness against himself and the unlawful seizure of private papers to be used as incriminating evidence against their owner at trial, the Court determined that both constitutional rights had been violated and ordered a new trial without the damaging evidence, thus foreshadowing the jurisprudential upheaval that was to come. However, the analysis used to bar the compelled production of Boyd's private papers was not developed by the Court in subsequent search and seizure cases.

Instead, nearly thirty years passed before the Court issued its watershed decision in *Weeks v. United States* (1914). Personal papers seized during two warrantless searches of the defendant's home had been used against Weeks in a successful federal criminal prosecution for conducting an illegal lottery through the U.S. mails. On review of the case, the Court determined that the admission of the illegal evidence was prejudicial error and reversed the conviction. This judge-made law came to be known as the Exclusionary Rule, because it *excludes* evidence deemed to have been acquired in violation of the Fourth Amendment. The rationale used to bar the admission of personal papers against the defendant in *Weeks* was gradually expanded by the Court to include contraband. However, the *Weeks* decision had no effect on criminal prosecutions in state courts for violations of state and local law.

Then the Court decided *Wolf v. Colorado* (1949), and, for the first time, the Fourth Amendment was held to apply to judicial proceedings in state courts as well as federal courts under the Due Process Clause of the Fourteenth Amendment. Still, *Wolf* appeared to exempt state courts from the constitutional obligation to bar the admission of illegally seized evidence in criminal trials, because a majority of the Court refused to require states to implement the Exclusionary Rule. Under *Wolf,* alternatives to the rule of exclusion, such as a civil suit against the offending law enforcement officer or a prosecution for criminal trespass, were still acceptable remedies under the Constitution for an illegal search and seizure.

Just six years later, in *Irvine v. California* (1954), the Court reconsidered the exemption of the state courts from the Exclusionary Rule announced in *Wolf.* However, the Court rejected the opportunity, advanced in a dissenting opinion, to authorize under a "totality of the circumstances" analysis the reversal of state court criminal convictions in particularly shocking cases. Significantly, the rationale for implementing the Exclusionary Rule, that of deterrence of police misconduct, which had first been introduced in *Wolf,* was also rejected in Justice Jackson's observation that the "disciplinary or educational effect of the court's releasing the defendant for police misbehavior is so indirect as to be no more than a mild deterrent at best."

Although some states voluntarily adopted the Exclusionary Rule, Ohio was one of the many states that did not. Then, in 1961, in the landmark decision of *Mapp v. Ohio,* the Court was presented with another opportunity to reconsider its holding in *Wolf.* Once again, the Court stared squarely into the face of the Fourth Amendment, and this time a 5-to-4 majority saw the Exclusionary Rule embedded firmly within it. For the first time, the Court viewed the Exclusionary Rule as being inextricably bound to the Fourth Amendment as a constitutionally required deterrent against police misconduct. The Court had decided to overrule its own legal precedent in *Wolf.*

Mapp imposed the Exclusionary Rule on all of the states. For the first time, the Court held that "all evidence obtained by searches and seizures in violation of the Constitution is, by that same authority, inadmissible in a state court." However, in keeping with this "prime purpose" of deterrence, the Court declined in *Linkletter v. Walker* (1965) to apply *Mapp* retroactively to state court convictions that had already become final through direct appeal.

What's Wrong with "the Right"?

American democracy is not strictly democratic. That is to say, our Constitution recognizes that there are some areas of life that should not be regulated by the majority, no matter how closely it approximates unanimity. In such areas, the public interest must give way to the personal freedom of the individual. Constitutional interpretation compels a balancing of these competing interests. In the case of the Fourth Amendment, the identifiable interests are the privacy rights of the individual (or deterrent effect on the conduct of law enforcement) versus the societal goals of preserving public safety, seeking the truth, and convicting the guilty.

Supporters of the Exclusionary Rule argue that its primary justification is the protection of the privacy rights of the individual, accomplished through the deterrence of police misconduct. However, the deterrence rationale has rendered the Exclusionary Rule vulnerable to persistent, heated attack from within and without because of the deep chasm that separates theory from practice.

Although it has never been demonstrated that the Exclusionary Rule has exercised its intended effect on law enforcement, it has certainly gotten the attention of criminal defendants. Every day, in courtrooms in state and federal courts throughout the country, the prophylactic effects of the Exclusionary Rule are routinely invoked. The sheer frequency with which the suppression of evidence is sought should call into question by its supporters the purported deterrent efficacy of the rule. Furthermore, the fact that most such motions may ultimately be determined to be meritless raises additional concerns over the waste of finite resources in an already overburdened criminal justice system.

A major defect in the deterrence rationale is the assumption that the Exclusionary Rule provides incentive for law enforcement to "follow the law" in the execution of searches and seizures. There are two fatal flaws in this assumption.

Supporters of the Exclusionary Rule continue to oppose its relaxation with "good faith" exceptions that, in their view, reward ignorance of the Constitution. However, there can be no incentive to "follow the law" unless law enforcement has a clear understanding of "what the law is" at the time a particular search or seizure is effectuated.

As we have already seen, the courts are constantly announcing evolutionary refinements in the decisional law. Furthermore, the law in effect at the time an appeal is decided controls the outcome of the appeal. In contrast to the law itself, this fundamental principle of appellate practice is unlikely to change significantly over time. Consequently, law enforcement and trial judges alike find themselves in the untenable position of being judged "guilty" of violating a defendant's constitutional rights under interpretations of the law pronounced many months or even years after the conduct under scrutiny occurred. Thus, deterrence under the Exclusionary Rule is dependent on the clairvoyance of those whose conduct the rule was intended to influence.

Even those supporters of the Exclusionary Rule who now question its deterrent effect continue to object to doing away with it all together in the absence of an adequate alternative. Civil lawsuits for money damages, they argue, are seldom brought and only rarely successful. Such reasoning highlights a second defect in the deterrence rationale, the assumption that the Exclusionary Rule provides some incentive, however tenuous, for law enforcement to consistently "follow the law."

Although proponents of the Exclusionary Rule laud its protection of the innocent against illegal activity by the authorities, the remedy of exclusion is only activated by the existence of inculpatory evidence. If a search or seizure uncovers no illegal activity on the part of its subject, there is nothing to be suppressed. Therefore, by its very definition, the Exclusionary Rule only benefits the guilty.

Supporters of the Exclusionary Rule also argue that its most compelling justification is the preservation of judicial integrity. According to this theory, the courts must not sanction unconstitutional conduct because the ends of justice cannot be separated from their means. By interpreting the Constitution to require the exclusion of highly probative, reliable evidence from a criminal defendant's trial, it has seemingly been determined that two wrongs can somehow be juxtaposed to make a right.

Supporters of this theory frequently argue that, just as there is no proof that the Exclusionary Rule benefits the system through deterrence of police misconduct, there is likewise no proof that it does any harm. Unfortunately, although the damage is undoubtedly subject to quantification, few meaningful statistics that would support or refute the claims of either side are available.

In reality, the Exclusionary Rule exacts a profound toll on our criminal justice system. The prospect of problems with evidentiary proof in the event that evidence is later suppressed plays a significant role in the charging decisions of prosecutors. Although a violation of the Fourth Amendment may ultimately be found in only a minority of charged cases, in each of those instances the prosecution's case against the defendant has either been weakened or completely destroyed by the suppression of highly probative, reliable evidence. Staleness may further jeopardize those cases while available appellate remedies that could take months or years are pursued.

Significantly, the Exclusionary Rule has been employed as a sanction for other types of constitutional violations such as the Fifth Amendment protection against compelled self-incrimination. Still, its most frequent application has been in the area of search and seizure. But, unlike a coerced confession, evidence obtained in violation of the Fourth Amendment is no less reliable than evidence obtained through legal means.

In every instance, the windfall goes to the criminal. But even if the common perception that criminals escape punishment under the Exclusionary Rule is an exaggerated one, such public opinion only serves to encourage criminal activity and undermine public confidence in the integrity of the judicial system rather than preserve it.

Evolutionary Refinements of the Right

Mapp v. Ohio was decided during a period of judicial activism by the United States Supreme Court. Under the leadership of Chief Justice Earl Warren, the Warren Court altered the nature of American criminal justice, substantially enlarging the rights of those suspected and convicted of crime and expanding the authority of the Court to enforce those judge-made changes in constitutional law.

Almost immediately, *Mapp* provoked a storm of public controversy. Critics of the decision decried its destructive effect on the truth-finding function, pointing out that, as a practical matter, only the guilty would enjoy its benefits. *Bivens v. Six Unknown Named Agents,* (1971), which recognized a federal cause of action for money damages for the violation of the Fourth Amendment by a federal agent, was decided just ten years after *Mapp.* In a dissenting opinion to that decision, Chief Justice Burger expressed skepticism over the judicial wisdom behind the Rule, arguing that its history

> demonstrates that it is both conceptually sterile and practically ineffective in accomplishing its stated objective. [Some] clear demonstration of the benefits and effectiveness of [the Rule] is required to justify it in view of the high price it extracts from society—the release of countless guilty criminals. But there is no empirical evidence to support the claim that the Rule actually deters illegal conduct of law enforcement officials....

Still, the Chief Justice did not propose abandoning the Rule without first replacing it with a "meaningful alternative."

However, five years later, in his concurring opinion in *Stone v. Powell* (1976) Chief Justice Burger voiced the concern that "the continued existence of the rule, as presently implemented, inhibits the development of rational alternatives." He argued that it was unlikely that other branches of government would act so long as judges continued to cling to their "Draconian, discredited device in its present form..., so long as persons who commit serious crimes continue to reap the enormous and undeserved benefits of the exclusionary rule."

Mapp v. Ohio is still the judge-made law of the land, but the political climate has changed significantly since the Warren era. Although the same forces that elevated the Exclusionary Rule to a principle of constitutional proportion are still active today, a proverbial shift in the wind is apparent. This subtle but significant change is perhaps best illustrated by the decisions made by the United States Supreme Court in the search and seizure area during the 1996–97 term. To law enforcement and prosecutors alike, they represent a welcome, refreshing breeze.

Maryland v. Wilson, decided in 1996, involved the issue of whether a passenger can be ordered from a vehicle by law enforcement once a lawful traffic stop is made. During a valid automobile stop for speeding (64 miles per hour in a posted 55 miles per hour zone), a Maryland state trooper ordered Wilson, one of two passengers, out of the car after noticing his apparent nervousness. As Wilson exited, cocaine fell to the ground in plain view. Wilson was arrested and charged with possession of cocaine with intent to distribute.

Wilson filed a motion to suppress, which was granted by the trial judge on the theory that the trooper's command that Wilson exit the vehicle constituted an unreasonable seizure under the Fourth Amendment. On appeal, the Maryland Court of Special Appeals affirmed on the authority of *Pennsylvania v. Mimms,* decided by the United States Supreme Court in 1977. *Mimms* held that an officer may, as a matter of course, order the driver of a lawfully stopped car to exit his vehicle. But *Mimms* did not apply to Wilson because *Mimms,* it was decided, did not apply to passengers.

After the Court of Appeals of Maryland declined to review the case further, the State of Maryland sought discretionary review before the United States Supreme Court. After accepting jurisdiction, the Court held that an officer making a lawful traffic stop may order passengers out of the vehicle pending completion of the stop. In a 7–2 decision delivered by Chief Justice Rehnquist, the Court concluded that the rule announced in *Mimms* should be applied to passengers as well as to drivers.

The *Wilson* decision first reiterates that the "touchstone" of Fourth Amendment analysis under *Mimms* is the "reasonableness in all the circumstances of the particular governmental invasion of a citizen's personal security." Such analysis requires striking "a balance between the public interest and the individual's right to personal security free from arbitrary interference by law officers."

The Court then concludes that, from the public interest perspective, the same legitimate and weighty interest in officer safety is present whether the occupant of the stopped vehicle is a driver, as in *Mimms,* or a passenger, as was Wilson. Indeed, an officer's exposure to danger in a traffic stop setting is likely to be greater when others in addition to the driver are present.

From the personal liberty perspective, the Court acknowledged that passengers are entitled to greater protection than are drivers because the stop itself is justified by the officer's belief that the driver, as opposed to the passenger, has committed a traffic offense. However, the decision recognizes that vehicle passengers in a valid traffic stop are already detained, so the additional intrusion is negligible.

In its decision to extend the rule of *Mimms* to automobile passengers, the *Wilson* Court felt compelled to address two of its recent prior decisions. In *Rakas v. Illinois,* decided in 1978, just a year after *Mimms,* the Court characterized its holding in that case as one that provided to passengers "no Fourth Amendment right **not** to be ordered from their vehicle, once a proper stop is made." In *Michigan v. Long,* decided in 1983, six years after *Mimms,* the Court characterized the holding in *Mimms* to apply to the more general category of "persons." The *Wilson* Court concluded that, because the statement in *Rakas* was made in a concurring opinion and because the language in *Long* was dictum, neither of these intervening decisions constituted binding precedent on the issue. Thus, after nineteen years, the rule of *Mimms* clearly applies to automobile passengers as well as drivers.

A second case, *Ohio v. Robinette,* also decided in 1996, involved the issue of whether a lawfully seized defendant must be advised that he is "free to go" before his consent to search will be recognized as voluntary. Robinette was stopped by a deputy sheriff on an Ohio interstate after being clocked at sixty-nine miles per hour in a posted zone where the speed limit was forty-five miles per hour because of construction. The deputy requested Robinette's driver license and ran a computer check, which indicated that Robinette had no previous violations. He then asked Robinette to step out of the vehicle, turned on his mounted video camera, issued a verbal warning to Robinette for speeding, and returned the license. At that point, the officer asked Robinette whether he was carrying any illegal contraband. When Robinette answered, "no," the officer requested consent to search the car, and Robinette consented. A small amount of marijuana and a film canister containing a pill determined to be a controlled substance were recovered.

Before trial, Robinette sought to suppress this evidence on the theory that his consent was not voluntary because he did not believe that he was free to refuse the deputy's request. After his motion to suppress was denied, he entered a "no contest" plea, was found guilty, and appealed.

On appeal, the Ohio Court of Appeals reversed Robinette's conviction, ruling that the search resulted from an unlawful detention. The Supreme Court of Ohio accepted discretionary review and affirmed, finding the search and seizure illegal under the Fourth Amendment as well as the Ohio Constitution.

The State of Ohio then sought discretionary review before the United States Supreme Court. After accepting jurisdiction, the Court rejected the notion of a per se rule or bright line test for determining whether a detention is appropriate, reiterating that voluntariness of a consent to search is a question of fact to be determined from all of the circumstances.

The *Robinette* Court first noted its recent holding in *Whren v. United States* (decided in 1996 after the Supreme Court of Ohio decided the present case) that the subjective intentions of law enforcement do not operate to invalidate their otherwise objectively reasonable actions. The Court then cited a number of cases in which it had rejected the application of bright line rules in Fourth Amendment analysis. One such case cited in the opinion is *Florida v. Bostick*. In that case, the United States Supreme Court disapproved a per se rule established by the Supreme Court of Florida that questioning bus passengers (for consent to search) always constitutes an illegal seizure.

Finally, the Court noted its rejection, in *Schneckloth v. Bustamonte,* of a per se rule for determining the validity of a consent to search. In that case, it was argued that a consent to search could not be valid unless the defendant knew he had a right to refuse the request. But the Court held that knowledge of the right to refuse consent is only one factor among all of the circumstances to be taken into account in determining voluntariness. Similarly, the Constitution did not, in the Court's view, require the authorities to warn Robinette that he was free to leave to render his consent to search voluntary.

The Future of the Right

Whether the judiciary is viewed as a proactive institution that foreshadows changing societal attitudes or as a reactive one whose decisions merely reflect those changes, the apparent shift in jurisprudential thinking on the issue of the wisdom of the Exclusionary Rule is clearly warranted. The Exclusionary Rule was a noble judicial experiment in constitutional interpretation that has failed with the passage of time to find any persuasive justification for its continued existence. Not only has it failed to fulfill its naive promise of deterrence; it also threatens to undermine confidence in the judicial system that it purports to preserve.

Whether the Exclusionary Rule will suddenly be completely overruled or only slowly modified over time remains to be seen. Furthermore, only time will tell whether a judicially created alternative to the Exclusionary Rule will accompany this inevitable evolution.

REFERENCES

Allen, F. A. (1975). The judicial quest for penal justice: The Warren Court and the criminal cases. Champaign: University of Illinois.
Bivens v. Six Unknown Named Agents, 403 U.S. 388 (1971).
Boyd v. United States, 116 U.S. 616 (1886).
Florida v. Bostick, 501 U.S. 429 (1991).
Irvine v. California, 347 U.S. 128 (1954).
Linkletter v. Walker, 381 U.S. 618 (1965).
Mapp v. Ohio, 367 U.S. 643 (1961).
Maryland v. Wilson, 117 S. Ct. 882, 137 L.Ed. 2d. 41 (1997).
Michigan v. Long, 463 U.S. 1032 (1983).
Marbury v. Madison, 1 Cranch 137, 2 L.Ed. 60 (1803).
Ohio v. Robinette, 117 S. Ct. 417, 136 L.Ed. 2d. 347 (1996).
Pennsylvania v. Mimms, 434 U.S. 106 (1977).
Rakas v. Illinois, 439 U.S. 128 (1978).
Schneckloth v. Bustamonte, 412 U.S. 218 (1973).
Stone v. Powell, 428 U.S. 465 (1976).
Weeks v. United States, 232 U.S. 383 (1914).
Whren v. United States, 116 S. Ct. 1769, 135 L.Ed. 2d 89 (1996).
Wolf v. Colorado, 338 U.S. 25 (1949).

Rejoinder to Ms. Coffman

MARK R. BROWN

As a prosecutor, Paula Coffman obviously knows a great deal about the costs of the Exclusionary Rule. Her firsthand experience in the trenches of the criminal justice system has undoubtedly placed her in a unique setting to judge the Exclusionary Rule's merits. One does not question the fact that many a shady criminal figure has benefited from the Exclusionary Rule since the time of *Mapp v. Ohio* (1961), and I do not purport to question Ms. Coffman's many experiences. Indeed, one need look no further than the local newspaper to stumble on Exclusionary injustices. Oliver North, for instance, escaped convictions for lying to Congress because of the legal technicalities of the Exclusionary Rule (See *United States v. North* [D.C. Cir. 1990]). Robert Williams, a lunatic who murdered a young girl in Iowa in 1968, had his conviction reversed because of the Exclusionary Rule (*Brewer v. Williams* [1977]). More examples certainly exist.

The trenches, however, do not necessarily offer the only (nor even the best) vantage point for judging the propriety and usefulness of legal rules and duties. Trees can get in the way of a bigger historical forest. History teaches that the rule of law is necessary to an ordered society. Any argument that excepts only a privileged few from the law's application ought to be carefully scrutinized.

Today's debate often focuses on the "profound costs" of the Exclusionary Rule and its marginal benefit. The problem with this argument is that it lacks empirical and logical support. Every study to date concludes that the Exclusionary Rule causes dismissals and acquittals in only a small fraction of criminal cases. Granted, there is a "cost" associated with any acquittal, at least if one assumes the defendant is guilty. But the aggregate cost, when compared with the number of successful prosecutions, is minute.

Proving that the Fourth Amendment Exclusionary Rule offers a true benefit to society is a more difficult and, perhaps, impossible chore. Suffice it to say that I, for one, believe it does. Police, I think, are honestly, professionally, and morally interested in fighting crime. The realization that evidence might be excluded at trial very likely causes police officers to adjust their behavior. This adjustment can be positive, conforming to Fourth Amendment norms, or negative, circumventing Constitutional rules. But nonetheless, I suspect that deterrence works, and I optimistically hope that it is more positive than negative.

My assumption that police turn to alternative crime control methods when confronted with enforced rules is buttressed by experience. Confessions, for instance, have long been a staple for proving guilt. In *Brown v. Mississippi* (1936), the Supreme Court told the states that no longer would brutally coerced confessions be admitted into evidence at criminal trials. This holding caused police around the country to modify their interrogation techniques. Rubber hoses, hot lights, and beatings were forced to the wayside, and less overt forms of coercion, such as "Mutt and Jeff" (good cop/bad cop) questioning and trickery, came into vogue (See *Escobedo v. Illinois* [1964]). When these approaches were questioned by the courts, police were again forced to adapt their behavior (See *Miranda v. Arizona* [1966]). The result is that police today rely more on physical evidence, such as DNA analysis, than they did sixty years ago. This evidentiary evolution has largely obviated the need for confessions in many types of cases, the OJ Simpson trial notwithstanding.

Of course, one can only hope that deterrence causes police to turn to lawful crime control methods as opposed to unlawful techniques. Perjury by police officers is not unknown, and police have been caught manufacturing confessions and evidence. Incidents such as these, however, are likely rare occurrences in the vast scheme of things. My studies lead me to believe that police are more likely to conform their conduct to announced rules than to risk sneaking around them. The reason for this, I believe, is their honest effort to enforce the law and punish wrongdoers. Successfully punishing criminals is partly a function of the Exclusionary Rule. Take away the disincentives of the Exclusionary Rule and this picture could very well change. Predicting what it might look like is impossible. But because I, like the Framers of the Constitution, continue to believe that discretion breeds abuse, I cannot help but believe that it would not be a pretty picture.

There is no moral to the Exclusionary Rule story. Reality is that bad things happen to good people. Innocents are victimized by criminals who are often not apprehended. Police are frustrated by budget cuts, politicians, and silly legal rules. But legal rules are what separate a civilized society from anarchy.

CASES CITED

Brewer v. Williams, 430 U.S. 387 (1977).
Brown v. Mississippi, 297 U.S. 278 (1936).
Escobedo v. Illinois, 378, U.S. 478 (1964).
Mapp v. Ohio, U.S. 643 (1961).
Miranda v. Arizona, 384 U.S. 436 (1966).
United States v. North (D.C. Cir. 1990).

AN UNFORTUNATE DEVOLUTION

MARK R. BROWN

A socially influential (and financially successful) movie of my youth was *Dirty Harry,* a Clint Eastwood thriller pitting Harry Callahan (Eastwood) against a deranged sociopathic killer, Scorpio, played by Andy Robinson. Against all odds, the police department, and several spineless municipal politicians, Dirty Harry brings Scorpio to justice the old-fashioned way, by blowing his brains through the back of his skull. Along with most of the hippy-hating, Nixon-loving "silent majority" in America at the time, I cheered Harry throughout the movie. I reeled in indignation when, after kidnapping and murdering a young girl, the killer had the audacity to whine to Harry, "I have my rights!" I applauded in moral satisfaction while Harry tortured Scorpio into disclosing the whereabouts of his victim. And I, along with the rest of America's cinematic public, gazed in astonishment as the chief of police informed Harry that Scorpio was to be released (sure to kill again) because of Harry's "technical" violations of the Fourth Amendment.

Dirty Harry was a product of its time. The year was 1971; Vietnam protestors were in full swing; the civil rights movement pressed its campaign for social equality; "black panthers" called for resistance to authoritarian oppression; and the economy spiraled into shambles. For many middle-class, white Americans, the country too was spinning toward anarchy. "Enough is enough," cried the silent majority, and President Nixon responded with "tough on crime" legislation and three "law-and-order" appointments to the Supreme Court: Chief Justice Warren Burger (1969), Associate Justice Harry Blackmun (1970), and Associate Justice William Rehnquist (1971). The "reformist," "judicially active," "liberal" Warren Court, which formally ended with Earl Warren's retirement in 1969, truly died.

Dirty Harry was fiction. Its rhetoric, however, accurately portrayed the arguments and views of millions of Americans. The literary license it took with the Exclusionary Rule—a real killer would not have been released under those circumstances—paralleled the imagination of Nixon's silent majority. Tough cops such as Harry were lionized at the expense of bleeding heart liberals. The Warren Court, that arrogant champion of rapists, murderers, and pushers, was mocked because of its detachment from the real world.

A quarter of a century later, the Fourth Amendment and its Exclusionary Rule are still under siege as antitheses to "law and order." And with this siege have come changes to the Fourth Amendment landscape. Today, police may stop motorists for pretextual traffic violations with the purpose of searching for illicit drugs (*Whren v. United States* [1996]). Police may legally force an unsuspected passenger out of an automobile and detain him or her pending the outcome of the officer's field investigation (*Maryland v. Wilson* [1997]). They may legally detain and question a tourist in an airport for no reason other than that he deplaned first, last, or somewhere in between (*United States v. Sokolow* [1989]). Unidentified and unknown tipsters may justify police detention and search with or without a warrant (*Alabama v. White* [1990]). Drug agents in helicopters legally hover over one's home and snap pictures of one's yard with constitutional impunity (*Florida v. Riley* [1989]). These photos can be enhanced with telephoto lenses (*Dow Chemical v. United States* [1986]) or infrared thermal imaging (*United States v. Cusumano* [10th Cir. 1995]) so that intimate details of one's home and life are put on open display. Video surveillance cameras can be legally placed on street corners. Parabolic microphones can be used to listen to ostensibly private conversations. A person's curbside garbage is readily accessible to search and seizure by police (*California v. Greenwood* [1988]).

Notwithstanding the wide constitutional latitude currently afforded police, the argument still is made that the Exclusionary Rule ought to be abolished. And the argument has not fallen on deaf ears. The Supreme Court has responded by carving out a significant exception to the Exclusionary Rule that allows even illegally seized evidence to be admitted into evidence at a criminal trial. Deemed the "good-faith exception" to the Exclusionary Rule, evidence that is obtained pursuant to an invalid and illegal warrant may still be used at trial (*United States v. Leon* [1984]). Most recently, the Supreme Court held that this exception also applies to evidence unlawfully obtained without a warrant (*Arizona v. Evans* [1995]). So long as the police reasonably rely on defective warrants or erroneous computers, the fruits of their reliance need not be suppressed.

What has often been lost in the debates over the Exclusionary Rule is that today evidentiary suppression provides the only remedy for unconstitutional police conduct. The Exclusionary Rule, like it or not, draws the sole line between proper crime control techniques and unbridled police license. Although civil suits and criminal charges against offending police officers are possibilities, they are much more theoretical than real. For reasons too numerous to quantify in this short discussion, juries, prosecutors and internal affairs departments are simply unwilling to discipline errant police officers. Better yet, just as the good-faith exception to the Exclusionary Rule has been enlarged over the last twelve years, so has police immunity to civil litigation (*Harlow v. Fitzgerald* [1982]). The result is that, without the Exclusionary Rule, the price of constitutional violations to police will be zero.

It is odd, I think, to place the Exclusionary Rule at the center of today's debate over societal disorder. The claims against the Exclusionary Rule are many and often profound. The Exclusionary Rule, it is argued, is an extraconstitutional evidentiary doctrine proactively, and hence illegitimately, developed by the Warren Court. It is a windfall to criminals and useless to law-abiding citizens. It cannot deter abusive police practices, in large part because the constitutional rules laid down by the courts are confusing moving targets. Lastly, and most importantly, as portrayed in *Dirty Harry,* the Exclusionary Rule puts criminals back on the street to kill again. The Exclusionary Rule therefore is to crime what police are to prevention. One cannot support the Exclusionary Rule without also supporting crime.

The Fourth Amendment Exclusionary Rule hardly supports this rhetorical praise. Crime and social ordering are complex phenomena that will not change dramatically one way or the other with new interpretations of the Exclusionary Rule. Society's substantive mores, criminal laws, and economic conditions have a lot more to do with crime and unrest in America than excluding or admitting evidence at criminal trials. Enforcement is only the tip of the iceberg. If one were truly interested in combating crime, arguments and resources could be directed more productively toward education and economic opportunities than by trashing the Exclusionary Rule. The Exclusionary Rule is just a strawman in the debate over crime in America.

Still, I would be remiss if I did not address the problem of police misconduct in today's society. Abuse of power is an important issue even if cast largely in the symbolic garb of the Exclusionary Rule. Our Founding Fathers knew long ago that power and discretion breed abuse. And today, believe it or not, police sometimes inadvertently break down the wrong door, shoot an innocent bystander, and arrest an innocent person. On occasion, these wrongs are more sinister; police have tortured suspects into involuntary confessions, mercilessly beat citizens who have done nothing more than violate local traffic codes, and have fabricated evidence to bolster a criminal case. Not all nor even most police, of course, have engaged in this type of activity. But enough have to give one pause. Studies conducted in the

1970s and 1980s, for example, found that although police use force in only about one in twenty police/citizen encounters, their force was excessive more than one-third of the time (Pate & Fridell, 1993, p. 1). The 1980s and 1990s are replete with unimaginable police practices, ranging from chokeholds (which have killed numerous Americans) to police canine attacks (which have crippled hundreds more). It does not stop with force. Just as police departments across the country have used illegal force, they have also engaged in illegal searches and seizures. The normative question that society must address is *at what price ought law and order be bought?* Should complete discretion be ceded to the police? If not, what control mechanism should be put in place?

Arguments against the Exclusionary Rule often cast it as a failed prophylactic. It was intended to deter, so the argument goes; it does not (or better yet, it cannot be proven to), and therefore it should be rejected. Several responses are in order. First, deterrence theory only partly explains the Exclusionary Rule. Corrective justice, restoring parties to their proper positions, is just as important as deterrence. Corrective justice directs that a party wronged by another be restored to his original position but for the wrong. The remedy, whether money, exclusion, or some sort of specific performance, retraces the moral relationship between the parties. In criminal cases, that moral relationship is between the state and the individual whose rights are offended.

Second, Chief Justice Marshall said in *Marbury v. Madison* (1803) that America is a "government of laws, and not of men." I believe that America is a better place because police are expected to operate under the rule of law. The Exclusionary Rule is merely one way to enforce this maxim. It is a remedy that seeks to restore both government and the individual to the positions they would have occupied but for a governmental violation of the Constitution. Where government breaks down a person's door and seizes evidence without a warrant, the Exclusionary Rule directs that the evidence be suppressed. The government is not allowed a windfall of evidence that it did not lawfully obtain. The Exclusionary Rule then is not any different from other judicially crafted rules requiring that government and its officials pay damages for unconstitutional injuries to person and property. If government takes property, it pays. Perfect remedies are impossible, so the courts do the best they can. Whether by money or exclusion, government is restored to the position it would have occupied but for its constitutional violation.

Third, far from being a simple windfall to criminals, the benefits of the Exclusionary Rule redound to the benefit of all citizens, innocent and guilty alike. Innocent citizens are sometimes criminally prosecuted. Not all searches, moreover, turn up evidence that is absolutely incriminating. Unlawfully seized evidence can be of an ambiguous nature, so that its exclusion might protect an innocent individual's privacy without altering the outcome of the criminal case. Even ignoring these possibilities, the bolder point is that it is the *threat* of exclusion that offers protection to innocent citizens. Police cannot know ex ante whether the person to be searched is a criminal. The threat of exclusion deters police from conducting illegal searches. Because society consists largely of law-abiding citizens, then, the Exclusionary Rule's benefit falls mainly to the innocent.

Of course, this opens the question of deterrent effect. The assumption is that a rational police officer will adjust his or her conduct to comply with the Constitution so as not to have evidence excluded from subsequent criminal proceedings. Several commentators, and Supreme Court Justices, have criticized this assumption. Indeed, in *United States v. Leon* (1984), a majority of Justices concluded that a police officer who cannot reasonably foresee that he or she is violating the constitution cannot be deterred. The Court thus refused to apply the Exclusionary Rule to evidence discovered with an unconstitutional warrant. Today this is called the "good-faith exception" to the Exclusionary Rule: so long as police reasonably believe their actions are legal, evidence will not be excluded even if their conduct was unconstitutional.

Proving the validity or invalidity of the Court's sociological conclusions about deterrence is a difficult task. Suffice it to say that there exists empirical evidence on both sides. Sociologists, criminologists, and legal scholars have argued, and continue to argue, over the deterrent effect of holding someone accountable for unforeseeable harm. Putting that difficult question aside, my immediate critique focuses on the lack of candor often exhibited in addressing the issue. The same Supreme Court that gave us *Leon,* for example, also created immunities for officials, including police officers, who unforeseeably engage in unconstitutional actions. See *Harlow v. Fitzgerald* (1982). Hence, a police officer who unforeseeably violates the Constitution cannot be held financially accountable for that wrong. A leading justification for this holding is the Court's avowed fear that personal liability for unforeseeable wrongs might "overdeter" official action, causing stale, listless government. One wonders how liability for unforeseeable wrongs can "overdeter" without at the same time "deterring" official action. This patent inconsistency in logic impeaches the Court's ostensible worries about proper deterrence in *Leon.* The Court was not dispensing with a useless remedy, but instead was embarking on a new policy of police permissiveness.

Even if deterrence is beyond proof, or perhaps even an illusion, society and its laws have always operated under its express assumption. The maxim "ignorance of the law is no excuse" permeates both criminal and civil law. A criminal is not excused because he failed to reasonably foresee the criminality of his actions. A homeowner who burns down his own house will not be heard to claim, "I thought it was legal." Such a defense invites obfuscation and ignorance. For this reason it must also be rejected as an excuse to the Exclusionary Rule. Whether deterrence works or not, principled law depends on the assumption that it does.

Opponents of the Exclusionary Rule often charge that it is the unpredictability of Fourth Amendment jurisprudence that proves unfair to police. How can police fairly be punished when no one could predict the outcome? The flaw in this argument is that it presumes that the Fourth Amendment is peculiarly difficult to understand and hence unpredictable. It assumes that judges so routinely strain legal principles in favor of criminals that Fourth Amendment rules are rendered unrecognizable. This is, of course, not the case at all. Instead, as is true throughout the legal landscape, Fourth Amendment law is applied and reapplied to changing fact patterns with differing conclusions. The results are not "new" and "unpredictable" any more than the result in any other type of case is novel and uncertain. Fourth Amendment principles evolve in the same way that all law evolves, through the application of settled norms to historic facts. Courts do not make "new" and "unpredictable" Fourth Amendment law any more than they make new property or contract law. Granted, one party always loses, and that person is never satisfied. To him the outcome is "unreasonable," "unpredictable," "surprising," and unfair. That, however, is the path of a neutral and detached legal system. If it is good enough for the common citizenry, it should be good enough for police.

One also often hears the story of the activist Warren Court's war on law and order. This story has it that the Warren Court warped the Constitution by engrafting onto it far-flung rules of criminal procedure. The Exclusionary Rule is perhaps the most obvious. There is some truth to this argument. However, if accepted, it ultimately proves too much. No, the Constitution of the United States does not mention an Exclusionary Rule. The Fourth Amendment speaks of people being "secure in their persons, houses, papers, and effects, against unreasonable searches and seizures," and the Fifth Amendment states that "[n]o person shall . . . be compelled in any criminal case to be a witness against himself," but neither mentions an appropriate remedy.

The dearth of language in the Constitution addressing appropriate rules of criminal procedure when measured against the many constitutional rules of criminal procedure should not seem startling. It certainly does not direct the conclusion that the Court's development of constitutional prophylactics is somehow illegitimate. The Constitution says virtually nothing about any important right, let alone mentioning remedies for legal wrongs. Still, today more than five hundred volumes of reports breathe life into the vague provisions of the Constitution. If the Exclusionary Rule is illegitimate, then so is virtually every other constitutional rule and remedy. Constitutional doctrine ranging from requiring compensation for state and local governments' taking property to treating corporations as persons are all suspect.

The related claim that the Exclusionary Rule is a product of the Warren Court's "liberalism" likewise smacks more of political rhetoric than reasoned observation. The open-ended language of the Constitution dictates that constitutional rules and remedies are—and must be—products of some Court's "activism." Viewed ahistorically and in a vacuum, rules can casually, and quite wrongly, be cast as products of either "liberal" or "conservative" judicial activism. For instance, long before the rise of Earl Warren, a very conservative Supreme Court adhered to the so-called *mere evidence* rule, which held that search warrants "may not be used as a means of gaining access to a man's house or office and papers solely for the purpose of making search to secure evidence to be used against him in a criminal or penal proceeding" (*Gouled v. U.S.*, [1921]). The *Gouled* rule was quite protective of a person's privacy and property. It meant that only contraband or instrumentalities of crime could be seized with warrants. One is hard-pressed to argue that *Gouled* was the result of the pre–New Deal Taft Court's liberal agenda. Viewed in historical context, constitutional scholars know that the pre-New Deal Taft Court was conservative, at least in the socioeconomic sense.

Likewise, the development of the Exclusionary Rule is just one piece of the Warren Court's varied patchwork of precedent. It cannot singularly identify the Warren Court as liberal or conservative. Better yet, the Exclusionary Rule cannot itself be identified as liberal or conservative because it is a simple piece in the chronological puzzle of "constitutional rights." It has value only as it stands relative to other rights and remedies. Although the Warren Court expanded the reach of the Exclusionary Rule, it overruled the holding in *Gouled*. In context, it appears more of a moderate compromise than a profound liberal invention.

Once the mythology is stripped away, one can judge the Exclusionary Rule and its impact in a more objective way. The truth behind the Exclusionary Rule is that it exacts a small price for controlling governmental lawlessness. Police do not go to jail because of the Exclusionary Rule, nor do they pay fines and compensate victims. Instead, evidence is excluded from a small portion of criminal cases, and in an even smaller fraction of these cases criminal defendants are acquitted or released. Even the most favorable studies for law enforcement have it that motions to suppress evidence are filed in only 10 percent of felony prosecutions and are successful only about 10 percent of the time. Acquittals and dismissals then occur in just over half of these cases, meaning that out of 200 cases only one criminal defendant prevails because of the Exclusionary Rule. Successful defendants, moreover, are largely skewed in favor of those charged with simple possession offenses, where the physical evidence is critical to the prosecution's case. Violent criminals rarely succeed using the Exclusionary Rule.

At this small price comes a proud benefit—government is held accountable under law. Granted, the constitutional victory is largely symbolic—it will not shelter the poor nor prove a panacea for the downtrodden—but it is still an important symbol. Relaxing all limitations on governmental power is dangerous business. The Constitutional Framers believed in checks and balances, and wisely so. They knew that absolute power corrupts absolutely. It may make for more efficient law enforcement (and make Dirty Harry's many movies shorter), but its cost is abuse. In the absence of realistic alternatives—which have yet to be discovered or developed—the Exclusionary Rule continues to prove its worth.

References

Alabama v. White, 496 U.S. 325 (1990).
Arizona v. Evans, 514 U.S. 1 (1995).
California v. Greenwood, 486 U.S. 35 (1988).

Dow Chemical v. United States, 476 U.S. 227 (1986).
Florida v. Riley, 488 U.S. 445 (1989).
Gouled v. United States, 255 U.S. 298 (1921).
Harlow v. Fitzgerald, 457 U.S. 800 (1982).
Maryland v. Wilson, 117 S.Ct. 882, 137 L.Ed. 2d. 41 (1997).
Marbury v. Madison, 1 Cranch 137, 2 L.Ed. 60 (1803).
Pate, A. M. and Fridell, L. A. (1993). *Police use of force: Official reports, citizen complaints, and legal consequences.* Washington, DC: Police Foundation.
United States v. Cusamano, 67 F.3d 1497 (1995).
United States v. Leon, 468 U.S. 897 (1984).
United States v. Sokolow, 490 U.S. 1 (1989).
Whren v. United States, 116 S. Ct. 1769, 135 L.Ed. 2d. 89 (1996).

Rejoinder to Professor Brown   PAULA C. COFFMAN

Like Professor Brown, I do not desire to live in a culture where the rules apply to only a few. Like most of us, I prefer American democracy to anarchy. After all, rules are the necessary means to the desired end of a civilized society. It is voluntary adherence to the rules, whatever they may be, by most of a society's members that creates and promotes social order.

I say *most* because not everyone is going to follow the rules. As we all know, crime represents a serious problem in this country and is a matter of significant concern to most Americans. Thus, if a society's rules are to be enforced, a collective response to rule-breaking must be agreed on by the law-abiding majority. Again, I say *majority* because crime is not a problem for criminals so long as their deeds remain undetected.

What constitutes an appropriate response to rule-breaking may itself be circumscribed by other rules. For instance, I share the view of most Americans that a man's hand is worth more than any wallet that hand could steal. Hence, although theft is a punishable offense in our society, chopping off the thief's offending member is not an available sentencing option. These rules too must be followed voluntarily by a majority of society's members. Otherwise, if enough people start breaking the rules, chaos ensues.

It is often said that our criminal justice system is built on the premise that it is better for one hundred guilty people to go free than for one innocent man to be wrongfully convicted. As a result of my experience defending the integrity of presumptively valid convictions and sentences in postconviction litigation, I am confident that the incidence of wrongful conviction among the thousands who are prosecuted in my own jurisdiction each year is infinitesimally small. Viewed from this perspective, the criminal justice system appears to be achieving its objective. But what if, instead of one hundred guilty people, the cost was one thousand? How many crimes would have to be left unpunished before the system of criminal justice would erode into a state of criminal injustice?

As a prosecutor, I often ponder the price of law and order, but from a vantage point where the amorphous rubber of constitutional theory meets the concrete road of daily life. Professor Brown contends that, without the Exclusionary Rule, the cost of constitutional violations to police will be zero. In a limited sense, he may be right. However, I question whether it is just law enforcement or, more accurately, the general public that law enforcement seeks to protect, who ultimately pays the bill for the Exclusionary Rule.

That having been said, I must take issue with the assertion that violent criminals only rarely capitalize on the Exclusionary Rule. Just as frequently as any other type of defendant, violent criminals at least *attempt* to capitalize on it. Although motions to suppress are commonplace in possession cases, because of the existence of physical evidence (contraband such as drugs or weapons) to be suppressed by the very nature of the offense charged, such motions are frequently encountered in murder cases as well.

Contrary to the suggestion that only petty criminals claim the benefit of the Exclusionary Rule, the potentiality for suppression of evidence exists in all criminal cases. For example, in many jurisdictions, defendants charged with driving under the influence (DUI) routinely seek suppression of all or part of the prosecution's case. Under the "fruit of the poisonous tree" doctrine, which expands the remedy of suppression for search and seizure violations beyond items of physical evidence (such as empty beer bottles) to include verbal evidence, the State's entire case is subject to exclusion.

What all of this means to you and me is that the motorist who is guilty of DUI cannot be successfully prosecuted if the court determines that there was insufficient legal justification for the traffic stop that led to his arrest. The irony here is that, in every single instance in which the defendant's argument that there was insufficient legal justification for a search and seizure prevails, incriminating evidence of some nature was actually seized. Under the Constitution, a reasonable suspicion is not always tantamount to an accurate suspicion.

So a drunk driver escapes justice to drive again. One can only hope that he has learned something from the experience and can resist the urge to celebrate his recent good fortune at the nearest bar. Most of us can live with that. I suspect that more than a few readers may conclude that this is a small price to pay for the assurance that their own use of the public highways may not be interrupted for even a minute by the authorities without a legally sufficient reason.

Most criminals use the highway (with or without a valid driver license). But let us suppose that, instead of a couple of empty "tall boys," a severed head is observed by the officer in plain view in the back seat of the murdering motorist's vehicle. This case too may fail. It bears noting that the remedy of suppression of all or part of the State's case is applied under the Exclusionary Rule without regard to the nature of the offense charged.

In answering Professor Brown's defense of the Exclusionary Rule, I have refrained from discussing specific cases in which I believe defendants have made a mockery of the truth-finding function of our criminal justice system. Ethical considerations generally prohibit such prosecutorial comment on pending cases. As to those closed cases resolved by dismissal, acquittal, or a plea to lesser charges after critical evidence was suppressed, there is always the possibility of a civil suit for slander to chill public comment.

Perhaps even better than the rest of us, criminal defendants know their rights and, like Dirty Harry's antagonist Scorpio, they do not hesitate to exercise them. Stripped of its lofty pretensions, the remedy of suppression plainly gives a defendant a license to lie. Insofar as the defendant and the criminal justice system are concerned, evidence not admitted at trial never existed. If the State cannot prove the defendant's guilt, then the defendant is innocent in the eyes of the law. Consequently, it could prove just too costly for a prosecutor to opine in public that Mr. So-and-so really was a child molester, for example, even though a jury, which did not have the opportunity to view certain excluded incriminating photographs, erroneously acquitted him.

Finally, I do not deign to suggest that adherence to the Exclusionary Rule "causes" crime. Like Professor Brown, I believe that the causes of criminal behavior are myriad, rendering the issue too complex for and outside the scope of our present discussion. The focus of our debate concerns how society should respond once a rule has been broken, once a crime has been detected. Some continue to see wisdom in failing to punish detected crime. Professor Brown argues that principled law depends on the assumption that deterrence works. But if we are to assume, as proponents of the Exclusionary Rule do, that negative sanctions imposed for violations of the rules positively affect the behavior of police, then how can we afford to ignore the unequivocally negative message we send to all criminals by allowing some of them to break the rules with impunity?

Civil Forfeiture in Law Enforcement: An Effective Tool or Cash Register Justice?

EDITOR'S NOTE: The changing nature of criminal conduct has necessitated innovative law enforcement responses. Patterns of criminal enterprise have heralded the advent of new criminal laws, especially federal and state Racketeer Influenced Corrupt Organizations (RICO) Acts, to attach greater penalties to ongoing offenses. The rewards available to modern-day criminals have led law enforcement officials and prosecutors to explore new methods of seizing the proceeds of criminal behavior. To this end, federal and state civil forfeiture laws have sprung up with a single purpose: to reduce the financial incentives associated with criminal conduct. But our dilemma: are these laws good business practices on the part of law enforcement or do they foster turnstile justice?

Carl W. Hawkins, Jr. is Captain with the Hillsborough County Sheriff's Office in Tampa, Florida. He has twenty-three years of law enforcement experience and has worked in every administrative and operational assignment at the sheriff's office. During 1996, he was awarded a Community Policing Fellowship to the National Center for State, Local, and International Law Enforcement Training at the Federal Law Enforcement Training Center, Glynco, Georgia. He holds a Doctor of Public Administration (1982) and a Master of Science in Criminal Justice (1977) from Nova Southeastern University and a Bachelor of Science in Criminal Justice (1974) from the University of South Florida. He is a graduate of the 18th Session of the Senior Management Institute for Police at the Police Executive Research Forum, the 76th Administrative Officer's Course of the Southern Police Institute at the University of Louisville, and the 77th Delinquency Control Course of the Delinquency Control Institute at the University of Southern California.

Thomas E. Payne began his career in public service twenty years ago when he was appointed Deputy Sheriff with the Harrison County, Mississippi, Sheriff's Department. During the course of his career, he has served as an agent with the Mississippi Bureau of Narcotics; a District Attorney's investigator; Director of the Public Advocacy Division of the Mississippi Attorney General's Office; chief counsel with the Mississippi Bureau of Narcotics; and Assistant United States Attorney for the Southern District of Mississippi. He currently coordinates the Criminal Justice Programs for all coast campuses for the University of Southern Mississippi. Dr. Payne has a Master of Science in Criminal Justice and a Ph.D. from the University of Southern Mississippi in Adult Education with an emphasis in Criminal Justice and a Juris Doctorate from the University of Mississippi.

AN EFFECTIVE TOOL

CARL W. HAWKINS, JR.

The only thing necessary for the triumph of evil is for good men to do nothing.
—Edmund Burke (1729–1797)

Forfeiture is a legal procedure in which the government may take, without compensation, property derived from or used in a criminal activity. Its use as a sanction aims to strip criminals such as racketeers and drug traffickers of their economic power because traditional forms of imprisonment and fines are inadequate to deter or punish immensely profitable illegal activity. The seizure of property or assets aims to reduce the profitability of crime and to curtail the financial ability of criminal organizations to continue their operations (Seigel, 1995).

There are two general types of forfeiture: criminal and civil. Criminal forfeiture is *in personam,* that is, against the person. It can only be used after the property owner has been convicted of certain crimes. Civil forfeiture, however, is *in rem,* or against the thing. It is directed at property and assets that have been used illegally. Civil forfeiture is normally based on the "guilt" of a piece of property and is separate from any criminal proceedings directed against the property owner. Therefore, the guilt or innocence of the property owner is not considered during the forfeiture process. The rationale for the use of civil law forfeiture is that property can be "guilty" if it was used directly in or in some way facilitated the commission of a crime. The property is then subject to "arrest," or seizure. Under many forfeiture laws, seizure of an item of property requires only probable cause that the property was involved in illegal activity (Aylesworth, 1992).

Property subject to civil forfeiture often includes vehicles used to transport contraband, equipment used to manufacture illegal drugs, cash used in illegal transactions, computer and technology used to further a crime, and property purchased with the proceeds of a crime. The government must always post notice of the seizure proceedings so parties with an interest in the property may contest the forfeiture (Seigel, 1995).

Forfeiture is not a new sanction. During the Middle Ages, "forfeiture of estate" was required in most felony convictions. The Crown would seize all of a felon's real and personal property. The common-law concept of "corruption of blood," or "attaint," prohibited the felon's family from inheriting or receiving the property that was obtained illegally because a criminal could have no power over the property because he never enjoyed it (Fried, 1988).

In this commentary, the advantages of having and continuing the use of civil forfeiture as an effective tool in law enforcement are examined. Even though many critics in the media and legal arena advocate the abolition of its practice, there are many effective uses for this law enforcement adjunct. This article presents a strong argument for its continued use, reviewing its many advantages, and concludes with a summary of some recommendations to prevent its abuse.

The Advantages of Civil Forfeiture for Law Enforcement

Civil forfeiture is an extremely effective tool in disrupting and dismantling an organized criminal enterprise. As the criminal justice system continues to focus criminal sanctions primarily on individual offenders, criminal networks remain untouched while retaining millions of dollars in profits. Though there are many critics of civil forfeiture, the huge profit-motivated transactions in drug and other forms of racketeering are abundantly clear. As of fiscal year 1994, forfeitures in net deposits to the United States Department of Justice's Asset Forfeiture Fund reached nearly $4 billion (U.S. Department of Justice, 1995). This money represents the goods and property typically retained in one form or another by a criminal enterprise. By dismantling the organization and removing the profit incentive to operate, many forms of illegal activity can be reduced in size and scope.

What are some of the advantages in continuing the use of civil forfeiture in law enforcement? The first is the deterrent effect on criminality. The basic idea of deterrence is that, by punishing one person, we dissuade others from committing future acts. Deterrence assumes that prospective offenders engage in a rational process of determining whether the expected costs associated with the punishment of a given crime are sufficient to offset its expected rewards and thus prevent its future commission (Wilson & Petersilia, 1995). Does the criminal justice system provide a deterrent effect on criminality? As a result of improvements in the record-keeping technology of prosecution over the past twenty years, we have learned a great deal about what happens between arrest and final case disposition. For adults arrested for felony crimes, of every one hundred cases considered for prosecution, an average of only thirty-three result in a conviction, and most of those are settled through reduced plea bargaining and jail terms of less than a year (Wilson & Petersilia, 1995). Most criminals arrested are not prosecuted or convicted, nor do they serve any length of time in prison.

So what deterrent effect does the criminal justice system have on criminality? It appears very little. By taking property and other goods through civil forfeiture, the deterrent effect of this action removes the rewards associated with crime and thus prevents such illegal activities in the future. According to Attorney Chris Sabella of the Hillsborough County, Florida, Sheriff's Office Forfeiture Unit, "These criminals will plead guilty to their criminal charges without hesitation but, on the seizure of their car, they'll fight with everything they have. They know that sometimes a plea in their criminal case will not affect their life as much as losing their means of committing the crime" (Personal interview, 1997).

Another advantage for continuing the use of civil forfeiture is the remedial effect on criminality. The underlying rationale for remediation is to create a financial disincentive, to protect the public from the harm of illicit monies, and to compensate public and private losses caused by conduct giving rise to forfeiture (U.S. Department of Justice, 1996). Civil forfeiture allows the court to take away the illegal tools used to commit crime. During the days of prohibition, removing the alcohol stills and liquor created a financial disincentive for bootleggers to operate. It cost the bootlegger additional money to continue the operation. The purchase of equipment and supplies to manufacture alcohol products financially cost the bootlegger *something*. The use of forfeiture was viewed as protecting the public from the harm of illicit alcohol. Even though prohibiting alcohol may have been very unpopular, the use of forfeiture was extremely effective in disrupting the criminal network. A more contemporary view of remediation occurs in New York, where persons arrested for drunk driving risk having their automobiles seized under the state's civil forfeiture law. The new law allows state prosecutors to confiscate cars involved in felony drunk-driving cases, sell them at auction, and give the proceeds to the victims of the crime; Texas enacted a similar law in 1984 (Seigel, 1995).

An additional advantage for continuing the use of civil forfeiture is the ability to save the taxpayer money in financing and equipping a police agency in its fight against crime. Most law enforcement agencies cannot afford to purchase the type of highly technical equipment needed to counter the technology of a criminal enterprise. The needs for sophisticated surveillance equipment, computers, motor vehicles for undercover operations, and other extraordinary purchases can explode a government budget. By using the criminal's property and money to finance the non-operating expenses of a police agency, criminal enterprises can be dismantled with the use of their own illegal resources and property. We can enhance the criminal investigation process by providing the tools needed to improve the investigation and subsequent prosecution of drug dealers and other racketeering enterprises.

Still another advantage for continuing the use of civil forfeiture is the improvement of officer morale and motivation. Most officers are frustrated by the criminal justice system and its lack of deterrent and remedial effect on crime and criminals. Officers see criminals arrested day after day, with very little, if any, punishment occurring to these criminals in our system of justice. Crime does pay, and it pays very well. By taking property and the illicit means for criminals to operate, officers can see the immediate effect their actions can have on the offender. Officers also can use the property seized to help investigate and dismantle the criminal enterprise. Police agencies now can be equipped to compete with the technology and equipment used by the criminal. Frustrated officers become satisfied officers. They see the immediate results of their action on crime.

The final advantage of continuing the use of civil forfeiture is the self-supporting nature and financial self-sufficiency of a forfeiture unit. By seizing property and other goods used by a criminal enterprise, a forfeiture unit can pay for itself without burdening the taxpayer for its continued operation and investigations. Salaries and equipment and vehicle purchases all can be paid out of the seized assets. Attorney salaries and time also can be reimbursed. If created properly, the forfeiture unit costs the taxpayer very little while supporting the agency in the battle it wages against crime and criminals.

Even with the advantages of civil forfeiture, there have been problems in its application. Some agencies confiscate large sums of property for minor offenses without considering the proportionality principle of the law. Other agencies use the incentive of obtaining property and goods as its goal, rather than dismantling and disrupting a criminal enterprise. All of these have occurred, and some safeguards are needed in practice. But the extent of reform called for by critics is not in line with the benefits derived from its current use and practice.

Ensuring the Future of Civil Forfeiture in Law Enforcement

To ensure the future of civil forfeiture, law enforcement should consider adopting some reforms to its current program and practice. What began as a good idea—and it still is—needs some small adjustments. These suggestions, I believe, will improve civil forfeiture for the future.

The first change is to improve the training of officers in the statutory requirements of civil forfeiture. This training should be conducted in conjunction with education about the agency's current procedure/policy on seizing property under this law. Consideration should be given to training the officer alongside the local prosecutor and forfeiture attorney to prevent improper seizures.

The second change is to encourage in-depth preseizure planning to identify and protect innocent owners and to avoid seizing assets that will ultimately be returned to the owner. By making this change, the innocent owner does not lose his or her property, and the effort should preclude the dismissal of weak cases.

The third change is to encourage the arrest of the offender, whenever possible, in addition to seizing the assets. This switch in policy direction eliminates the claim of seizure without arrest and wards off the charge of asset hunting.

The fourth change is to develop a publicized policy for the use and disposal of the proceeds of the forfeiture. Included in the policy is a regularly scheduled, independent audit of the program, with the reporting of the findings released for public inspection.

The final change is to develop an accurate database on all seizures and forfeitures, as well as an articulated justification for confiscating criminal assets. This information is extremely helpful during an audit of the program and can answer immediately any allegations of abuse of forfeiture.

By making these adjustments to civil forfeiture, law enforcement will stem the tide of complaints leveled against this effective tool. It is much wiser to improve on civil forfeiture than to totally remove this practice from law enforcement's arsenal. Crime should never pay, and civil forfeiture has many advantages for law enforcement in disrupting and dismantling a criminal enterprise. Fix it, don't eliminate it!

REFERENCES

Aylesworth, G. N. (1992). Forfeiture of real property: An overview. *Police Executive Research Forum, 14,* 1–64.

Fried, D. J. (1988). Rationalizing criminal forfeiture. *Journal of Criminal Law & Criminology, 79,* 328–436.

Sabella, C. (1997). Personal interview. July 31, Tampa, Florida.

Seigel, L. J. (1995). *Criminology: Theories, patterns and topologies.* St. Paul, MN: West Publishing Company.

U.S. Department of Justice. (1995). *Audit report: Asset forfeiture program—Annual financial statement.* Washington, DC: Criminal Division, Asset Forfeiture and Money Laundering Section.

U.S. Department of Justice. (1996). *State and local law enforcement asset forfeiture training curriculum module 1: Introduction to forfeiture.* Washington, DC: Criminal Division, Asset Forfeiture and Money Laundering Section.

Wilson, J. Q., & Petersilia, J. (Eds.). (1995). *Crime.* San Francisco, CA: Institute for Contemporary Studies.

Rejoinder to Dr. Hawkins

THOMAS E. PAYNE

> Power [to govern] is delegated and must be exercised according to the judgement of the individuals to whom it is delegated . . . [but] *the public has a right to spell out the criteria by which the judgements should be made, and to insist on both competence and good faith in the application of those criteria* [emphasis added] (Reiman, 1985).

Before we can fix the problem, we must come to terms with realistic processes and procedures that establish a true change in course. It is a far too simplistic solution to merely call for a fix. The issue is not the need for the fix; that is a much too obvious and by now a foregone conclusion. What we need now is the methodology designed to truly change the offending characteristics of the law.

In his treatise on moral issues in police work, Reiman points out that the citizen not only has the right to demand this change but also a right to "both competence and good faith" in the process of change. Therefore, the concern that must be addressed is who should be the change agent. If law enforcement is to take this role, as proposed, then what guidelines can we put into place to ensure the public's trust? Can we legitimately claim professional privilege and "police ourselves" with the inherent conflict of interest present in our current civil forfeiture procedures? Can we guarantee to the public "good faith" efforts when we have so much at stake economically?

The answers to these questions are beyond the scope of this discussion, but they are answers that we in public law enforcement should be the first to address. We cannot allow the contentment with special units and cash-filled war chests to blind us to this critical juncture in our continuing evolution. Are we to be perceived as for-profit law enforcement agencies dedicated to the public good, as long as we are well financed through the "booty" we recover from the criminal? If this perception holds true, we run a very real risk of changing our historical identity. We will no longer be identified as the new centurions, but rather as the pirates of the Caribbean. A humorous analogy, but one too close for comfort.

The call for change must come from public law enforcement, and we should be willing to sit down at the table with all groups interested in the freedom of the citizen. As a group, our goal would be to craft the process and procedure necessary to insure constitutional rights of all citizens and, as importantly, restore the trust that we have lost over the course of our recent history. The public should expect no more, and we should demand no less. The worst mistake we could make at this important juncture in our history is to do nothing. "But if the watchman sees the sword coming and does not blow the trumpet, and the people are not warned, and the sword comes and takes any person from among them . . . his blood I will require at the watchman's hand" (Ezekiel 33:6). Just as the watchman, our cost for not sounding the call for reform is too great a price to pay.

REFERENCE

Reiman, J. (1985). The social contract and the police use of deadly force. In F. A. Ellison and M. Feldberg (Eds.), *Moral issues in police work.* Savage, MD: Srowman & Littlefield Publishers.

CASH REGISTER JUSTICE

THOMAS E. PAYNE

The worm does not his work more surely on the dead body than does this slow creeping fire upon the living frame.

—Charles Dickens, *Oliver Twist*

I can find no better analogy to describe the state of our civil forfeiture laws than that used by Dickens in describing the fever that raked the body of young Oliver Twist. The living frame of our democracy and the Constitution on which it is nourished are being devoured by a "slow creeping fire"...a fever that has invaded our criminal justice system and spread across our nation's courts and law enforcement agencies. A fever caused by our own creation, designed as a statutory antibody, carrying out the dual mission of retribution and restitution, it quickly mutated into a means of revenue production unsurpassed in the annals of law enforcement history. Never before had we in law enforcement found so easy and direct a method of making money, production so prolific that it became a cash cow for agency heads and soon the opiate of the whole body politic. What began as a tool in the arsenal of this nation's war on drugs has too quickly degraded into a money grab, pitting one agency against another, leaving private property strewn across the jurisprudential landscape, much wasted and far too much innocence lost in the quest for justice, a quest that today can only be described as Cash Register Justice.

Asset forfeiture has grown into a multi-million dollar revenue source for local, state, and federal police agencies. Estimates place the income generated at over $500 million in the federal system and millions more in state and local (Murphy, 1991). In its early use, asset forfeiture held the sensible attributes expounded by its proponents, but the lure of ready cash has changed the focus from banging the bad guy to clanging the register. Officer and prosecutors are no longer looking at the offender as the target of their enforcement efforts but rather are looking beyond the offender to his pocketbook, car, or villa. The result of this perversion of original intent is an outcry by the innocent owner, courts, and defense bar. "Failure to strictly enforce the Excessive Fines Clause inevitably gives the government an incentive to investigate criminal activity in situations involving valuable property, regardless of its seriousness, but to ignore more serious criminal activity that does not provide financial gain to the government" (*United States v. Real Property Located at 6625 Zumeriz Drive*, 845 F. Supp. 725,735 [C. D. Cal. 1994]). The Supreme Court recognized the government's financial interest in forfeiture proceedings. As it described:

> The extent of the Government's financial stake in drug forfeiture is apparent from the 1990 memo in which the Attorney General urged United States Attorneys to increase the volume of forfeitures in order to meet the Department of Justice's annual budget target: "We must significantly increase production to reach our budget target...Failure to achieve the $470 million projection would expose the Department's forfeiture program to criticism and undermine confidence in our budget projections. Every effort must be made to increase forfeiture income during the remaining three months of [fiscal year] 1990." (*United States v. James Daniel Good Real Property*, 510 U.S. 43 [1993]).

The outcome is the perception that the cure is worse than the bite. "What I most fear is that the actions of governments will become so oppressive to inno-

cent people that the bulk of innocent humanity will start to see the drugs [sic] bar-
ons as a lesser evil than governments" (Abaci, 1997). The fear of government
overreaching has spread across the nation; the fear is not limited to the arena of
asset forfeiture, but it is clearly one of the symptoms fueling a national debate.

One merely has to listen to the discussion that occurs daily on the information highway to sense the anger and frustration directed toward the government
over the civil forfeiture issue. "The Supreme Court has legalized **governmental
robbery** of 'innocent owners' by police forces with their March decision on property forfeiture" [emphasis added] (Simac, 1996)... Steve Dasbach, chairman of
the Libertarian Party, said. "*Cops have become robbers* with a *license to steal,* under the new ruling" [emphasis added] (Simac, 1996).

Those groups, often characterized as "fringe," are not the only entities that
have joined in this debate. In an Internet article questioning whether indigent defendants are afforded the same justice as those who could afford a lawyer, Martin
Schaffer, a public defender, captured the current feeling among the defense bar
when addressing issues of civil forfeiture:

> In the wake of the U.S. Supreme Court's opinion in *Bennis v. Michigan,* 116
> S. Ct. 944 (1996), civil asset forfeiture has lately been getting increased atten-
> tion. Many observers believe that the system requires additional safeguards,
> such as: ensuring actual notice of forfeiture proceedings; eliminating incen-
> tives that create "contingent fee" law enforcement; authorizing release of cer-
> tain property pending disposition of the case; and providing counsel for the
> indigent." (Shaffer, 1997)

Expressing concern over the burden of proof in civil forfeiture cases, one
author explained that "the government may rely on hearsay, circumstantial evidence or facts learned after seizure. The standard effectively leaves the claimants
with the burden of proving their innocence or losing their homes and other property" (Stahl, 1992).

The perception that government overreaching is trampling the property and
due process rights of the citizen has also reached the Halls of Congress. Congressman Henry Hyde, Chairman of the House Judiciary Committee, has sponsored
House Bill 1916 in direct response to the concern over abuse by law enforcement
agencies in the administration of civil forfeiture laws. In testimony before the
House Committee on the Judiciary, E. E. Edwards spoke in favor of H. R. 1916
and on behalf of the 39,000 direct and affiliated members of the National Association of Criminal Defense Lawyers (NACDL). In what by now is a clarion call for
reform, Edwards testified:

> the unchecked use of over-broad civil forfeiture statutes has run amok. Law
> enforcement agencies, in their zeal, have turned the War on Drugs into a
> War on the Constitution.... It is the civil forfeiture law... which concerns
> us the most, due to the utter lack of Constitutional safeguards and the unfair

procedural advantages it affords the government at the expense of law-abiding citizens. (Edwards, 1997)

In summarizing a previous attempt at legislative reform, NACDL Forfeiture Abuse Task Force Co-Chair David B. Smith, of Alexandria, Virginia, extolled the virtues of the Hyde bill and pointed out the need for reform:

The Hyde bill changes the burden of proof, clarifies the definition of an "innocent owner," eliminates the cost bond requirement, sets a reasonable time period for property owners to challenge forfeitures, and permits appointment of counsel to represent indigent claimants. It will provide greater fairness and due process in the otherwise Byzantine procedural labyrinth—inherited from Draconian customs laws—that often overwhelms innocent forfeiture victims." (Smith, 1995)

The asset forfeiture laws must be reformed to prevent even the perception of government overreaching and profiteering. Hanging in the balance are the constitutional rights of the citizen and, just as importantly, the citizens' trust of their government. The silver star of law enforcement has been tarnished by the rush to profit. Our steps must be toward meaningful reform designed to eliminate the perception of conflict that result from direct economic incentives in civil forfeiture cases. The forfeiture of ill-gotten gains by criminals and criminal organizations is an appropriate and laudable law enforcement goal. But the use of the civil law to water down the procedural safeguards of citizens has proved a nemesis more than an ally to criminal justice agencies. The costs in negative citizen perception and the chance of constitutional violations far outweigh its gains. The moves to reform must encompass a procedural change designed to protect the property and due process rights of the citizen. In short, the same safeguards afforded a criminal defendant when being seized by the government should also be given to the defendant's property. The loss in revenue that these added safeguards will inevitably bring pales in comparison to the loss of the liberty of our citizens.

REFERENCES

Abaci, J. (1997). Internet Home Page. Retrieved September 1997 from the World Wide Web: http://www.abaci@dircon.co.uk.

Dickens, C. (1996). *Oliver Twist: The Collectors Library of Classics.* Nashville: Thomas Nelson, Inc.

Edwards, E. E. (1997). Testimony before the United States House Committee on the Judiciary, July 22, Washington, D.C. Retrieved September 1997 from World Wide Web: http://www.criminaljustice.org/TESTIFY/test 0003.htm

Murphy, S. P. (1991, March 8). 10 Sites Are Seized in U.S. Drug Sweep. *Boston Globe,* p. 17.

Shaffer, M. L. (1997). Indigence, civil forfeiture and double jeopardy: Equal justice for all? Retrieved September 1997 from the World Wide Web: http://co.lake.il.us/pubdef/shaffer.htm

Simac, S. (1996). Supreme court agrees cops are robbers. Retrieved September 1997 from the World Wide Web: http://coastalpost.com/96/4/1.htm.

Smith, D. B. (1995). Civil forfeiture laws trash the Constitution. NACDL News Release. Retrieved September 1997 from the World Wide Web: http://www.criminaljustice.org/MEDIA/pr000028.htm

Stahl, M. B. (1992). Asset forfeiture, burdens of proof and the war on drugs. *Journal of Criminal Law & Criminology, 83,* 274–337.

United States v. James Daniel Good Real Property. (1993). 510 U.S. 43.

United States v. Real Property Located at 6625 Zumeriz Drive. (1994). 845 F. Supp. 725, 735 (C. D. Cal).

Rejoinder to Dr. Payne
CARL W. HAWKINS, JR.

Dr. Payne is theoretically correct in calling for some reform to the current practice of civil forfeiture. What began as a good idea—and it still is—needs some revision to its application. The only problem with Dr. Payne's analysis is the hysterical dialogue he quotes from the information highway and the extent of his proposed changes.

Suggesting that the police are engaged in "legalized governmental robbery of innocent owners" and have a "license to steal" goes beyond criticism to outrageous statements in support of reform. There is absolutely nothing wrong in removing illicit money and property from a criminal enterprise. Criminals should not be able to keep any property obtained through illegal ways. Dr. Payne appears to support these statements by reflecting that "the forfeiture of an ill-gotten gain by criminals and criminal organizations is an appropriate and laudable law enforcement goal."

Where we differ is our approach to the amount of reform needed. Dr. Payne suggests that "the costs in negative citizen perception and the chance of constitutional violations far outweigh the gain." He adds, "the moves to reform must encompass a procedural change designed to protect the property and due process rights of the citizen. In short, the same safeguards afforded a criminal defendant when being seized by the government should also be given to the defendant's property." Is Dr. Payne suggesting that the burden of proof shift from a probable cause determination for the illegal property to a higher standard of beyond a reasonable doubt? Civil proceedings have a different threshold of proof than do criminal proceedings. By suggesting these safeguards, Dr. Payne may in effect be advocating the elimination of civil forfeiture for future use by law enforcement, because the criminal forfeiture laws already have the procedural requirements he recommends.

The proposed changes I advocate remove the negative perceptions and the chance of constitutional violations without eliminating the use of civil forfeiture. A posted notice of the proceeding is currently required so that any party who has an interest in the property may contest its forfeiture. The reforms to training, pre-seizure planning, arrest of the offender, audit of the assets, and creation of an accurate database should answer many of the concerns by the critics. Crime does pay well, and the use of civil forfeiture provides law enforcement with an effective tool to disrupt and dismantle crime and criminals. Again: fix it, don't eliminate it!

A Police Officer's Bill of Rights: A Needed Protection for Cops?

EDITOR'S NOTE: The control of police misconduct is a major issue facing American law enforcement. As part of the professionalization process, agencies have structured their organization to prevent inappropriate or illegal behavior by officers; have attempted to define appropriate behavior through written policies, voluminous procedures, and codes of conduct; and have aggressively pursued perceived violators through internal affairs investigations and, at times, the use of undercover police officers. Some officers would hold that, at times and in many agencies, the police organization's response to perceived misconduct has been too aggressive and has violated the rights of individual officers. As a result, in a number of states, the last two decades have witnessed the promulgation of legislatively mandated police officer bills of rights, designed to clearly define protections for officers under investigation. Yet the debate now rages: Is such legislation really necessary? Do we give police officers more protection than we give the bad guys?

Hal Johnson currently serves as General Counsel of the Florida Police Benevolent Association and has held that position for over eighteen years. As General Counsel, Mr. Johnson oversees a legal staff that represents law enforcement and correctional officers on a statewide basis. He personally handles numerous labor negotiations, disciplinary hearings, and decertification matters throughout the State of Florida. Mr. Johnson has also assisted in legislation that substantially affects law enforcement in Florida. Mr. Johnson has served as the Chairman of the Labor and Employment Law Section of the Florida Bar and has lectured at many seminars dealing with law enforcement officers or employee rights. He previously served as a staff counsel for the Florida Public Employees Relations Commission (PERC). Mr. Johnson received his B.A. from Drake University and his J.D. from The Florida State University.

Michael Scott is an independent police management consultant and a member of the adjunct faculty at Armstrong Atlantic State University in Savannah, Georgia. He formerly was Chief of Police of the Lauderhill, Florida Police Department, having founded that municipal police department in 1994 in a transition from contracted police services. Scott previously served as Special Assistant to the Chief of Police of the St. Louis Metropolitan Police Department, where he was primarily responsible for implementing problem-oriented policing throughout the department. He has served as the Director of Administration for the Fort Pierce, Florida Police Department; a Senior Researcher at the Police Executive Research Forum; the Legal Assistant to the Police Commissioner of the New York City Police Department; and a police officer in the Madison, Wisconsin Police Department. Scott holds a B.A. from the University of Wisconsin–Madison and a J.D. from Harvard Law School. He is the author of *Managing for Success: A Police Chief's Survival Guide* and coauthor of *Deadly Force: What We Know. A Practitioner's Desk Reference to Police-Involved Shootings in the United States.*

YES

HAL JOHNSON

Over the past several years there has been an increasing debate between the nation's police associations and police administrators about the need for the adoption of federal or state legislation establishing a standard Law Enforcement Officer's Bill of Rights. The debate should now end. With the United States Supreme Court's recent decision in *LaChance v. Erickson* (1998), a bill of rights for law enforcement is no longer a need; it is a necessity.

The Rules of Play

In January, 1998, the United States Supreme Court issued a decision in the case of *LaChance v. Erickson,* which deals with untruthfulness during an internal investigation. When coupled with the Supreme Court's decisions in *Garrity v. New Jersey* (1966) and *Gardner v. Broderick* (1967), the *LaChance* case makes the law enforcement officer's bill of rights a basic necessity for officers who are subject to investigation and interrogation. Without the protections it will afford officers, Rudyard Kipling's sage advise on having the "truths you have spoken twisted by knaves to make a trap for fools" may take on new meaning for officers—the officer's truths may become the officer's grounds for dismissal.

As most everyone involved in law enforcement is aware, the *Garrity* and *Gardner* decisions formed the cornerstone of disciplinary investigations. These decisions, rendered by the United States Supreme Court, eliminated an officer's ability to invoke the Fifth Amendment protection against self-incrimination during an internal disciplinary investigation. As a result, an officer involved in a disciplinary interrogation must answer questions specifically, narrowly, and directly related to the alleged employment misconduct under investigation.

Today, officers are routinely advised of their "Garrity rights" (a misnomer of sorts) and the fact that their "failure to cooperate" (answer the questions) in an internal investigation can lead to disciplinary action "including dismissal." Simply put, an officer has the option to answer the questions during the internal investigation, resign, or be dismissed. Thus, *Garrity* and *Gardner* make up the first part of the disciplinary "rules of play" that confront an officer.

The second part of this disciplinary "rules of play" is now set forth in the *LaChance* case. The *LaChance* case (actually six consolidated cases) involved the issue of whether governmental employees could be disciplined both for alleged misconduct that was the subject of an internal investigation and arguably untruthful statements *given* during an interrogation of an officer about the alleged misconduct. The lead case involved an officer under investigation for allegedly making a series of harassing telephone calls. The officer denied the general charge, making harassing calls, but the investigation determined that he had encouraged another person to make the calls. The agency fired the officer for both his participation in the harassing phone calls and giving a false statement, that is, denying his involvement in making the calls, during the internal investigation. When a merit review board reviewed, it reduced the punishment to a fifteen-day suspension. The merit review board concluded that the officer could not be charged separately for untruthfulness because it was not the subject of the investigation, and the officer's denial of the alleged misconduct during the investigation was general in nature.

It was the board's position that the officer should be able to deny charges of misconduct without the denial itself becoming the basis of a more severe charge of untruthfulness. In fact, this rationale proved persuasive when the matter was reviewed by a federal circuit court. As that court noted: if employees were not allowed to make inaccurate statements, they might be "coerced into admitting the misconduct, whether they believed they are guilty or not, to avoid the more severe penalty of removal possibly resulting from a falsification charge."

The Supreme Court disagreed. In a unanimous decision it held that an employee could be disciplined and dismissed both for the misconduct that was the subject of the investigation and "willful falsehoods" made by the employee in denying the specific charges of misconduct made against him.

In upholding the dismissals, the Supreme Court rejected the primary argument of the employees that to allow an agency to add an untruthfulness charge for statements given in an internal affairs investigation could have a chilling effect on the employee's participation in the investigation. The Court dismissed this argument as "entirely frivolous." It found that "the opportunity to be heard does not include the opportunity to lie" and that "if an employee feared that answering a question could subject the employee to criminal prosecution he had the right to remain silent and suffer the consequences of his silence."

After *LaChance,* the rules of play for a police disciplinary investigation are as follows: (1) during a disciplinary interrogation, the officer must answer all questions specifically, narrowly, and directly related to the alleged employment misconduct under investigation, and (2) if the officer's responses or general denial of the misconduct during the investigation is found to be untruthful, such denials or responses can, and probably will, become the basis of an additional disciplinary charge. Who controls these determinations affecting the professional status of the officer? The police administration, of course.

Ensuring the Rules Are Fairly Applied

The reason many states have adopted a law enforcement officer's bill of rights is the result of real and perceived abuses of the disciplinary rules of play by police administrators and internal affairs investigators. Although these administrators and investigators could, and can, require an officer to truthfully answer questions related to specific allegations of misconduct, abuses did occur. Officers under interrogation were mistreated or treated like criminals. Officers were subject to "fishing expeditions," verbal abuse and threats, and exhaustive interviews and were double-teamed by investigators. Access by an officer to a representative or attorney was routinely denied. Officers were cross-examined on fabricated evidence or statements. Confessions or admission were reported when none had occurred.

Certainly, the techniques (noncoercive, of course) were used by police administrators and internal investigators under the banner of "rooting out police corruption and abuses." Unfortunately, it became clear to many police associations and state legislatures that such techniques were misguided and, in many cases, merely a bad means to support a preordained decision about an officer's conduct. The result was the legislative imposition of a law enforcement officers' bill of rights—to protect officers—internally—from overzealous administrators and investigators.

From the comments of various police administrators, one would think that adoption of a law enforcement officers' bill of rights has spelled and will spell the end of a law enforcement agency's ability to investigate and discipline officers for misconduct. That is simply not true!

Set out below is the Florida Law Enforcement Officer's Bill of Rights originally adopted in 1974. Read it—please! It is simple and straightforward. It has not led to a lot of litigation. It has not cost agencies significant money for compliance. It has not led to the inability of supervisors and subordinates to communicate and solve problems. And, I can assure you, it has not prevented law enforcement agencies from investigating and disciplining officers for alleged misconduct. On the contrary, in my experience, agencies that fully comply with the rights set out below have, generally, more professional officers with higher morale because officers are treated fairly, and discipline is not viewed as arbitrary. More importantly, these agencies tend to have a higher success rate when discipline is contested because they have gathered the facts *before* a disciplinary decision is made and not after the decision is made.

112.532   Law enforcement officers' and correctional officers' rights.— All law enforcement officers and correctional officers employed by or appointed to a law enforcement agency or a correctional agency shall have the following rights and privileges:

(1)   RIGHTS OF LAW ENFORCEMENT OFFICERS AND CORRECTIONAL OFFICERS WHILE UNDER INVESTIGATION.—Whenever a law enforcement officer or correctional officer is under investigation and subject to interrogation by members of his or her agency for any reason which could lead to disciplinary action, demotion, or dismissal, such interrogation shall be conducted under the following conditions:

(a)   The interrogation shall be conducted at a reasonable hour, preferably at a time when the law enforcement officer or correctional officer is on duty, unless the seriousness of the investigation is of such a degree that immediate action is required.

(b)   The interrogation shall take place either at the office of the command of the investigating officer or at the office of the local precinct, police unit, or correctional unit in which the incident allegedly occurred, as designated by the investigating officer or agency.

(c)   The law enforcement officer or correctional officer under investigation shall be informed of the rank, name, and command of the officer in charge of the investigation, the interrogating officer, and all persons present during the interrogation. All questions directed to the officer under interrogation shall be asked by and through one interrogator at any one time.

(d)   The law enforcement officer or correctional officer under investigation shall be informed of the nature of the investigation prior to any interrogation, and he or she shall be informed of the name of all complainants.

(e)   Interrogating sessions shall be for reasonable periods and shall be timed to allow for such personal necessities and rest periods as are reasonably necessary.

(f)   The law enforcement officer or correctional officer under interrogation shall not be subjected to offensive language or be threatened with transfer, dismissal, or disciplinary action. No promise or reward shall be made as an inducement to answer any questions.

(g)   The formal interrogation of a law enforcement officer or correctional officer, including all recess periods, shall be recorded, and there shall be no unrecorded questions or statements.

(h)   If the law enforcement officer or correctional officer under interrogation is under arrest, or is likely to be placed under arrest as a result of the interrogation, he or she shall be completely informed of all his or her rights prior to the commencement of the interrogation.

(i)   At the request of any law enforcement officer or correctional officer under investigation, he or she shall have the right to be represented by counsel or any other representative of his or her choice, who shall be present at all times during such interrogation whenever the interrogation relates to the officer's continued fitness for law enforcement or correctional service.

(2)   COMPLAINT REVIEW BOARDS.—A complaint review board shall be composed of three members: One member selected by the chief administrator of the agency or unit; one member selected by the aggrieved officer; and a third member to be selected by the other two members. Agencies or units having more than 100 law enforcement officers or correctional officers shall utilize a five-member board, with two members being selected by the administrator, two members being selected by the aggrieved officer, and the fifth member being selected by the other four members. The board members shall be law enforcement officers or correctional officers selected from any state, county, or municipal agency within the county. There shall be a board for law enforcement officers and a board for correctional officers whose members shall be from the same discipline as the aggrieved officer. The provisions of this subsection shall not apply to sheriffs or deputy sheriffs.

(3)   CIVIL SUITS BROUGHT BY LAW ENFORCEMENT OFFICERS OR CORRECTIONAL OFFICERS.—Every law enforcement officer or correctional officer shall have the right to bring civil suit against any person, group of persons, or organization or corporation, or the head of such organization or corporation, for damages, either pecuniary or otherwise, suffered during the performance of the officer's official duties or for abridgment of the officer's civil rights arising out of the officer's performance of official duties.

(4)   NOTICE OF DISCIPLINARY ACTION.—No dismissal, demotion, transfer, reassignment, or other personnel action which might result in loss of pay or benefits or which might otherwise be considered a punitive measure shall be taken against any law enforcement officer or correctional officer unless such law enforcement officer or correctional officer is notified of the action and the reason or reasons therefore prior to the effective date of such action.

(5)   RETALIATION FOR EXERCISING RIGHTS.—No law enforcement officer or correctional officer shall be discharged; disciplined; demoted; denied promotion, transfer, or reassignment; or otherwise discriminated against in regard to his or her employment or appointment, or be threatened with any such treatment, by reason of his or her exercise of the rights granted by this part.

112.533   Receipt and processing of complaints.—

(1)   Every law enforcement agency and correctional agency shall establish and put into operation a system for the receipt, investigation, and determination of complaints received by such agency from any person.

(2)(a)   A complaint filed against a law enforcement officer or correctional officer with a law enforcement agency or correctional agency and all information obtained pursuant to the investigation by the agency of such complaint shall be confidential and exempt from the provisions of s. 119.07(1) until the investigation ceases to be active, or until the agency head or the agency head's designee provides written notice to the officer who is the subject of the complaint, either personally or by mail, that the agency has either:

1.   Concluded the investigation with a finding not to proceed with disciplinary action or to file charges; or

2.   Concluded the investigation with a finding to proceed with disciplinary action or to file charges.

Notwithstanding the foregoing provisions, the officer who is the subject of the complaint may review the complaint and all written statements made by the complainant and witnesses immediately prior to the beginning of the investigative interview. If a witness to a complaint is incarcerated in a correctional facility and may be under the supervision of, or have contact with, the officer under investigation, only the names and written statements of the complainant and nonincarcerated witnesses may be reviewed by the officer under investigation immediately prior to the beginning of the investigative interview.

(b)   This subsection does not apply to any public record which is exempt from public disclosure pursuant to s. 119.07(3). For the purposes of this subsection, an investigation shall be considered active as long as it is continuing with a reasonable, good faith anticipation that an administrative finding will be made in the foreseeable future. An investigation shall be presumed to be inactive if no finding is made within 45 days after the complaint is filed.

(c)   Notwithstanding other provisions of this section, the complaint and information shall be available to law enforcement agencies, correctional agencies, and state attorneys in the conduct of a lawful criminal investigation.

(3)   Any person who is a participant in an internal investigation, including the complainant, the subject of the investigation, the investigator conducting the investigation, and any witnesses in the investigation, who willfully discloses any information obtained pursuant to the agency's investigation, including, but not limited to, the identity of the officer under investigation, the nature of the questions asked, information revealed, or documents furnished in connection with a confidential internal investigation of an agency, before such complaint, document, action, or proceeding becomes a public

record as provided in this section commits a misdemeanor of the first degree, punishable as provided in s. 775.082 or s. 775.083. However, this subsection does not limit a law enforcement or correctional officer's ability to gain access to information under paragraph (2)(a).

112.534 Failure to comply.—If any law enforcement agency or correctional agency fails to comply with the requirements of this part, a law enforcement officer or correctional officer employed by or appointed to such agency who is personally injured by such failure to comply may apply directly to the circuit court of the county wherein such agency is headquartered and permanently resides for an injunction to restrain and enjoin such violation of the provisions of this part and to compel the performance of the duties imposed by this part.

Conclusion

After reviewing Florida's law, the reader should inquire whether any of the rights provided an officer subject to interrogation are unreasonable. The obvious answer is "no." Candidly, the average legislator or law-abiding citizen would probably expect to be granted such rights when volunteering a statement during a police investigation. Thus, it is clearly reasonable to grant these protections to an officer forced to "volunteer" to participate in the interrogation.

Do the rights outlined in the law prevent investigation of alleged misconduct by an officer? Again, the answer is "no." Police administrators and investigators can investigate alleged misconduct by an officer. The bill of rights merely ensures the officer under investigation knows the subject of the investigation and is afforded rights and protections against certain interrogation techniques subject to abuse. Remember, *Garrity, Gardner,* and *LaChance,* which define the "rules of play," mandate that the officer answer the investigator's questions, and the answer must be truthful or the officer faces dismissal. It is therefore crucial, and now a necessity, that the officer has a level playing field, where the officer understands the factual substance and nature of the alleged misconduct. This is especially true after *LaChance,* where a mistake or misstatement by an officer can become a separate ground for discipline as "untruthfulness." Internal investigation should not be a matter of "trick" techniques or gamesmanship, but a fair and impartial determination of the facts surrounding alleged misconduct.

Still, many police administrators object to being required to afford these basic protections to their officers. Their objections fall into two categories. The first objection from police administrators is: "police have more rights than a common criminal." The answer is that police officers are not common criminals and should not be treated as common criminals. Furthermore, common criminals are not required to participate in an interrogation, answer all the questions, and answer them truthfully. Law enforcement officers are.

The second objection from police administrators is: "police have more rights than other public employees." That is true, but police officers' jobs are not like those of other employees. Any police administrator will tell you law enforcement officers are held to a higher standard of conduct than other employees. Furthermore, other employees are not generally interrogated under oath over the minute details of a traffic stop, use of force, or the discharge of a weapon, with the consequences of a wrong statement being dismissal for untruthfulness. It is ironic that law enforcement agencies train their officers to be prepared and review their reports before a criminal or civil deposition but object to such preparation before an interrogation on which an officer's professional career may rest.

In closing, I must confess I have never understood why police administrators object so vociferously to the law enforcement officer's bill of rights. It merely requires them to treat their officers in a professional, fair, and reasonable manner when required to submit to a mandatory interrogation on an allegation of misconduct. That is not unreasonable when an officer's professional career is on the line. It is an absolute necessity!

CASES CITED

Gardner v. Broderick, 392 U.S. 273, 88 S. Ct. 1913, 20 L.Ed. 2d 1082 (1968).
Garrity v. New Jersey, 385 U.S. 493, 87 S. Ct. 616, 17 L.Ed. 2d 562 (1967).
LaChance v. Erickson, 118 S. Ct. 753 (1998).

Rejoinder to Mr. Johnson
MICHAEL SCOTT

In Mr. Johnson's view, the United States Supreme Court's recent ruling in *La-Chance v. Erickson* represents the death knell for fairness in police disciplinary actions, which fairness can only be restored by a federally legislated police officer's bill of rights. According to Johnson, what was once merely a "need" is now a "necessity" occasioned by this court decision. This very reliance on the *LaChance* case as proof positive that police officers need special employment protections actually suggests that bill of rights proponents do not seek a level playing field at all, but rather one that is decidedly tilted in favor of dishonest police officers.

A fairer reading of the *LaChance* decision is that it corrected an outrageous holding by the lower court, a holding that would have given federal employees the legal privilege to lie to administrators about alleged misconduct. The Supreme Court's decision was unanimous, an indication that it sought to correct bad law rather than to settle a reasonable difference of legal opinion. In *LaChance,* the Supreme Court held that the United States Constitution (nor existing federal statutes) does not preclude a federal agency from sanctioning an employee for making false statements in an internal investigation. As the Court noted, not even criminal suspects enjoy the legal right to tell lies without fear of sanction. The argument to the contrary implies that employees lying to employers about alleged misconduct is simply part of the labor relations game. Particularly in the context of policing, where a police officer's veracity lies at the heart of his or her capacity to be effective, and where the public's interest in controlling abuses of police authority is so keen, the internal investigation of police misconduct should not be viewed as but a game. The adversarial notions of a fair fight in the context of police misconduct must take into account the public's overriding interest in having police officers tell the truth about their actions, whatever the consequences.

The question is not merely whether police administrators and police internal investigators have made or continue to make mistakes, intimidate police officers, or violate basic principles of fairness in investigating misconduct. To be sure, some have and some still do, more so in some departments than in others. The real questions are whether this occurs sufficiently frequently and egregiously to warrant special legislatively granted rights as a remedy, and whether such a remedy would make matters worse than the original ailment. Mr. Johnson simply asserts that police administrators abuse, threaten, and otherwise mistreat police officers during internal investigations, but offers no evidence of the scope or seriousness of the problem. So too does Mr. Johnson assert that the Florida experience with a state legislated law enforcement officer's bill of rights has not led to excessive litigation, added administrative costs, fewer internal investigations, and ineffective supervisory communications, but his assertion is not buttressed by any evidence.

Mr. Johnson posits that Florida police agencies that comply with the provisions of the bill of rights tend to have more professional officers with higher morale because police administrators treat the officers fairly and do not discipline them arbitrarily. His clear implication is that the bill of rights statute is responsible for that fair treatment of officers. The relationship between the fair treatment of officers and the statute may be a spurious one, however, and Johnson's own argument suggests that it is. Although the statute binds all municipal police agencies in Florida, Mr. Johnson acknowledges that the professionalism and fair treatment of officers vary from department to department in the state. It is the police administrators' willingness to fully comply with the provisions of the statute that accounts for the variation, according to Mr. Johnson. It cannot, therefore, be the language of the statute that makes administrators more or less willing to fully comply with its provisions and to treat officers fairly. More likely, it is the police chief executives' own character, sense of fairness, and embodiment of professional ethics that cause them to treat police officers either fairly or unfairly. Police chiefs in Florida who treat officers fairly would do so in the absence of the bill of rights. Those who treat their officers unfairly and discipline them arbitrarily either circumvent the statute or find other means to achieve unfair results.

Mr. Johnson's argument that police officers should not be treated like common criminals is one that appeals more to popular emotions than to reason. Few people would disagree that the position of police officer should be accorded greater respect than the status of criminal offender. When police officers commit crimes, however, they should be treated exactly like criminals, with all the opprobrium reserved for criminal status, but, as important, with all the rights and privileges accorded criminal suspects and defendants. This much the law already guarantees. Neither the common criminal, invoked to generate the reader's antipathy, nor the legislator or law-abiding citizen, invoked to generate the reader's sympathy, enjoys the sorts of legal protections contemplated by a police officer's bill of rights, however. Few citizens indeed, law-abiding or otherwise, enjoy the protection of special statutes that govern and limit their employers' prerogative to enforce the rules of employment and to discipline and dismiss unfit employees.

The holdings of the Supreme Court in the cases Johnson cites in support of a legislated police officer's bill of rights (*Garrity, Gardner, LaChance*) are misconstrued and overstated. In none of those cases did the Supreme Court mandate that employees answer investigators' questions, truthfully or otherwise, or prescribe what penalties employees will face for failing to respond or be truthful. Those matters the Court left up to the employer. It is the employer's rules that determine whether the employee under investigation must answer questions and the consequences for failing to answer truthfully. The Court only said that the Constitution does not prohibit public employers from imposing such requirements and that the state could not exploit the less restrictive rules of employment to circumvent the rules of criminal process. Just as the Supreme Court takes care not to overstep its appropriate authority and unnecessarily dictate matters of employment, so too should legislatures exercise caution in regulating matters better left to employers and employees.

Far from being an "absolute necessity," a legislated police officer's bill of rights represents an extraordinary measure of special employment protection for a select sector of the labor market, a sector that has demonstrated more than ample capacity to safeguard its own legitimate interests at the local political and organizational level. However reasonable or benign its proponents make the legislation sound, a statutory police officer's bill of rights is at best unnecessary and at worst a threat to the checks and balances against abuses of authority by the police.

CASES CITED

Gardner v. Broderick, 392 U.S. 273, 88 S. Ct. 1913, 20 L. Ed. 2d 1082 (1968).
Garrity v. New Jersey, 385 U.S. 493, 87 S. Ct. 616, 17 L. Ed. 2d 562 (1967).
LaChance v. Erickson, 118 S. Ct. 753 (1998).

NO

MICHAEL SCOTT

A police officer's bill of rights is a collection of guarantees and prohibitions regulating how police officers are investigated and disciplined for administrative rule violations. It is a set of employment rights. At least seventeen states have enacted such legislation, and Congress has deliberated a federal bill for over twenty years (U.S. House of Representatives, 1993; Chiuchiolo, 1981). Each of these state bills of rights and the many federal bills that have been proposed vary in the scope of protection they offer and in the remedies for violations of those rights (Illinois Law Enforcement Commission, 1981). It is not possible, therefore, to characterize all of this legislation unilaterally. However, the basic premises of such legislation only confound an already complex area of public policy without substantially improving police labor-management relations. Plainly stated, a legislated bill of rights for police officers is bad public policy.

Applying the Principle of Equal Treatment

Police officers should be protected against arbitrary and unfair disciplinary procedures. I have argued against such policies and drafted and adopted policies granting some of these very protections while serving in various policy-making positions. Where others, including some police unions, have argued in favor of random drug testing of police officers, I have argued against it. The main underlying argument in favor of safeguarding police officers from arbitrary or excessively intrusive disciplinary practices is that police officers should be accorded the same protections they are expected to accord citizens in the course of their duties. Police officers tend to treat the public in the same measure they themselves are treated by their supervisors and managers. If police administrators do not respect police officers' rights and privileges, they should not be surprised to find that officers view citizens' rights and privileges with cynicism and disrespect. This argument is reciprocal, though, and it is under this equal treatment principle that legislated police officers' bills of rights fail.

Most versions of police officers' bills of rights grant far greater protections to police officers than are legislatively mandated for the average worker. Extending police officers greater rights and privileges than other similarly situated workers will inspire in the public cynicism and disrespect of police officers. Police officers have unique responsibilities and liabilities that other workers do not, but they also have unique power and authority. To the greatest extent possible, police officers should be treated the same as other workers, with no fewer rights and protections, but no more.

In the American constitutional framework, rights and privileges are fashioned by courts and legislatures, taking into account the balance of interests at stake. In the context of policing, the predominant public interest is in safeguarding against abuses of police authority. It is at least as important as the public interest in effective policing and more important than individual police officers' employment rights. This is asserted not to trivialize the significance of employment rights in the constitutional framework, but to elevate to the highest constitutional level the public's interest in curtailing police abuse of authority.

Where police officers face unique and unusual exposure, they should be accorded unique protection. For example, some states appropriately restrict the release to the public of the home addresses and other personal information about police officers because the nature of police officers' work creates unusual risks for officers if this information were readily available to the public. Police officers are not, however, uniquely or unusually exposed to complaints, administrative investigation, or discipline in the course of their work. All workers are subject to these employment hazards, up to and including the potential loss of their employment. Every occupation presents a somewhat distinct pattern in the motives for and nature of administrative complaints and investigations, but the distinctiveness of a pattern does not in and of itself make the pattern so unusual as to warrant special protection.

Existing statutory and case law adequately protects police officers' employment rights as it protects the employment rights of similarly situated workers. Police officers enjoy all of the constitutional rights and privileges granted to every citizen, with respect to both criminal and administrative investigations. The United States Supreme Court has issued a number of rulings that make clear that police officers and other public employees do not forfeit these rights and privileges simply by accepting public employment. In *Garrity v. New Jersey* (1967), the Court's ruling safeguarded police officers' Fifth Amendment privilege against self-incrimination in criminal proceedings. In *Pickering v. Board of Education* (1968), the Court asserted that public employees do not forfeit all their rights to freedom of speech. In *Garcia v. San Antonio Metropolitan Transit Authority* (1985), the Court extended the Fair Labor Standards Act to state and municipal employees. In *Cleveland Board of Education v. Loudermill* (1985), the Court recognized certain procedural due process rights of tenured public employees, including the right of the employee to notice of charges, an explanation of evidence, and the opportunity to be heard. These latter rights are some of the same sorts of rights included in police officer's bills of rights. In sum, the United States Supreme Court and state supreme courts have demonstrated a willingness and ability to safeguard the constitutional protections of public employees, including police officers.

The U.S. Supreme Court has, however, made clear that not every protection contemplated by police officer's bills of rights are constitutional matters. The Court limited its holding in *Loudermill* by asserting, "To require more than [notice, explanation of evidence, and opportunity to be heard] prior to termination would intrude to an unwarranted extent on the government's interest in quickly removing an unsatisfactory employee." The Court had already cautioned in *Bishop v. Wood* (1976) that "The federal court is not the appropriate forum in which to review the multitude of personnel decisions that are made daily by public agencies." The federal courts are already in danger of being overwhelmed by litigation involving the routine matters of state and local governance. A federal police officer's bill of rights would unnecessarily add to this burden. The Court's rulings do not, of course, prohibit the Congress or state legislatures from legislatively creating additional rights and privileges for police officers, but the rulings should be instructive and caution-ary to legislatures about maintaining an appropriate balance of interests in matters of public employment.

Much of the American constitutional framework rests on the principle of bal-anced powers. The powers of the police must be governed and abuses of that power corrected and curtailed. Although there exist a number of legal, political, and ad-ministrative mechanisms for correcting and curtailing police abuse of authority, the most consistently effective mechanism is internal administrative discipline (Presi-dent's Commission, 1967; Perez and Muir, 1995). Police administrators are prima-rily responsible for administering this discipline. To effectively meet this obligation, they must be granted sufficient authority to investigate misconduct and take appro-priate corrective action. Any proposal that limits police administrators' authority in this regard must consider the degree to which such limitations threaten the public interest in controlling abuse of police authority.

The patterns of police abuse of authority have been reasonably well docu-mented at various times and places throughout the country (Goldstein, 1977). No single pattern holds throughout all jurisdictions, but few jurisdictions have not witnessed some widespread abuses at some point in their police departments' his-tories. The problem is as pervasive as it is enduring. The patterns of abuse of ad-ministrators' power in administering discipline is no doubt real, but considerably less well documented. Perhaps this is because far fewer persons are directly af-fected by the abuses of police administrators' authority in personnel matters than are affected by police officers' abuse of authority, but a compelling statistical case has yet to be made that the problem of abusive police administrative authority is a national crisis. Absent such a crisis, the interest of protecting police employment rights ought to remain subservient to the public interest in controlling police abuse of authority.

Applying the Principles of Federalism

The principle of federalism argues that governmental power ought to be central-ized in matters of national concern and decentralized in matters of local or state concern. In no other realm has the principle of local control been more jealously guarded than it has been in policing. The American antipathy toward federal po-licing is legendary. Despite all the confusion, redundancy, and inefficiency of having tens of thousands of police forces throughout the country, no effort to cre-ate a single federal or even state police force with exclusive jurisdiction has ever succeeded. Even more modest proposals to establish national standards for police administration have produced only voluntary programs and standards (e.g., the Commission on Accreditation of Law Enforcement Agencies, Inc.). The police, like other sectors of the labor force, are governed by such federal laws as the Americans with Disabilities Act, the Fair Labor Standards Act, and the Age Dis-

held accountable. Inasmuch as accountability is a local, or at best a state concern, then police administrators' authority to investigate and respond to misconduct must also be a local, or at best a state concern.

Of primary concern to the local jurisdictions that operate police forces are unfunded federal mandates. A federal police officer's bill of rights will present yet another unfunded mandate to the states and localities. Any set of rights and privileges, particularly ones as comprehensive as most versions of police officer's bills of rights, carries with it fiscal obligations to fund the procedural mechanisms for enforcing these rights. The costs of a comprehensive system are substantial, and most will be borne by the local jurisdiction (Chiuchiolo, 1981). These costs include the direct costs to the local jurisdiction in attorneys' fees, document production, hearing board expenses, and administrators' time, as well as indirect costs such as lost opportunities (what police supervisors and administrators might do more productively with their time and attention). As any police administrator can attest, contested personnel matters can become enormously time consuming, crowding off the administrator's calendar many otherwise important duties. Depending on the specific remedies for bill of rights errors and the forum in which they are to be heard, the amount of additional time consumed by personnel matters could well become significantly greater. This would be particularly true in the first few decades after enactment of a federal police officer's bill of rights, when litigants would challenge the "substantial similarity" of existing state protections with the new federal mandates. (State provisions of law must generally be "substantially similar" to corresponding federal provisions for the state to be exempt from the specific provisions of the federal law.) A related concern to local jurisdictions is the likely expansion of liability for due process claims that a federal police officer's bill of rights would bring.

The laws of the various states pertaining to the rights of public employees vary considerably. For example, some states recognize police officers' rights to collective bargaining, and other states expressly prohibit such bargaining. Within each state there exists a framework of statutes, case law, collective bargaining agreements, arbitration decisions, and administrative rulings under which police personnel matters are resolved. Each state's framework has evolved to provide for its police officers a set of rights and responsibilities that reflect the public policy of that state. The federal constitution does not require all states to have a uniform public policy on labor relations. Indeed, the federal system of government is strengthened by diversity of law, which fosters experimentation and progressive legislation. In the absence of a compelling national interest to establish uniformity, the public policies and corresponding legal framework of the states should be respected.

Balancing Employment Interests with the Public Interest in Controlling Police Misconduct

It is not the case, as some might claim, that a police officer's bill of rights is a good idea that is merely too expensive or abstractly offensive to states' rights. The substance of some of the common provisions of police officer's bills of rights are mis-guided policy as well. A number of provisions are oversolicitous of police officers in the internal investigative arena. These provisions extend greater legal protection to police officers than the law recognizes for criminal suspects. For example, most versions of police officer's bills of rights preclude police administrators from using more than one person to interview the police officer, presuming that multiple inter-viewers are inherently coercive or confusing to the officer. No similar flat prohibi-tion on multiple interviewers is to found in criminal case law when police officers are interviewing suspects. One is hard-pressed to imagine why police officers, trained in the techniques of interviewing and the laws governing interrogations, should be seen as more vulnerable than the least intelligent and resourceful private citizen facing even more threatening circumstances. Indeed, police officers often use multiple interviewers in criminal cases, for a variety of reasons. The technique can prove effective without being impermissibly coercive. It defies logic that police administrators should be precluded from using similarly effective, noncoercive in-terviewing methods. Similarly, many versions of police officer's bills of rights pre-clude police administrators from questioning officers while off duty or anywhere other than the workplace, restrictions that have no counterpart in the criminal in-vestigation context.

Some versions of police officer's bills of rights preclude police administra-tors from initiating an investigation of a police officer on the basis of an anony-mous or unsigned complaint, presumably because such complaints are regarded as inherently unreliable. Again, no similar flat prohibition exists when police of-ficers investigate criminal suspects. There the courts inquire into the totality of the circumstances to determine the reasonableness of the police response to anon-ymous and confidential complaints against private citizens. In the criminal con-text, one can hardly imagine how the police could effectively investigate serious criminal activity without at least occasionally using confidential informants and anonymous tips. As the seriousness of the offense increases, so too do the reason-able fears of witnesses for retaliation. This is no less true with respect to police misconduct than crime. Police administrators' abilities to investigate serious po-lice misconduct would be compromised if they were not permitted to proceed on the basis of anonymous or confidential information. If citizen witnesses to police misconduct were compelled to identify themselves to the offending police offi-cers, they would understandably be more reluctant to provide any information at all.

The most expansive versions of police officer's bills of rights that invoke all procedural safeguards for any questioning that might lead to disciplinary action will also have a chilling effect on the relationship between police supervisors and their officers. Good police management practices vest supervisors with responsi-bility to correct police officers' bad performance and minor misconduct and suf-ficient disciplinary authority to do so. Supervisors often cannot know precisely what consequences will follow from inquiring into police officers' actions. A supervisor's inquiry often satisfies the supervisor that the officer's actions were reasonable and justified, but if the supervisor is not so satisfied, the inquiry could lead to warnings or reprimands. The supervisor might subsequently learn that the officer's disciplinary record warrants more severe corrective action such as suspension from duty. In such instances, the supervisor could inadvertently have initiated questioning of the officer without all of the procedural protections guaranteed by the police officer's bill of rights. A prudent and cautious supervisor, faced with the possibility of jeopardizing an internal investigation or risking supervisory liability, will be hesitant to inquire too deeply into police officers' actions without formalizing the interview process. This inevitable formalization of the supervisor–officer relationship will transform the relationship into an adversarial one, and supervisors will be less inclined to resolve minor rule infraction informally (Chiuchiolo, 1981). Much of the potential for informal teaching and mentoring by supervisor of officer will be stifled. Even if police officer's bills of rights are carefully worded to allow some informal questioning, the maze of rules and restrictions will be complicated enough to discourage supervisors from questioning the actions of their officers. The net effect of complicating the supervisor–officer relationship will be that police officers will be even less likely to have to explain and justify their actions than they are now. This will erode a critical mechanism by which police officers are held accountable (Vaughn, 1992).

The remedies for violations of the various rights and privileges incorporated in police officer's bills of rights are not always clearly defined. Some bills provide for declaratory or injunctive relief. Some violations might yield claims for monetary damages. Courts might, as they did in the criminal law field, impose an exclusionary rule on police administrators that would preclude the use any testimony or evidence derived in violation of a provision of the police officer's bill of rights. Were this to occur, the public would be asked to pay an inordinately high price to keep police administrators faithful to the technicalities of the administrative process. An exclusionary rule would create an even greater risk that incompetent, brutal, or corrupt police officers would remain employed as police officers with the full knowledge of police administrators. The U.S. Supreme Court acknowledges the high price of the criminal law exclusionary rule but is mindful that this price is balanced against a fundamental public interest in guarding against police abuse of authority.

In holding that the suspension without pay of a police officer who had been arrested for a felony before a hearing did not deny the officer due process of law under the Constitution, the Court explicitly acknowledged the significant interest of the government in disciplining "employees who occupy positions of great public trust and high public visibility, such as police officers" (*Gilbert v. Homar,* 1997). In the context of the police officer's bill of rights, it is that fundamental public interest in guarding against police abuse of authority that is sacrificed for the employment interests of police officers. To elevate employment rights above the public interest in preventing the overreach of government would surely be a perversion of the principles of democracy.

Conclusion

On one level the concept of a police officer's bill of rights seems fair and just. Police officers are, in the main, society's good guys. If criminal defendants have special rights by virtue of their status, then it might seem fair for police officers to have some rights by virtue of their status as well. Increasingly, victims of crime are being granted rights by legislatures. If we endow them with special rights, why not also endow their guardians, the police? Expanding the notion of rights in a democracy to an ever wider range of activities, however, does not honor the notion but trivializes and marginalizes it.

A police officer's bill of rights tries to equate the balance of power between police employees and police employers with the balance of power between the government and the individual citizen. These sets of relationships are not equal. The American Constitution, through the Bill of Rights, exists largely to give the individual citizen a fighting chance when confronted by the enormous power of the state. Police officers as employees are not so otherwise powerless when confronted by their employer, even if that employer is the government. Police officers in many jurisdictions have, through collective action, become powerful enough to protect their own interests in their relations with their employers. Some police unions have successfully negotiated police officer's bills of rights into the collective bargaining agreements (Burpo, 1972). This is proof enough that police officers do not need the special protection of the legislature. Moreover, most professional organizations of police administrators have track records of endorsing fair personnel practices that include some, though not all, of the procedural requirements contemplated by a police officer's bills of rights (Vaughn, 1992). Police officers as employees are today better viewed as a relatively powerful group confronting an adversary in labor relations that accedes to some, and shares some, of the police officers' interests in administrative fairness.

Police officers do hold a unique place in society and in the government. In an almost paradoxical way, police officers have as much or more discretionary authority than do many higher ranking government officials. Certainly, the authority they have is more profound. To a large degree, a police officer's value to the community and to society depends on that officer's integrity, especially on the officer's judgment, competence, and honesty. Where those traits are found to be lacking, the officer is of little value, even of negative value, to the community. In this respect, police services are personal services, the value of which is heavily dependent on the unique abilities of the individual officer. The communities that employ police officers have a right to select and deselect those individuals who can and cannot provide the desired personal services. The converse is not true: Individuals do not have the right to be police officers (see Justice Holmes in *McAuliffe v. Mayor of New Bedford* [1892]). Police officers have certain rights to be judged fairly and perhaps on occasion to be compensated for losing their employment as police officers. Under a democratic form of government, however, it makes little sense to create an artificial set of rights that makes it unnecessarily difficult for a community to exercise its right to choose and retain those individuals in whom it will vest its most precious trust. In this way, a police officer's bill of rights makes little sense.

REFERENCES

Bishop v. Wood, 426 U.S. 341, 96 S. Ct. 2074, 48 L. Ed. 2d 684 (1976).

Burpo, J. (1972). The policeman's bill of rights. *Police Chief, 39* (9), 18.

Chiuchiolo, M. (1981). The law enforcement officer's bill of rights: Panacea or problem? *Police Chief, 68* (12), 70–72.

Cleveland Board of Education v. Loudermill, 470 U.S. 532, 105 S. Ct. 1487, 84 L. E. 2d 494 (1985).

Garcia v. San Antonio Metropolitan Transit Authority, 469 U.S. 528, 105 S. Ct. 1005, 83 L. Ed. 2d 1016 (1985).

Garrity v. New Jersey, 385 U.S. 493, 87 S. Ct. 616, 17 L. Ed. 2d 562 (1967).

Gilber v. Homar, 117 S. Ct. 1897 (1997).

Goldstein, H. (1977). *Policing a free society.* Cambridge, MA: Ballinger Publication. (Reprinted by the Board of Regents of the University of Wisconsin, 1990).

Illinois Law Enforcement Commission. (1981). *A guide to data sources on police bills of rights.* Springfield, IL: Illinois Law Enforcement Commission.

McAuliffe v. Mayor of New Bedford, 155 Mass. 216, 220, 29 N. E. 517 (1892).

Perez, D., & Muir, W. K. (1995). Administrative review of alleged police brutality. In W. Geller and H. Toch (Eds.), *And justice for all: Understanding and controlling police abuse of force.* Washington, DC: Police Executive Research Forum.

Pickering v. Board of Education, 391 U.S. 563, 88 S. Ct. 1731, 20 L. Ed. 2d 811 (1968).

President's Commission on Law Enforcement and the Administration of Justice. (1967). *The challenge of crime in a free society.* Washington, DC: U.S. Government Printing Office.

U.S. House of Representatives. (1993). *Rights of police officers during internal investigations: Hearing before the Sub-committee on Crime and Criminal Justice.* Washington, DC: U.S. Government Printing Office.

Vaughn, C. R. (1992). The police officer's bill of rights: A needless intrusion. *Police Chief, 59* (5), 6.

Rejoinder to Mr. Scott Hal Johnson

I read with some interest the comments of Michael Scott and his assessment of various forms of proposed federal legislation establishing a police officer's bill of rights. Contrary to Mr. Scott's commentary, I do not agree that its passage will recrimination in Employment Act. Few federal statutes or regulations, however, uniquely govern police personnel matters.

Proponents of police officer's bills of rights claim that federal legislation is necessary to ensure uniformity across jurisdictions in the regulation of police officer disciplinary matters. They further claim that a full panoply of rights must be included in a federal bill of rights because of the interrelatedness of the several issues attendant to internal investigations and discipline. If these two arguments are valid, then they argue for creating a uniform federal code for all police personnel matters. Just as surely as rights of appeal are interrelated with rights to counsel in police internal disciplinary matters, so too are police disciplinary matters interrelated with police selection standards, training standards, and supervision standards. If it makes sense to ensure uniformity in how police officers are investigated and disciplined, it logically makes sense to ensure uniformity in matters that influence the need for officers to be investigated and disciplined in the first instance. A federal code of regulations for police personnel matters might then dictate minimum national standards for employment, training, promotion, and so forth. Yet, local control of policing means little if it does not place police personnel matters within the control of local officials. It is through these very personnel mechanisms that local communities, through their local officials, exert great influence on local police practices and priorities. To abrogate police personnel matters to the federal government is in essence to abrogate local control of policing.

To make the case for the importance of uniformity in the area of police internal investigations and discipline, proponents claim that local political pressure can improperly influence police administrators' decisions in these matters. They claim that a set of federal standards will mitigate such untoward influence. This claim seems fanciful in that those who exert improper political influence are chiefly interested in the final disposition of an internal investigation, a matter not addressed by any police officer's bill of rights. Moreover, local political influence cuts in several ways. Police officers accused of misconduct are as likely to be the beneficiaries of political influence as its victims. Surely as many police officers have been spared discipline by the benevolence of a political patron as have been unjustly punished for political expediency. The tenure provisions and accountability mechanisms of the local police administrators account for local political influence far more than could a police officer's bill of rights.

Police administrators are held accountable by a wide range of mechanisms, some legal and some political. The mechanisms vary across jurisdictions. There is no federal statute or national standard of any sort that governs these accountability mechanisms. If police administrators are to be held accountable at least partly for the manner and extent to which they control their officers' use of authority, as well they should be, then it stands to reason that the specific provisions governing their authority to investigate and discipline wrongdoing should correspond to those specific mechanisms for accountability. In other words, police administrators should have authority commensurate with the measures by which they will be

sult in the end of the free world as we know it, in the financial ruin of states, cities, or counties that must comply with its terms, or the absolute inability of police agencies to investigate and discipline their officers. You must understand, however, I know better because I represent police officers in a state that has had police officers' bill of rights since the early 1970s.

No, Mr. Scott, granting police officers a uniform set of rights while they are under investigation is not an attack on motherhood, apple pie, and the American way. It is merely a reasonable set of guidelines for investigating individuals charged with the difficult task of enforcing our laws and dealing with the criminal element in our society. If you cannot provide police officers with a reasonable set of rights while they are under investigation, then why expect them to honor the basic rights of individuals who they have reasonable grounds to believe are criminals?

Let me get off my soapbox and back to Mr. Scott's commentary. His first reason for rejecting a uniform police officers' bill of rights is succinctly summarized as "equal treatment under the law." Mr. Scott is apparently offended that police officers are seeking a bill of rights that are not available to other public employees because "[p]olice officers are not, however, unique or unusually exposed to complaints, administrative investigation, or discipline in the course of their work."

Where did Mr. Scott do his police work? How many secretaries do you know who are interrogated under oath and subject to possible criminal charges about the manner in which they effected an arrest, the use of force, or their pursuit of a fleeing felony? How many secretaries are expected to recall in specific detail how a traffic stop was handled, the tone of voice used during the stop, and whether something was said by them that could be interpreted as offensive? How many secretaries are subject to lose their employment, and possibly their career, if their responses are determined to be "untruthful"? No, Mr. Scott, police officers are not like other public employees. If they are, then those employees need a bill of rights too.

Mr. Scott's next rationale for rejecting a federal police officer's bill of rights is that law enforcement agencies "must be granted sufficient authority to investigate misconduct and take appropriate corrective action" to prevent "police abuse of authority." Such a statement sounds reasonable, but the simple fact is the police officer's bill of rights does not in any manner prevent the investigation or discipline of police officers. It provides minimal safeguards for ensuring that the interrogation of an officers is done under reasonable circumstances. Can Mr. Scott argue with a straight face that allowing an officer under interrogation time for "personal necessities" will impede an agency's ability to conduct a full investigation of an officer and take disciplinary action?

Furthermore, *Garrity v. New Jersey* requires a police officer subject to an administrative interrogation to answer all questions reasonably related to the complainant under investigation. The officer cannot refuse to answer such questions without being subject to disciplinary action. With such a requirement in place, any competent law enforcement agency and its investigators should be able to ferret out "police abuse" and still comply with the minimal safeguards afforded to police officers by a bill of rights. Let's not forget that the reason various states have adopted a police officer's bill of rights is because the various legislatures were convinced that abuses of police authority were occurring against police officers during internal investigations.

The next reason advanced by Mr. Scott for rejecting a uniform bill of rights is that it "will present yet another unfunded mandate to the states and localities." Mr. Scott advises this includes direct costs of compliance—bathroom breaks are expensive—and other costs that result from an agency's failure to comply with the safeguards outlined in the bill of rights.

Well, Mr. Scott, you should know that Florida has had a police officer's bill of rights for almost twenty-five years. The litigation over it has been minimal. To date, I am unaware of the "state and localities" bankrupted by compliance with it. Furthermore, having handled disciplinary cases on behalf of officers for twenty years, I can recount only a handful of instances in which discipline was not sustained against a officer for violations of the bill of rights—and in those instances the punishment was usually reduced, not overturned.

My experience is that a law enforcement agency that complies with the police officer's bill of rights is far better prepared to defend the disciplinary action it metes out against an officer, because the agency has done a thorough investigation and has the appropriate evidence and necessary witnesses to support its disciplinary case. I do not have any empirical data to support my position, but my experience indicates that compliance with the bill of rights by an agency saves it money because it can successfully defend the disciplinary action it takes.

The final reason advanced by Mr. Scott for rejecting adoption of a police officer's bill of rights appears to be that the safeguards provided will prevent agencies from utilizing various police techniques that are effective and used in the interrogation of criminal suspects. The response to this contention is found in the contention itself: police officers are not criminals and should not be treated as criminals.

As previously stated, police officers in an administrative investigation are required to answer questions reasonably related to the subject of the complaint under investigation. The officer cannot refuse to answer. The officer cannot claim the privilege against self-incrimination. The officer cannot get up and leave. Simply put, Mr. Scott's claim that law enforcement agencies need to treat their officers as criminals to get the facts is not true. All the agency has to do is ask the officer the questions it wants answered after complying with certain procedural safeguards.

In closing, it is my experience that good, well-administered law enforcement agencies do not have a problem with the police officer's bill of rights. Those agencies treat their officers as officers and not criminal suspects. When they take disciplinary action, there is usually some basis for it (not always), and the discipline is generally sustainable on appeal. I guess that is the real purpose of the police officer's bill of rights: to treat officers fairly and objectively during a disciplinary investigation. I guess Mr. Scott has a basic problem with that purpose.

CASE CITED

Garrity v. New Jersey, 385 U.S. 493, 87 S. Ct. 616, 17 L.Ed. 2d 562 (1967).

Are Juvenile Curfews a Legal and Effective Way to Reduce Juvenile Crime?

EDITOR'S NOTE: Especially over the last several years, the issue of escalating juvenile crime has confronted political leaders, law enforcement officers, and citizens. Adults search for methods to control criminal and delinquent behavior and reduce the opportunity for crime to occur. Programs such as the Serious Habitual Offender Comprehensive Action Program (SHOCAP) focus on the worst juvenile criminals, and Drug Abuse Resistance Education (DARE) and Gang Resistance Education and Training (GREAT) attempt to strengthen the resolve of the "good kids." Yet crime and delinquent acts committed by juveniles still occur, and frustrated citizens and politicians look for new, more effective means of protecting society. One approach adopted in a number of cities is the curfew law, designed to keep minors off the streets after certain nighttime hours.

Lee Freeman O'Brien has served since 1991 as Police Legal Advisor to the City of Orlando Police Department. She, along with others from the City Attorney's Office, successfully defended against the ACLU's challenge to the Orlando Youth Protection Ordinance. Ms. O'Brien has prior experience as a state prosecutor and as the state's legal representative in child abuse, neglect, and abandonment proceedings. She received her Juris Doctorate in 1985 from The Florida State University and has been a member of the Florida Bar since 1986.

Professor Paul Joseph teaches law at the Shepard Broad Law Center of Nova Southeastern University, in Fort Lauderdale, Florida. He is a past-president of the Florida American Civil Liberties Union (ACLU) and a former member of the ACLU national board. Professor Joseph received his B.A. from Goddard College, his J.D. from the University of California at Davis, and his LL.M. from Temple University Law Center.

YES

LEE FREEMAN O'BRIEN

Communities nationwide have experienced an alarming increase in youth-related offenses. Graffiti, vandalism, and property crimes are on the rise. Violent acts committed by minors are unacceptably high. Organized gangs, once thought to exist only in certain areas of the largest cities, have found their way to smaller cities, towns, and suburban areas. The number of children falling victim to acts of violence is horrifying. Many parents seem to have lost control over their children or to have abdicated responsibility out of fear, disinterest, or naiveté.

The ability of government to "get tough" with runaways, habitual truants, and ungovernable children is virtually nonexistent in light of federal and state laws limiting the actions permitted against so-called status offenders. Traditional system resources available for juvenile delinquency intervention, punishment, and rehabilitation are stretched beyond their limits.

Communities must now find more creative ways to deal with the problems presented by minors who aimlessly roam our streets at all hours of the night. Local governments correctly assess the combination of unsupervised idleness and the normal impulsiveness of teenagers as a recipe for disaster.

Although some major metropolitan cities have had juvenile curfews for decades, the use of curfews as an effective crime prevention and citizen protection tool did not become popular until the 1990s. According to one study, as many as 146 of the largest 200 cities in the United States had curfew laws on their books by mid-1995 (Ruefle and Reynolds, 1996). The latter half of this decade has witnessed many smaller cities, towns, and boroughs following this trend.

Critics argue that any kind of curfew aimed at minors is an infringement on constitutional rights. More emotionally, they accuse local governments of enacting these laws as a cosmetic effort to quell community fear of juvenile delinquency.

In fact, few government officials would choose to be faced with the prospect of enacting juvenile curfews. Many have children, and each remembers his or her own teenage years. Some may recall the daunting prospect of facing selective service during the Vietnam War and wonder whether curtailing the nighttime activities of today's sixteen- and seventeen-year-olds seems fair. Few governmental officials are naive enough to believe that a curfew, standing alone, is the great panacea to their crime problems. Instead, they arrive at a decision to enact curfews only after studying their community's unique situation, assessing possible alternatives, and putting in place a multifaceted approach to curb the problem of juvenile crime and juvenile victimization. Most naysayers fail to mention the fact that a curfew keeps a child in a safe environment, thereby preventing that child from becoming another crime statistic.

The harsh reality, however, is that times have changed. A good look at the news reveals that our youths are no longer the "innocent children" we think of when we wax nostalgic. Instead, there are alarming incidents of murder, rape, robbery, aggravated assaults, firearms violations, and more. Sophisticated, illegal drug use among teens is prolific. Not all children are involved, but all children are affected. Society in general is profoundly impacted by this appalling trend. Communities, through their elected officials, have the right to protect themselves from the impetuous nature of juvenile offenders. Parents often need laws to assist them in keeping their children at home. Moreover, the community has the right to ensure the safety of citizens of every age.

For any juvenile curfew to withstand legal challenge, it is imperative that it be constitutionally sound. A curfew law must be able to pass a "strict scrutiny" test by demonstrating (1) that there is a compelling governmental interest and (2) that the legislation is narrowly drawn to achieve the governmental objective.

The city of Dallas passed this critical test in federal court in 1993 by showing that it had a vital interest in reducing juvenile crime and juvenile victimization, while ensuring that its ordinance was carefully drafted to meet those goals and still respect the interests of its minor citizens (*Qutb v. Strauss*). City officials compiled and studied powerful statistical information regarding crimes committed by and on children. The city was also able to establish that the vast majority of these crimes occurred in the late night and early morning hours. Dallas ensured that specific exceptions for constitutionally protected activities were incorporated into their ordinance. These exceptions included minors who are accompanied by an adult; engaged in interstate commerce or First Amendment–protected activities; traveling to or from work; responding to an emergency; attending activities sponsored by a school, religious organization, or civic group; or married.

Many large cities and small towns have followed Dallas's example. Additionally, some states have adopted legislation enabling their political subdivisions to adopt curfew legislation.

Other communities have taken a more limited, but also effective, approach. The success of a limited approach depends largely on the nature, scope, and location of the juvenile problem in a community. By way of example, the city of Orlando enacted a Youth Protection Ordinance in 1994 after a citizen board determined that an inordinate number of youths were committing, or falling victim to, crimes committed in its downtown entertainment district. That district is composed of approximately twelve square blocks of commercial property, where the nighttime establishments cater primarily to an adult crowd. Children drawn to this area at night had no place to go and had become a menace to many and potential prey to the criminals. Instead of a citywide curfew, the city ultimately passed a curfewlike protection ordinance applicable only in the downtown entertainment district. On initial contact, officers issue unaccompanied minors a written trespass warning. A child who subsequently returns to the restricted area during the prohibited hours is subject to arrest for misdemeanor trespassing. In the two years after enactment of the ordinance, more than three thousand written warnings were issued to offending juveniles in the restricted area. During that same period, fewer than 140 arrests were made for trespassing in violation of those warnings. Orlando was fortunate to be able to curb a large portion of its juvenile crime and victimization problem without having to impose a citywide curfew.

Research shows that the vast majority of communities do not enact a curfew and expect their youth-related problems to simply vanish. Officials and civic leaders also look at other community-based resources to assist them in creating programs or other means through which to channel their children's interests. Among the many creative solutions nationwide are nighttime sports and recreational programs; incentives and challenges issued to private industry to create diversionary and mentoring programs for teens; drug and crime education, awareness and prevention programs; coalitions with other youth-oriented community groups; identifying at-risk children at younger ages to implement intervention efforts; and other community programs limited only by imagination and resources. These programs not only deter juvenile crime and victimization during their respective curfew hours, but also identify vulnerable children with drug abuse and alcohol problems, mental heath concerns, and other behaviors that may lead to criminal behavior or victimization. These programs, in conjunction with curfew laws, enable the community to employ resources to prevent more serious problems in the future.

REFERENCES

LeBoeuf, D., & Brennan, P. (1996). Curfew: An answer to juvenile delinquency and victimization? *Juvenile Justice Bulletin.* Washington, DC: U.S. Department of Justice, Office of Juvenile Justice and Delinquency Prevention.

Ruefle, W., & Reynolds, K. M. (1996). Keep them at home: Juvenile curfew ordinances in 200 American cities. *American Journal of Police, 15* (1), 63–84.

CASE CITED

Qutb v. Strauss. 11 F. 3d 488 (5th Cir. 1993).

Rejoinder to Ms. O'Brien   PAUL JOSEPH

A careful reading of the "procurfew" essay reveals that its arguments rest on fundamentally inconsistent premises. It suggests that kids today are vicious thugs who prey on society. However, it also suggests that curfews are needed to protect these vulnerable young innocents from the terrors of the big city. Under both views, parental responsibility is almost casually dismissed in favor of government control. The "procurfew" side cannot have it both ways.

Make no mistake: curfews are punitive. They turn children into criminals merely for using the public streets and sidewalks. Curfews do not differentiate between the class president returning home from a late movie with parental permission, a child afraid to go to his home because of abuse, and the young criminal. All are treated the same. All are made into criminals. The "crime" for all is merely being out at night. That's what's so bad about curfews!

The "procurfew" side makes sweeping generalizations about crime and the character of kids and parents. These sweeping statements, offered in emotionally charged language and without any proof, then become the basis for a proposal to ban all kids from the streets and to treat them as criminals should they be found outside after some arbitrarily chosen time.

Let's drop the rhetoric and get serious. Society has a right to protect itself from kids who commit crimes, but society has no legitimate right to treat *all* kids as criminals merely because they use public streets and sidewalks. Society has a right to intervene when parents cannot or will not raise their children, but society has no legitimate right to punish the *kids* for the neglect of parents. Society has a right to provide help and support to kids in trouble, but society has no legitimate right to treat every kid as though they require extensive government control absent any reason to believe that this is so.

Rather than making innocent conduct criminal, why don't we focus on detecting and counteracting those people—kids or adults—who actually commit crimes? Rather than sweeping aside parental decisions about what their children can and cannot do, why don't we start out trusting the parents to know what's best for their children, saving government intervention for actual cases of neglect or abuse? Rather than treating all kids alike, why don't we recognize that they are individuals and should receive individual treatment based on their conduct?

Curfew proposals give politicians many opportunities to proclaim that they are getting "tough" on crime without actually doing anything or spending any money. Verbally bashing curfew opponents may be a great way to win votes. Curfews are great politics, but they are bad public policy.

NO

PAUL JOSEPH

Banning children from the public streets is not the way to reduce juvenile crime. Kid curfews may seem appealing, but the more you think about them, the worse they look. Juvenile curfews are bad for at least six reasons:

1. Curfews shift the responsibility for raising and disciplining kids from the parents to the government.

2. Curfews criminalize status instead of bad conduct.
3. Where child neglect is present, the law should penalize the parent, not the child;
4. Curfews may not be enforced or may be selectively enforced.
5. Curfews teach bad citizenship lessons to children.
6. With limited exceptions, curfews are unconstitutional.

Who has the primary responsibility to make decisions about raising children, the parents or the government? In a free society such as ours, the answer is that parents have the primary say. We recognize that parents are in the best position to judge the maturity and abilities of their children. We live in a very diverse society, with many races, religions, and cultural differences. We support the right of parents to make basic decisions about raising their children with their religious and moral values. We definitely do not believe that the government can make such decisions; nor do we believe that government should rigidly mandate one model for all parents and children. Yet this is exactly what juvenile curfews do. As one court explained in striking down a curfew, "the curfew interferes with parental control because it prohibits parents from allowing their children to participate in beneficial programs or groups which may keep them out after curfew hours" (*Washington v. J. D.,* 1997).

Now, I can hear someone saying, "But what if parents neglect their children or do something really terrible to them, can't the government step in?" Of course! But we are not talking about child neglect or abuse; we are talking about an absolute ban on kids being able to use the public streets and sidewalks during certain hours, even with parental approval. This is hardly the kind of extreme situation in which the government should override the parent's judgment.

Also, look at whom the curfews penalize—most target the child, not the parents. If we really have a case of child neglect or abuse, it is the parents who should be the focus of the law. And, as importantly, such a decision should be made on a case-by-case basis. Juvenile curfews don't do that. They impose a "one size fits all" criminal sanction on children—for using the public streets. Another court, striking down a curfew law, explained that whatever the problems caused by juveniles, they were not sufficient to allow "the wholesale nullification of the fundamental right to move freely about for the thousands of law-abiding minors of the District " (*Hutchins v. District of Columbia,* 1996).

Some kids commit crimes. In our society, those who do so are the legitimate target of law enforcement. But juvenile curfews don't focus on kids who commit evil acts. Rather, they make all kids criminals for the most innocent of behaviors— walking down the public sidewalk.

The fact is that many juvenile curfews will not be enforced at all or will be enforced only selectively. Although we like to pretend that police enforce all laws whenever a violation is seen, this is not realistic. There are too many laws and too few police. Minor laws are often ignored because police have their hands full with more serious matters. Enforcement may be more stringent where a curfew applies only to a few blocks that can be easily patrolled, but, where they apply to the whole town, it is likely that juvenile curfew laws will often be ignored by law enforcement. Furthermore, where the target area of enforcement is only a few blocks, the kids can merely move to another part of town.

Where an officer does decide to enforce the curfew law, will he or she do so evenhandedly or selectively? That is, will the officer pick and choose whom to stop? Will the decision to intervene be based on race, gender, or other inappropriate criteria?

Imagine a curfew that requires all juveniles to be off the streets by 11:00 P.M. On two different nights, at 11:30 P.M., an officer is driving through an upper-middle-class, largely white residential area. One night, the officer spots a clean-cut white youth in a suit and tie walking up the block. Another night, the officer sees an African American youth, wearing tennis shoes and a tee-shirt, whose hair is worn in dreadlocks. Both youths would be breaking the law—they are both walking on the public sidewalk after 11:00 P.M. Will the officer stop neither, both, or one of the youths? Which one do you think is more likely to be stopped by the officer? If you suspect that the African American is more likely to be stopped, even though both were committing exactly the same "crime," you understand the meaning of "selective enforcement" and what is so bad about it. Juvenile curfews turn masses of young people into "criminals," leaving it to the police to decide which violators to stop and which to ignore. For example, according to figures reported by the Pittsburgh Chapter of the ACLU, during the first three-and-one-half months of a New Orleans curfew, 93 percent of the kids detained were African American.

It is a basic proposition of our society that people are free to go about their business without police intervention. Unless the officer has "reasonable suspicion" that a person is breaking the law, the officer cannot stop a person even briefly (*Terry v. Ohio,* 1968). The officer can ask a person to stop and talk with him, but the person can politely refuse and walk on. With "reasonable suspicion," however, the officer can "seize" a person briefly for investigation and sometimes even conduct a limited search for weapons. Under the curfew law, very few kids will be out legally. It will be impossible for the officer to know that a particular child is, for example, "engaged in interstate commerce" (*Ashton v. Brown,* 1995) until that child is seized and subjected to questioning. Therefore, police will have "reasonable suspicion" to believe that *any* youth on the streets is violating the curfew, and the officer will have the right to seize all of them for investigation. Many of our children will have the experience of being treated as presumptively guilty when they are innocent of any wrongdoing.

We pride ourselves on being a free society. Our schools prepare the next generation of leaders. What message does a juvenile curfew send? I believe that it tells kids that we distrust them as a group, that we judge them not by their conduct but by their status as kids. It is a lack of basic trust and respect both for our children and for their parents. It also teaches that when we fear or distrust a group of people, we can make even their most innocent activities—such as using the sidewalks—an opportunity for police scrutiny. An ACLU Press Release, posted on its website, for example, recounted the story of a youth in San Diego who was arrested at 10:20 P.M. while eating in a Mexican restaurant, after water polo practice. The curfew that was the subject of this story was struck down as unconstitutional in *Nunez v. City of San Diego* (1997). Will children who have learned this lesson, that they can be stopped by police at will, grow up to respect the ideas of freedom and individual rights? Is this the right educational lesson for our future adults?

It is true that curfews have sometimes been upheld by the courts, but they have also been struck down. Curfews are judged on a "strict scrutiny" standard, and the burden of proof is on the government. The government must demonstrate a "compelling" interest in having the curfew, and the particular law must be narrowly drawn to accomplish that compelling goal. In general, if a curfew is to be upheld, there must be no "less restrictive" way of accomplishing the goal. Therefore, the legal fate of any particular curfew law is likely to turn on the specific facts involved.

When evaluating any particular curfew, it is important to closely examine the government's arguments to see whether they make sense. For example, if a curfew that applies from 11:00 P.M. until 6:00 A.M. is justified as necessary to stop juvenile crime, but it turns out that most juvenile crime actually is committed just after school, during times not covered by the curfew, then is the curfew really narrowly tailored to address issues of juvenile crime? *Nunez v. City of San Diego* (1997), for instance, cites a Justice Department study that "shows that juvenile crime peaks at 3 P.M. and again around 6 P.M."

There is no doubt that many children need our help and assistance. More supportive programs and opportunities should be a high priority. This is absolutely true. But there is no requirement that a teen curfew exist before a night basketball program can be started. These are two wholly separate issues. We can say "Yes" to night basketball while we "Just Say No" to curfews.

Our society has basic choices to make. We can judge each individual by his or her conduct *or* we can stigmatize entire groups. We can value parental decision making in child rearing *or* we can replace parental judgment with government judgment. We can teach our belief in freedom through our actions *or* we can talk about freedom while acting to abridge it. We can focus on those individual children in need of our help and those individual children who require law enforcement attention *or* we can treat all children like criminals—making them "trespassers" in their own towns. Juvenile curfews embody bad social policy choices and should not be adopted.

REFERENCES

Ashton v. Brown, 660 A.2d 447 (Md. 1995).
Correspondence from the Pittsburgh ACLU chapter to city officials; posted on the ACLU Website, which can be found at http://www.aclu.org/.

Hutchins v. District of Columbus, 942 F. Supp. 665 (D. D.C., 1996).
Nunez v. City of San Diego, 114 F. 3d 935 (9th Cir. 1997).
Terry v. Ohio, 92 U.S. 1 (1968).
Washington v. J. D., DOB 5-22-79, 86 Wash. App. 501, 937 P. 2d 630 (1997).

Rejoinder to Professor Joseph   Lee Freeman O'Brien

Professor Joseph declares that curfews are not the way to reduce juvenile crime. Curfew laws, and the enforcement of those laws, however, remove an essential element of crime: opportunity. More important, curfew laws prevent juveniles from victimization.

Professor Joseph is correct when he states that parents should be responsible for rearing their children. Unfortunately, many parents are either unaware of the actions of their offspring or have abdicated parental responsibility. In these instances, it is both the right and the obligation of government to intervene. Hopefully, this intervention will occur before the child's situation is beyond control. When parents cannot or will not rear and discipline their children in a reasonable manner, the consequences affect all of society.

Curfews do not prohibit children from participating in beneficial postcurfew activities. Every successful curfew law provides exceptions and exclusions for participation in activities protected by the First Amendment, activities enjoyed with a parent or guardian, and beneficial activities sponsored by the community.

Status stigmatization is a valid concern for every citizen. Children are no longer stigmatized with a criminal label for truancy, ungovernability, or habitually running away. Neither are they labeled in cases of many curfew violations. Many of the newer curfew laws provide for civil sanctions or a progressive handling of violations, from civil fines to criminal misdemeanor sanctions. Even when these violations are criminal in nature, the stigma is minimal, at best. It is much better that a child have a curfew violation on his or her record than a burglary or assault charge, and it is certainly better to have a curfew violation than to fall prey to some unspeakable crime. The public policy served by curfew laws is to protect children and society at large and to provide assistance to parents. This is one device available in the law that actually provides for the prevention of crime and victimization, rather than simply providing for prosecution after commission.

I agree with Professor Joseph that child neglect calls for penalizing parents, not children. However, our underfunded and understaffed social service agencies are woefully ill equipped to deal with protective services intervention in cases where Johnny is out at all hours of the night. These agencies fight an uphill battle to keep up with the numerous serious abuse, neglect, and abandonment cases. Certainly, parents of repeat curfew violators should be referred to an appropriate social service agency and to the criminal courts much in the same fashion as those who flaunt compulsory school attendance laws. Unfortunately, by the time these referrals are made, it is usually much too late for the child, who by then has been victimized or enveloped in the criminal justice system.

It is speculative to assert that curfews may not be enforced or may be selectively enforced. Officers indeed have their hands full with a myriad number of serious matters. That explains why every speeder is not ticketed; why every truant is not picked up; why every jaywalker is not vigorously prosecuted. Nowhere is it written that officers should not exercise discretion in the performance of their field duties. Discretion does not constitute selective enforcement. Selective enforcement is that which targets minorities, or the poor, or other persons based on their race, class, ethnicity, and so forth. That is an abhorrent practice that must not be condoned by any local government. Such conduct is not endorsed by reputable police departments or their officers. If it occurs, the wronged juvenile may mount a defense to the charge and a civil suit against the agency for this unconstitutional practice as applied to his or her circumstances. That being said, the mere possibility of selective enforcement is not a basis to conclude that these laws are improper or unconstitutional. Absent specific allegations of discriminatory purpose, any speculative failure by law enforcement to treat equally all persons who violate curfew laws does not constitute denial of equal protection. The specter of selective enforcement alone is not unconstitutional.

Law enforcement officers do, however, employ common sense on the streets. A child of sixteen or seventeen years of age walking in a residential neighborhood with a basketball under his arm is not likely to be stopped at all, or, if stopped, it will be merely to confirm that he is late getting home. A fourteen-year-old child in a downtown nightclub district at 3:00 A.M. will undoubtedly draw the immediate attention of a law enforcement officer, as will a group of kids in a high-crime area in the middle of the night. That is not selective enforcement; it is smart policing.

I absolutely disagree that curfews teach bad citizenship lessons to children. Laws designed in children's best interests are like rules in a family structure. These laws are no less inclined to make a child feel presumptively guilty than are parental rules imposing dating restrictions, chore assignments, or punishments for failing to meet family expectations. Teens are eager to declare that society distrusts them as a group, but I fear that misplaced belief transcends every generation of teenagers.

Curfew laws are, for the most part, constitutionally drawn and enforced. It is incumbent on local governments to ensure that any curfew law be drafted within a constitutionally permissible framework. Curfews nationwide have passed constitutional muster time and again, under state and federal constitutional analyses. Regardless of the standard applied, both federal and state courts have consistently determined that the constitutional rights of juveniles are not coextensive with that of adults, especially when the legislation is designed to protect the well-being of minors.

Local governments, if their geographical framework provides, may want to examine enacting curfew-type ordinances in specific areas where juvenile crime and victimization is highest. This is particularly appropriate in areas where teens have no legitimate business, such as nightclub areas, commercial entertainment districts that cater to an adult crowd, daytime commerce centers, and the like. Predictions of displacement into other areas have been generally unrealized. Should displacement occur, local governments have the authority and option to expand curfew areas.

Conclusion

Societal circumstances require ever-creative solutions. Curfews are merely a sound, proactive response to very real problems that affect our communities and the health, safety, and welfare of each member thereof.

Should a College Degree Be Required for Today's Law Enforcement Officer?

EDITOR'S NOTE: As society continues to change at a tremendous rate, it seems clear that the organizational, societal, and technological demands placed on law enforcement officers are greater than ever before. With these increasing expectations comes a dilemma that has been subject to years of debate and only limited progress: must police officers be college-educated? The issue is critical enough that two sets of debates will be presented, each with a slightly different perspective, yet both with arguments overlaid by individuals characterized as "pracademics," recognized for their academic expertise and professional experiences.

Max L. Bromley is Associate Professor in the Department of Criminology at the University of South Florida. He has previously served as Associate Director of Public Safety at the University of South Florida and worked as a law enforcement officer for almost twenty-five years. He was senior coauthor of *College Crime Prevention and Personal Safety Awareness,* has coedited a volume entitled *Hospital and College Security Liability Awareness,* and is coauthor of the fifth edition of *Crime and Justice in America; Department Self-Study: A Guide for Campus Law Enforcement Administrators* is used at over 1000 institutions of higher education. Dr. Bromley received his B.S. and M.S. in Criminology from The Florida State University and his Ed.D. from Nova University.

Michael J. Palmiotto is Associate Professor of Criminal Justice and Coordinator of the Criminal Justice Graduate Program within the Hugo Wall School of Urban and Public Affairs at Wichita State University. He received his master's degree in Public Administration from John Jay College of Criminal Justice and his

Ph.D. from the University of Pittsburgh. He has written numerous articles as well as three books on criminal investigation and policing.

YES

Michael J. Palmiotto

Higher education for police officers can be traced to 1929, when the University of Southern California offered an advanced degree in public administration with a specialization in law enforcement. Michigan State University initiated its Bachelor of Science Degree in Police Administration in 1935. Higher education programs for the police grew slowly until the 1960s.

During the 1960s, prominent groups, such as the International Association of Chiefs of Police and the International Association of Police Professors (now the Academy of Criminal Justice Sciences), began to issue public statements in support of higher education for law enforcement personnel (Kobetz, 1977, p. 7).

The President's Commission on Law Enforcement and Administration of Justice provided further impetus in its report, *The Challenge of Crime in a Free Society*. The Commission recommended that all police officers be required to have two years of college education at a minimum and that all future police personnel be required to possess a bachelor's degree (President's Commission, 1967). As they explained:

> The police personnel need that the Commission has found to be almost universal is improved quality. Generally, law enforcement personnel have met their difficult responsibilities with commendable zeal, determination, and devotion to duty. However, Commission surveys reflect that there is substantial variance in the quality of police personnel from top to bottom.
>
> ...The Commission believes that substantially raising the quality of police personnel would inject into police work knowledge, expertise, initiative, and integrity that would contribute importantly to improved crime control.
>
> The word "quality" is used here in a comprehensive sense. One thing it means is a high standard of education for policemen...A policeman today is poorly equipped for his job if he does not understand the legal issues involved in his everyday work, the nature of the social problems he constantly encounters, the psychology of those people whose attitudes toward the law differ from his. Such understanding is not easy to acquire without the kind of broad general knowledge that higher education imparts, and without such understanding a policeman's response to many of the situations he meets is likely to be impulsive or doctrinaire. Police candidates must be sought in college....
> (p. 107)

The 1960s was a decade of social disruption and violence. Police confrontations with students at universities and with anti-Vietnam war protesters were common events. Police inability to cope with the ghetto riots and their apparent helplessness to curtail the spiraling crime rate led both liberal and conservative politicians to believe that higher education was desirable. The National Advisory Commission on Civil Disorders and similar commissions of this period reflect these views (Jacobs & Magdovitz, 1977).

The police were charged not only with being ineffective in controlling disorder, but also with aggravating and precipitating violence through harassment of minority ghetto dwellers, student dissidents, and other citizens. The National Advisory Commission on Civil Disorders discovered that, in America's cities, aggressive police patrolling and harassment resulted from society's fear of crime. This practice created hostility and conflict between the police and minorities. Finally, President Johnson's Commission on Campus Unrest also advocated the belief that education for police might assist in decreasing police/citizen confrontations. That Commission found:

> Law enforcement agencies desperately need better educated and better trained policemen.... There should be special monetary incentives for all who enter the police service with college degrees or who obtain degrees while in police service. (p. 154)

The consensus was that, to improve law enforcement, the quality of police personnel had to be upgraded through higher education. There is little doubt that law enforcement personnel had limited education. The median educational level of police officers in 1966 was 12.4 years. In December 1968, *Fortune* magazine estimated that fewer than 10 percent of American police officers had been to college; in October 1968, *Time* reported that Detroit police recruits were from the bottom 25 percent of their high school graduating classes (Jacobs & Magdovitz, 1977).

The 1960s focused on the need of criminal justice education. This need is determined by "an analysis of the criminal justice system and by an assessment of the manpower requirements of the system's agencies (Sienna, 1974). Today, the need of the criminal justice field is for personnel with advanced degrees. New developments and techniques making criminal justice activities more sophisticated demand more sophisticated, well-prepared, well-schooled officers. Technology for policing has advanced by leaps and bounds to a point that a police officer in the 1960s would consider his role in the 1990s to be science fiction!

Education is usually based on a solid foundation of liberal arts. A law enforcement practitioner—or a potential practitioner—must perceive policing as it relates to American society and the democratic process. Higher education exposes students to ideas, concepts, and problem-solving techniques. The educational process aims to develop individuals who know how to live within a group, individuals who understand conflicts in our society and who possess an understanding of motivation, stress, and tension of other people in our society. An individual with this knowledge and understanding has the ability to apply past information to new situations (Anderson, 1967)

A college education will not transform an intellectually wanting person into an accomplished one. But, all things being equal, the college-educated individual is more qualified and better prepared than the high school graduate. The college-educated person has more experience with people and new situations. His or her responsibility and adaptability to new surroundings have been tested. In addition, he or she has been exposed to various cultural characteristics and ethical and racial backgrounds. This exposure should eliminate or reduce prejudice and bias. More importantly, a formal education should teach individuals to check their judgments regarding prejudices in favor of more tranquil analysis (Hewitt, 1964).

A basic concern of higher education in law enforcement is the need to study and improve the system. Academic study of policing is needed to identify problems and to identify ways in which problems can be solved. Persons interested in research careers in criminal justice need higher education (Sienna, 1974).

As already noted, during the 1960s, the importance of high-quality personnel was finally recognized; the drive to upgrade personnel began. However, in the 1970s, the National Advisory Commission on Criminal Justice Standards and Goals stated:

> Police agencies have lost ground in the race for qualified employees because they have not raised standards. College graduates look elsewhere for employment. Police work has often come to be regarded by the public as a second class occupation, open to anyone with no more than a minimum education, average intelligence, and good health (1973; p. 367).

The Commission on Criminal Justice Standards and Goals found it ironic that educational levels were not increased for the police, because studies found that police officers with a college education generally performed significantly better than officers without a college education. According to the Commission, upgrading the educational level of police officers should be a major challenge facing policing. Professions require a higher educational degree and, if the police hope to be recognized as a profession, they need to take notice of the professional criteria. The Commission recommended that all police officers be required to possess a bachelor's degree no later than 1982 (p. 367); in 1997, the police, as a universal standard, do not yet require an undergraduate degree. This is at a time when we are entering a new millennium with more college graduates than ever in our society, and still the police still do not require a college education. However, it should be noted that a study sponsored by the Police Executive Research Forum (PERF) found that approximately 62 percent of policing agencies serving jurisdictions with populations of more than 50,000 people had some form of incentive program to encourage education. This same study found that only approximately

14 percent of these departments had a *mandatory* requirement of a college degree as a prerequisite for employment (Carter, Sapp, & Stephens, 1988b).

In the last thirty years, police education has increased but not to the point where all entry-level police officers are required to have an undergraduate degree as a requirement for employment. If the police are to increase their professionalism and if they have any expectations of meeting the demands placed on them by their communities, they must improve the educational level of all police officers. The 14 percent of departments requiring a mandatory college education has to rise to 100 percent of all departments requiring a college education for all of their sworn police personnel. American society is becoming increasingly more complex, sophisticated, better educated, multicultural, and multilingual; its police should do no less.

It is critical that the police be familiar with the socioeconomic and cultural makeup of the community they serve. They must identify the cultural diversity among the people they protect. America's communities are heterogeneous, and a police officer with an adequate educational background should function better in the community than an officer unaware of various cultural differences among the numerous ethnic and racial groups. The police need to continue their pledge toward professionalism. In some areas the police have made great strides; in other areas they have not. Excessive use of force, as in the Rodney King fiasco, is one area that needs to be addressed and amplified. Police corruption, including police officers buying and selling drugs, stealing, and robbing, must be curtailed. Our newspapers have an overabundance of police officers being criminally involved with illegal drug activity. The police pledge of professionalism has to become more than rhetoric. It is time it became a reality.

Yet professionalism implies standards and proficiency. Have the police nationally recognized uniform standards and proficiency? Who can respond "yes" to this question? Do those individuals who believe that a college education is unnecessary for police officers realistically believe that the police are professional? How can anyone in our society recognize the police as a profession without the formal requirement of a college degree as a minimum prerequisite for professional recognition? The Police Executive Research Forum study (Carter, Sapp, & Stephens, 1988) hypothesized several advantages of college education for police officers:

- It develops a broader base of information for decision making.
- Course requirements and achievements inculcate responsibility in the individual and a greater appreciation for constitutional rights, values, and the democratic form of government.
- College education engenders the ability to flexibly handle difficult or ambiguous situations with greater creativity or innovation.
- Higher education develops a greater empathy for diverse populations and their unique life experiences.
- The college-educated officer is assumed to be less rigid in decision making and more readily accepts and adapts to organizational change.

- The college experience will help officers better communicate and respond to crime and service needs of a diverse public in a competent manner with civility and humanity.
- College-educated officers exhibit more "professional" demeanor and performance.
- The college experience tends to make the officer less authoritarian and less cynical with respect to the milieu of policing.

It should be obvious to all rational thinking individuals that not all college graduates are eligible to be police officers. There will always be individuals who will be considered unsuitable or unsuited for police work based on physical abilities, physical illness, and emotional temperament. Of course, individuals with felony records or a history of violence should be barred from the police field. However, all things being equal, the college graduate has to be considered the more qualified to perform police work. The PERF list of advantages for a college education for sworn police officers is both logical and rational. This is especially true in a period in which politicians and police administrators are claiming to support problem-solving and community-oriented policing as crime control strategies. To operate successfully, these strategies require that first-line police officers be decision makers and work closely with their communities. The police organization has to be less bureaucratic and less authoritarian if the community-oriented and problem-solving strategies are to be successful. College-educated officers will function better under a system in which they are given the opportunity to use their problem-solving skills. Community-oriented policing will be more successful with a college-educated police officer who has the proven ability to be trainable and who should be more readily open to new ideas and concepts.

The 1960s gave a major impetus to the college education movement. This trend continues into the 1990s. It will not be achieved until every police agency in this country requires, as a prerequisite to employment, that all police officers have, at a minimum, a baccalaureate degree. With the twenty-first century upon us, our politicians, police managers, and police officers, along with their professional organizations, must throw the dinosaur back to antiquity and open a new page for policing in America. The American citizen has the right to be policed by professionally educated police. More importantly, how can the police expect to be viewed or treated as professionals when they lack the minimum prerequisite of a profession . . . preparatory advanced education?

References

Anderson, W. R. (1967). The Law Enforcement Education Act of 1967. *The Congressional Record,* H. R. 188, January.

Carter, D. L., Sapp, A. D., & Stephens, D. W. (1988a). Higher education as a bona fide occupational qualification (BFQ) for police: A blueprint. *American Journal of Police, 7* (2), 16–18.

Carter, D. L, Sapp, A. D., & Stephens, D. W. (1988b). *The state of police education: Police direction for the 21st century.* Washington, DC: Police Executive Research Forum.

Hewitt, W. H. (1964). The objectives of formal police education. *Police, 9*(2), 25–27.

Jacobs, J. B., & Magdovitz, S. B. (1977). At LEEP's end? A review of the law enforcement education program. *Journal of Police Science and Administration, 5*(1), 1–18.

Kobetz, R. W. (1977). *Law Enforcement and Criminal Justice Education Directory, 1975–76.* Gaithersburg, MD: IACP.

National Advisory Commission on Criminal Justice Standards and Goals (1973). *The Police.* Washington, DC: U.S. Government Printing Office.

Sienna, J. J. (1974). Criminal justice higher education—Its growth and directions. *Crime and Delinquency, 20*(4), 389–397.

The President's Commission on Law Enforcement and Administration of Justice. (1967). *The Challenge of Crime in a Free Society.* Washington, DC: Government Printing Office.

U.S. President's Commission on Campus Unrest (1968). Washington, DC: Government Printing Office.

Rejoinder to Professor Palmiotto Max L. Bromley

Professor Palmiotto's argument in support of requiring a college degree for today's law enforcement officers revisits the formative years of the modern era of criminal justice in our nation. The period falls generally between the mid-1960s and the late 1970s. Ironically, this timeframe roughly corresponds to the existence of a federal agency that was largely responsible for supporting the growth of higher education in policing, namely, the Law Enforcement Assistance Administration (L.E.A.A.). As we know today, more money was made available from L.E.A.A. in support of higher education for police than at any time before or since its inception. With the demise of L.E.A.A. in the early 1980s, the support for college-educated police officers became less of a federal priority as other issues came to the forefront. Significantly, universal acceptance of college-educated requirements for entry-level police officers was never achieved.

On the surface, it appears difficult to argue against a college degree requirement for entry-level police officers in our country. As Professor Palmiotto points out, the President's Commission of 1967, the President's Commission on Campus Unrest in 1968, and the National Advisory Commission on Criminal Justice Standards and Goals of 1973 each supported requiring college education for police officers. The National Advisory Commission on Criminal Justice Standards and Goals actually recommended that all police officers be required to possess a bachelor's degree no later than 1982.

The recommendations of these well-intentioned commissions were just that —recommendations made without any real legislative or regulatory means to carry them out. Although our society generally places high value on higher education and ascribes additional status to those professions requiring college education, the linkage has not apparently been made to policing.

In his argument, Professor Palmiotto notes that, in the study by Carter et al. (1988) conducted for the Police Executive Research Forum, 62 percent of the responding agencies had some form of incentive programs that encourage employed police officers to attend college. Ironically, only 14 percent of these same departments had a mandatory college requirement for new hires. Likewise, in a nationwide demographic study of police agencies for the Bureau of Justice Statistics, Reaves (1996) found that only 12 percent of the local police departments require new recruits to have some college education. In addition, only 8 percent require "some type" of degree, with only 1 percent requiring a four-year degree (Reaves, 1996). These data would appear to indicate less than substantial support at the local level for college education for police officers entering the workforce. One of the legitimate questions to be asked in light of these findings is, why is that the case?

Professor Palmiotto suggests that the demands placed on today's police officers are becoming greater as this country becomes more diverse in its population. For police personnel to be more professional and for officers to behave more appropriately in dealing with citizens, he argues that a college education is a necessity. Some thirty years ago, the earlier listed commissions made these same arguments. As I will point out later, with respect to the effect of college education on the performance and attitudes of police officers, research results have been, at best, mixed.

Professor Palmiotto also offers a list of advantages of a college education for police officers. Intuitively, it is difficult to refute many of the points appearing on this list. However, as noted, the limited research conducted in this area over the last twenty-five years is less than conclusive in supporting college education for police officers. Professor Palmiotto concludes by noting that, as police departments employ new strategies such as community-oriented policing and problem-solving policing, a greater number of college-educated officers will be required. He assumes that the evolving police organizations will be less bureaucratic and less authoritarian than the current ones. Although not totally discounting Professor Palmiotto's suggestion, I will propose a different way to resolve some of these issues.

REFERENCES

Carter, D. L., Sapp, A., & Stephens, D. (1988). *The state of police education: Police direction for the 21st century.* Washington, DC: Police Executive Research Forum.

National Advisory Commission on Criminal Justice Standards and Goals. (1973). *A national strategy to reduce crime.* Washington, DC: U.S. Government Printing Office.

President's Commission on Law Enforcement and Administration of Justice. (1967). *The challenge of crime in a free society.* Washington, DC: Government Printing Office.

Reaves, B. (1996). *Local police departments 1993.* Washington, DC: U.S. Department of Justice, Bureau of Justice Statistics.

U.S. President's Commission on Campus Unrest. (1968). Washington, DC: Government Printing Office.

NO

Max L. Bromley

Responding to this question in a negative fashion may at first appear to be a suggestion that policing as a profession move backward. The "no" response to this critical question also may be viewed as strange coming from someone who had been a campus police administrator for over two decades and now serves as a university professor in a discipline that encourages its graduates to enter police work and the criminal justice field. However, the "no" response is provided to critically review the college education requirement within the context of the last thirty years experience and is meant to serve as a catalyst to develop a more realistic approach to enhancing police professionalism as we enter the next century.

The remainder of my position will review results of some of the research conducted with regard to college-educated police officers; raise questions regarding the vagueness of the college education requirement; discuss whether a college degree is a realistic requirement for entry-level police officers; and question why there isn't more obvious support for such a degree requirement from political leaders and citizens. In addition, I'll raise concerns regarding the obstacles to requiring college degrees that exist within police organizations, as well as offer some suggestions as to what needs to be done with this issue in the very near future.

Prior Research

Ideally, policy decision making in the public sector (e.g., policing) should be based at least in part on research findings. This is of particular importance if the policy change involves human resources and ultimately is linked in some fashion to public funding. It is difficult to imagine a Fortune 500 company making a major modification in its requirements or practices for personnel hiring without first obtaining data from research that would substantiate the change. As noted earlier, the impetus for adopting a college degree requirement for police officers was based primarily on the recommendations of several national commissions. Most empirical studies regarding the performance of college-educated police officers were conducted after many departments across the country had acted on such commission recommendations.

Perhaps the fairest way to characterize the results of the various research studies is to describe them as mixed. For example, Hudzik (1978) noted that,

"Existing research findings cannot be accepted as conclusive evidence that a college education should be a prerequisite to law enforcement employment. The lack of sufficient research controls in the projects measuring the effects of college education results in our being unable to conclude which effects are attributable to college education." (p. 78)

Others have also questioned the effects of college education on police officer performance. For example, Lewis (1970) and Livermore (1971) questioned the value of college education as well as the actual relevance of college course offerings. Wilson (1974) found college-educated officers to be resistant to authority within the command structure and more likely to leave police service within the first few years when compared with non–college-educated officers. Griffin (1980) found an inverse relationship between patrol officer education level and performance evaluation ratings, noting that it was not until college education and years of practical experience were combined that patrol officers attained higher performance evaluation ratings.

Eisenberg and Reinke (1973) noted that the relationship between a college degree and better job performance on the part of police officers was inconclusive. Similarly, in 1981, Sherman and Blumberg conducted research regarding the impact of higher education on use of force by police officers. Once again their findings were mixed. Their study of police officer use of weapons covering a seven-year period in the Kansas City, Missouri, Police Department, led to inconclusive results. "In short, the present study is far from conclusive about higher education and the use of deadly force. It is even less conclusive about the value of higher education for improving police performance, the many components of which are not necessarily consistent for individual officers" (Sherman & Blumberg, 1981, p. 328).

In the late 1980s, Carter and Sapp conducted research regarding the effect of higher education on police civil liability. Theoretically, better-educated officers are less likely to be involved in cases of civil liability. They found no prior research that directly addressed the effect of higher civil liability lawsuits. With regard to their own findings Carter and Sapp (1989, p. 154) stated: "While the evidence is indirect, the arguments suggest that higher education may reduce liability risks." They conclude their study by suggesting that further policy research is necessary (Carter & Sapp, 1989).

Vagueness of the College Requirement

A second issue is relative vagueness of requiring a college degree for entry-level police officers. In American society, a certain aura of professionalism is granted to those individuals who have obtained a college degree. It is generally accepted that persons having college degrees will make more money in their lifetime and secure a better quality of life as compared with non–college-degree holders. In addition, certain occupations, such as teaching, accounting, nursing, medicine, and the law, are viewed as professions. For these occupational specialties, college training and even postgraduate degrees (in the case of law and medicine) are necessities, and specific curricula must be mastered before one can be employed as a professional.

It is hard to imagine that the American public would accept services from an accountant whose degree was in fine arts or accept health assistance from a nurse whose college degree was in banking and finance. Yet, in discussing the requirements for upgrading the professionalism of law enforcement on the basis of requiring higher education, terms such as "some college," "two years of college," or a "four-year degree" are used to describe minimum-level entry requirements for police officers. The lack of specificity with regard to not only the level of degree but also the curriculum content does little to enhance policing as a profession. If college education is to be a requirement for entry-level police officers, questions regarding the nature of the curriculum and the preferred level of degree (i.e., A.A., B.A., etc.) need to be raised, debated, and settled.

With respect to curriculum content, one of the problems that has been raised in the past is the differentiation between what is to be taught in the police academy training curriculum versus what should be included in an academic college curriculum. College programs that include academic credit courses on crime scene investigation and firearms use are not consistent with the traditional expected content of college academic courses. To not clearly differentiate between the two types of programs (training versus academic) creates even more ambiguity with respect to requiring a college degree for police officers. Recommending a generic college degree requirement for all law enforcement officers assumes that the impact of such a degree will have a positive effect on *all* degree holders. Yet there is little evidence and support of this assumption. Furthermore, as noted by Sherman and Blumberg, "The impact of higher education may be less homogeneous than some have suggested" (1981, p. 318).

Obstacles within the Police Organization

Historically, the police organization has been described as paramilitary and bureaucratic in nature. This implies characteristics such as a formal rank structure, a chain of command, emphasis on discipline, and a rule-oriented approach to managing operations on a day-to-day basis. There is little evidence that this will change in the near future (Swanson, Territo, & Taylor, 1993). This style of organization may be conducive to responding to major emergencies, but it does not necessarily foster individuality or creative problem solving on the part of college-educated employees. It tends to produce a type of organizational setting within which college-educated officers may become frustrated. As noted by Maslach (1982), "People with higher levels of education have higher expectation for what they want to do in life" (1982, p. 61). Dantzker (1990) also suggested that, although police officers may have high expectations, they often experience a difference between reality and theory in their jobs.

In an hierarchical organization in which there are relatively few supervisory or administrative positions, promotions are relatively infrequent, and this may further frustrate college-educated officers. In their study of veteran police officers, Fischer, Golden, and Heininger (1985) found that those officers with higher levels of education often desired to be promoted but were frequently frustrated when they were not able to achieve a higher rank within their organization. Swanson (1977) also noted that there are relatively few promotional opportunities for officers with most police organizations, which in turn leads to frustration on their part. He also described a lack of career paths available for college-educated police officers (Swanson, 1977). According to Scott (1986), even in departments that have higher education requirements, it is the police culture itself that inhibits the development of police officers as change agents. Smith (1978) suggests that the key to changing police officer attitudes may have less to do with college requirements and training curricula and more to do with the police organizational working environment.

The placement of college police officers within a rigid bureaucratic environment that tends to stifle their creativity may do little to actually enhance police officer performance within the community. Swanson (1977) noted that police agencies are essentially line and line and staff organizations. This type of structure assumes that persons at the lower level of the department "must be closely controlled and often coerced to achieve agency objectives." (Swanson, 1977, p. 314). He goes on to note that college-educated officers are "Quite capable of being self-controlling and creative" (Swanson, 1977, p. 314). Thus there may be a lack of congruence between organizational structure and college-educated officer desires and abilities.

Breci (1997) provided another more recent example of a lack of organizational support for higher education. In this study of 915 police officers in Minnesota, the majority of officers indicated a lack of support on the part of their departments for them to continue their higher education. For example, "80 percent of the departments did not provide pay incentives for a return to college, 62 percent did not offer tuition assistance and 67 percent failed to adjust their work schedules to allow attending college classes." (Breci, 1997, p. 55).

Is the College Degree Requirement Realistic?

A final area that I would like to address regarding the requirement of a college degree for police officers is the question as to whether such a requirement is realistic. This is both a political and budgetary question within the criminal justice system. Does the public place such emphasis on the value of higher education for police personnel that they are willing to invest the tax dollars necessary to fund the proposed requirement? Are political leaders and police executives willing to divert dollars from other portions of their budgets to financially support higher education initiatives? Weirman and Archambeault (1983) raised these and related questions in their assessment of the demise of L.E.A.A. funding in the 1980s. At present, federal level budgetary support under the Clinton administration is directed at simply placing more police officers on the street through the C. O. P. S. program, with little emphasis on enhancing services through requiring higher educational standards for police officers.

Powell (1986) noted a variety of reasons that a bachelor's degree requirement for police personnel has not yet been implemented:

> First is the time that would be involved for those non-degree police officers already in the system to obtain baccalaureate degrees. Second is the geographic inaccessibility of colleges and universities to many areas, combined with the cost of tuition and books. Third is the minimal manpower resources available to police agencies to allow schedule adjustments for education. Finally, there is the ever present ambivalence within the police agencies on the real need for higher education. (Powell, 1986, p. 2)

In his survey of police supervisors, criminal justice educators, non–criminal justice higher education faculty, and citizens in the state of Michigan, Powell (1986) found general support for improving the quality of policing through higher education but did not find conclusive evidence that the majority of those surveyed supported the need for mandatory implementation of such a requirement.

In their nationwide study of police agencies serving populations of 50,000 or greater, Carter, Sapp, and Stephens (1988b) found that only 20 percent of the departments had a "formal or informal promotion policy requiring some form of higher education" (Carter et al., 1988b, p. 23). Therefore, most of these agencies serving large populations do not include higher education as a promotional requirement. This indicates a lack of commitment to higher education on the part of police executives or the political leadership within those communities.

Finally, the question of agency size must be raised regarding the plausibility of requiring a college education for police officers. According to Reaves (1996), there are approximately 9400 police agencies serving populations of less 10,000, and there are 6400 departments (or 52 percent of all departments) who employ fewer than ten officers in our country. With regard to the budget of these smaller police agencies, "departments serving populations of 2,500 to 9,999 persons spend an average of $45,800 per year on each officer" and those agencies serving populations of less 2500 spend $29,000 annually on each officer (Reaves, 1996, p. 7). By way of comparison, "police agencies who serve populations of 50,000 up to 1 million or more, spend between $67,800 and $77,200 on each officer" (Reaves, 1996, p. 7). Without a dramatic increase in the police budgets for the smaller departments, it does not appear realistic to expect them to be able to attract college-educated officers. Further, even if college-educated officers were hired, the smaller agencies who have limited potential promotional opportunities would in all likelihood experience additional officer turnover at the entry level.

What Needs to Be Done First?

Although my position in this chapter has been negative with respect to the appropriateness of requiring a college degree for police officers, that does not imply that this issue should not be examined further. The goal of requiring a college degree for police officers may be worthwhile within the context of an ever-changing society. However, there needs to be additional discussion, serious debate, and effective political leadership as characterized by new legislation and fiscal support before change can occur. I propose that a number of steps need to be taken to more comprehensively examine the proposed educational requirement.

First, additional research should be conducted on a nationwide basis with respect to the effect of higher education on police officer performance. Sophisticated sampling techniques need to be employed to control for a variety of variables, including agency size, populations served, and other appropriate variables or demographic features. In addition, a survey of police executives, political leaders, and citizens should be conducted to determine their perceptions of the need for college-educated police officers. I also suggest that there be a thorough examination of the current criminal justice curriculum in higher education for police practitioners. Clear distinctions must be made between skill development training taught in police academies and academic course work that is part of a college or university curriculum. Higher education professionals in criminal justice and police executives should collaborate to develop the framework for a content-specific curriculum that produces college graduates who possess the intellectual skills necessary to be successful as police officers. For any curriculum to be successful, it cannot be developed in a vacuum and certainly needs critical input from all parties effected.

Next, I argue that the emphasis on requiring a college degree for entry-level police personnel has focused on the wrong stage or step in the organizational ladder. Instead, it would seem more appropriate that a higher education requirement first be enacted at the managerial/executive levels of police organizations. As noted by Witham (1985, p. 70), "Some advocates of police professionalism have argued that all officers should be required to possess a minimum of a bachelor's degree. Many people would argue that college level education is even more important for the police managers than patrol officers."

In police agencies where it is financially feasible, alternative entry-level career opportunities, such as community service officers or police aides, should be developed. This would allow non–college-educated individuals a chance to work for a police department, gain experience, and work toward a college degree. Departments could phase in these persons as fully certified, degree-holding police officers on completion of their college coursework and police academy training.

Finally, it appears that changes must be made to the typical police organizational culture and its traditional hierarchical structure. Traditional police bureaucracies are not sufficiently flexible to attract and retain large numbers of college-educated officers. The lack of an adequate number of career-enhancing opportunities and the failure to support officers in their efforts to continue their higher education are perceived as negatives for college-educated officers. Although authorities have argued that the traditional police organization must be altered for community-oriented policing to be successfully implemented, a similar case could be made with respect to requiring a college education for police officers. To change the police organization and its culture, police executives, with the support of their political leaders, must exert strong leadership. Police departments should attempt to hire college-educated officers and encourage current personnel to continue their education; however, it is not realistic at this time to require all police officers to have a college degree.

REFERENCES

Breci, M. (1997). What motivates officers to continue their college education? *Journal of Criminal Justice Education, 8*(1), 51–60.

Carter, D., & Sapp, A. (1989). The effect of higher education on police liability: Implications for police personnel policy. *American Journal of Police, 8*(1), 153–166.

Carter, D. L., Sapp, A., & Stephens, D. (1988a). *The state of police education: Police direction for the 21st century.* Washington, DC: Police Executive Research Forum.

Carter, D., Sapp, A., & Stephens, D. (1988b). Higher education as a bona fide occupational qualification (BFOQ) for police: A blueprint. *American Journal of Police, 7*(2), 1–27.

Dantzker, M. (1990). Examination of a college degree on the perceived stress of patrol officers. *Journal of Police and Criminal Psychology, 6*(2), 26–36.

Eisenberg, T., & Reinke, R. (1973). The use of written examinations in selecting police officers: Coping with the dilemma. *Police Chief, 40*(3), 24–28.

Fischer, R., Golden, K., & Heininger, B. (1985). Issues in higher education for law enforcement officers: An Illinois study. *Journal of Criminal Justice, 13,* 329–378.

Griffin, G. (1980). *A study of the relationship between level of college education and police patrolman's performance.* Saratoga, NY: Twenty One Publishing.

Hudzik, J. (1978). College education for police: Problems in measuring component and extraneous variables. *Journal of Criminal Justice, 6,* 69–81.

Lewis, A. (1970). Police halt push for college grads. *The Washington Post* (December 17): D-1.

Livermore, J. (1971). Policing. *Minnesota Law Review, 55,* 649–730.

Maslach, C. (1982). *Burnout: The cost of caring.* Englewood Cliffs, NJ: Prentice Hall.

Powell, D. (1986). An assessment of attitudes toward police education needs. *Journal of Police and Criminal Psychology, 2*(1), 2–8.

Reaves, B. (1996). *Local police departments 1993.* Washington, DC: U.S. Department of Justicer, Bureau of Justice Statistics.

Scott, W. (1986). College education requirements for police entry level and promotion: A study. *Journal of Police and Criminal Psychology, 2*(1), 10–28.

Sherman, L., & Blumberg, M. (1981). Higher education and police use of deadly force. *Journal of Criminal Justice, 9,* 317–331.

Smith, D. (1978). Dangers of police professionalization: An empirical analysis. *Journal of Criminal Justice, 6,* 199–216.

Swanson, C. (1977). An uneasy look at college education and the police organization. *Journal of Criminal Justice, 5,* 311–320.

Swanson, C., Territo, L., & Taylor R. (1993). *Police administration: Structures, processes and behavior.* New York: Macmillan Publishing Company.

Weirman, C., & Archambeault, W. (1983). Assessing the effects of LEAA's demise on criminal justice higher education. *Journal of Criminal Justice, 11,* 549–561.

Wilson, J. (1974). "Is college necessary for police." *Washington Post,* October 31.

Witham, D. (1985). *The American law enforcement chief executive: A managerial profile.* Washington, DC: Police Executive Research Forum.

Rejoinder to Professor Bromley   MICHAEL J. PALMIOTTO

Professor Max Bromley makes a valiant effort to attempt to explain in a logical and rational manner why police agencies should not mandate a college education for all police officers. To his credit, he presents several rational arguments against the requirement that all police officers be required to have a college degree. Many of Professor Bromley's points have a definite appeal to those police officers who are anti-education. However, Professor Bromley raises several key issues related to a college education for police officers. What is more important, he raises basic issues pertaining to police organizations. The concern he raises regarding education and police organizations evokes the question "Which comes first, the chicken or the egg?" In this rejoinder, I hope to respond to Professor Bromley's major premise.

Professor Bromley emphasizes that the impetus for adopting a college degree requirement for police officers was "based primarily on the recommendation of several commissions." Although he is correct in stating that national commissions were major stimuli for advancing higher education for police officers, he fails to recognize that the educational movement can be traced to a single, progressive individual—August Vollmer—in the 1920s. The movement to require a college education for police officers has occurred throughout most of the twentieth century. This movement will not go away.

According to Professor Bromley, research pertaining to the value of a college education is mixed. The studies he cites are studies from the 1970s, with one from the late 1980s. Can a true assessment of a college education be obtained when the research probably included officers in various stages of their college educations? Can accurate evaluations of college-educated officers be expected when supervisors and administrators may not be supportive of college education for police officers? Does not the individual with the greater education stoop to the standards of the less-educated individual? If college-educated officers have a limited impact on policing, is it because they are a minority in the organization with limited authority and power to influence the organization? It should be recognized that the noncollege police officer often feels intimidated and threatened by the college-educated officer. That noncollege officer will often debase the performance of the college officer. Noncollege supervisors have been known to give college-educated officers poor annual evaluations simply because of their anti-education attitude.

It appears to be Professor Bromley's contention that a college education is an unnecessary requirement because police organizations are "paramilitary and bureaucratic in nature." Are not federal law enforcement agencies, such as the FBI, Secret Service, and U.S. Marshal Service, paramilitary and bureaucratic organizations? Yet, these policing agencies require a college education for employment. Are not municipal, county and state policing as important to the welfare of citizens? Should local police officers be less educated than their federal counterparts?

The argument that, because of limited promotions in police agencies, a college education should not be required for the police field is weak. When we examine all of the professions and fields that require a college education, we find that the same argument can be made for every other field. For example, are all accountants in a CPA firm promoted? Are all lawyers in a law firm made partners? Do all FBI agents become supervisors? We all know that promotion in any organization is limited. Some individuals who fail to obtain a promotion may leave the organization, others who are not promoted will remain, and some individuals do not want to be promoted.

In a period of problem-oriented policing and community-oriented policing, there is a greater expectation of creativity and problem solving by police officers. If police organizations give more than lip service to community policing, then, for this philosophy to be successful, the rigidity of the police organization needs to decrease and disappear. An officer with a college education should be better able to cope with the changing philosophy of policing than a non–college-educated police officer.

The survey of the Minnesota police officers, in which most indicated that they did not support their department's continuing higher education policy, should not come as a surprise. Police officers are not known for their ready acceptance of change. Usually, when change occurs, the city "fathers," state legislative branch, state or federal laws, and the courts will dictate it to the police organization. How many police chiefs would require recruit training if state law did not require it? How many police departments would employ ethnic or racial minorities? How many police departments would hire female police officers? Police departments are usually content with the status quo and resist change. It is the rare police administrator who implements change and the even rarer organization that supports it.

The college degree requirement is realistic, and, perhaps more important, a sufficient number of college graduates are willing to enter the field for a police officer's salary. Currently, college graduates are being recruited along with high school graduates. In many areas of the country, police officers with high school diplomas are receiving higher salaries than elementary and secondary school teachers with college degrees. College graduates are attracted to the teaching field because they want to work with children and not necessarily because of the salary. Should we not expect college graduates inclined toward police work to become police officers?

Professor Bromley makes an excellent point that small police agencies with fewer than ten officers may not be able to employ a college graduate. The salaries of very small police agencies are often so low that one has to wonder why anyone would accept these positions. With extremely low salaries, the caliber of the people employed is often subject to question. With a college education requirement, many of these departments may have to be eliminated or, at least, consolidated. The emphasis should be on quality and not just having a "good old boy" as a police officer. Rural, suburban, and urban police departments should recruit quality people. Only with quality police officers will a community have an effective police agency.

According to Professor Bromley, we need "additional discussion, serious debate, and effective political leadership." Over the last several decades, there have been enough discussion and debate about the value of a college education for police officers. What has been lacking is police *leadership*. If there had been police leadership supporting college education, a college education would be a requirement today. Not only have police administrators shown a lack of leadership, but heads of police organizations and unions have failed to live up to their responsibility.

According to Professor Bromley, additional research on the issue of college education for police officers should be conducted. It is difficult to support this position. New research will not reveal any new findings. It will only rehash what already is known. The police field first must determine whether it is on the path toward professionalism. If the answer is yes, then police agencies should immediately put in place the college education requirement. The suggestion by Professor Bromley that criminal justice professors and police executives should collaborate to develop a curriculum for college graduates interested in police work is an excellent recommendation. There definitely must be dialogue between the academic profession and the police field. The police practitioner should understand the academic field if he or she is to appreciate the value of a college education. The academician should understand where the police are "coming from" and what the police consider to be important issues to their field.

No reason exists for only advocating a college education for police managers, as Professor Bromley proposes, and not for the line officer. Although the police manager may need a formal college education emphasizing management principles and concepts, this in no way should detract from the college education requirement for the line officer. Police managers most frequently are taken from the ranks and, eventually, a line officer can become a manager.

I strongly disagree with Professor Bromley that it is not realistic at this time to require all police officers to have a college degree. Professor Bromley does not provide a timetable to require all police officers to have a college degree. If one is to accept Professor Bromley's assumption about college education for police officers, then there never will be a realistic time to require college education for all police officers!

College-Educated Cops: Is the Time Now?

EDITOR'S NOTE: Professors Palmiotto and Bromley have argued the need for college-educated police officers forcefully and from a firm theoretical perspective. At the center of this complex issue is change... in the police organization, in the technology its personnel use, in the community it serves. In this debate, Dr. Garner and Mr. Lynn move us to the next practical level. If higher education is a desirable prerequisite for entry-level police officers, is it needed NOW? And, if not now, WHEN?

Dr. Randall Garner holds a B.S., an M.A., and a Ph.D. in Psychology and currently is Assistant Professor of Criminal Justice at Sam Houston State University and Director of the Texas Community Policing Institute. Dr. Garner began his law enforcement career in 1976 and has served at all levels of command, most recently as Chief of Police for a Houston-area agency. During his tenure as Chief, he was active in national, state, and local law enforcement organizations. Dr. Garner is an honors graduate of both the FBI National Academy (139th Session) and the Southern Police Institute (66th Administrative Officers Course, University of Louisville).

R. Lynn has been in law enforcement for more than sixteen years and has held numerous supervisory positions. He is currently an instructor at a regional police academy where he teaches courses on Police–Community Relations, Cultural Diversity, First Line Management, and other related areas. Mr. Lynn has been active in police policy issues and has served as the president of a local police officers association. Mr. Lynn holds a degree in Police Administration and has taught several college courses as an adjunct professor of criminal justice.

YES

RANDALL L. GARNER

Unarguably, policing is becoming more complex in today's ever-changing society. What was once described as maintaining order and keeping the peace has developed into problem-solving, statistical analysis, technological innovation, and innumerable social intervention strategies. The information one must possess to become a police officer appears to be increasing exponentially. Additionally, the level of scrutiny police officers receive has never been greater. The quickly advancing societal landscape, as well as a few high-profile events, have rekindled the drive to increase the educational requirements of police officers.

The idea of requiring police officers to obtain a college education is not new. During his tenure as Berkeley, California's, police chief in the early 1900s, August Vollmer, known as the father of police professionalism, was a staunch supporter of increased educational requirements for officers and encouraged the hiring of degreed applicants (Walker, 1992). Vollmer required his officers to attend classes at the University of California at Berkeley and designed a sequence of courses he believed were important to an officer's education and professionalization. Because he believed so strongly in the importance of education, the cadre of college students he recruited for police service became known as "Berkeley's college cops" (Carte, 1973).

Vollmer's thinking, however, was not widely embraced at a time when "professionalism" was more a consideration of reducing outside political influences than increasing the standards and requirements of those in policing. It was not until the latter 1950s and early 1960s that a minimum requirement of a high school or general equivalency diploma (GED) was established and minimal training standards begun.

With the widespread civil unrest of the 1960s, a renewed call for increasing officers' formal education was reestablished. As Palmiotto discussed in an earlier debate, the President's Commission on Law Enforcement and Administration of Justice (1967) identified the need for college-educated personnel to address the increasing complexities of society.

One government "solution" to address this issue was to infuse educational funds through programs such as the Law Enforcement Educational Program (LEEP), professedly to increase the educational standards of officers throughout the nation. Unfortunately, with little oversight or program evaluation, LEEP became a total "*leap* of faith." Some officers did benefit from a college degree, but the curricula were often inadequate to meet the Commission's goals, and some were little more than "advanced" academies. Researchers suggest that the colleges' and universities' rush to acquire the flowing federal funds overshadowed proper consideration of the Commission's ideals, that is, to provide a broadened educational background that would facilitate present and future officers in their changing and increasingly challenging roles. The National Advisory Commission on Higher Education for Police Officers (1979), in fact, found that many criminal justice college programs were simply extensions of academy-based courses. This was contradictory to the broad-based social sciences approach to understanding and dealing with human behavior that Vollmer and the President's Commission had envisioned.

Research conducted during the early 1970s and 1980s addressing the benefits of college-educated police officers was equivocal at best. Some researchers found the college experience to be of little value, and others supported the notion that a college-educated police officer was better able to handle rapid changes, increased diversity, and technological innovations that were becoming more prevalent in law enforcement (Buckley, McGinnis, & Petrunik, 1992; Carter & Sapp, 1990; Radelet & Carter, 1994). It is not surprising that these contradictory findings developed. Proper analysis was virtually impossible, given the large curriculum variances, the few officers who actually attained baccalaureate degrees, the naturally occurring delay between attaining increased education and its impact on the profession, and the spate of confounding variables that could not be experimentally controlled. Additionally, those officers who did obtain a college degree were often viewed as suspect by fellow, nondegreed officers, and few if any organizational changes occurred to attract or retain college-educated individuals. Only now are we seeing those with higher education becoming the chiefs and administrators of police agencies and the resultant impact they can have on the policy and philosophy of law enforcement.

Unfortunately, the ongoing debate over the potential benefits of receiving a college education dominated the 1970s and 1980s. Rather than moving forward to enhance entry requirements and modify curriculum, decision makers continued to struggle over the merit of higher education. There seemed to be an interminable argument over the training versus education issue, a debate long ago resolved for other professions in favor of college degree requirements. Yet, critics of enhanced police college education requirements continued to reference the problems encountered in the early 1970s and 1980s to de-emphasize the potential importance of a college degree. Only now, possibly because of the increased attention on the philosophy of community policing and the need to have educated officers who are better communicators and better able to handle diverse situations and populations, is there a renewed call for increased educational standards.

This author contends that the time has come to put an end to this protracted debate. While decision makers have been wallowing in a quagmire of semantic conflict, the complexities of policing have continued to burgeon. The state of college education for police officers has improved significantly over the years. Most of the programs created in the mid-1970s, primarily in pursuit of federal dollars, have been discontinued, however, the more carefully planned and encompassing programs have survived. This is not to suggest that more improvement is not warranted; however, many of the past decade's mistakes have resulted in a natural "course correction" as a consequence of demanding increased standards and reduced discretionary funding.

From a research standpoint, as enough time has elapsed to examine the role of the college educational experience, a more well-rounded scenario has emerged. Recent studies, many of which are cited by Dr. Palmiotto in the previous debate, have, in spite of some detractors, emphasized the benefits associated with a college education.

Of course, many decision makers would prefer the debate to continue, seeking an absolute answer as to whether a college education is beneficial for police officers. Unfortunately, such an absolute is not possible in law enforcement—as it is not in medicine, law, psychology, teaching, counseling, or other professions that require such education. Some argue that one could become an adequate surgeon, forgoing all of those "pesky" college requirements, with ample technical training—as was once practiced in the armed forces. Yet, as medicine becomes more complex, few of us today would want to be exposed to a "technically" trained surgeon. We cannot quantify everything, and many other professions do not question the value of a college education in preparing to meet the challenges of their chosen field. A quote often attributed to Einstein suggests that "everything that counts cannot be counted, and everything that can be counted may not count."

The bottom line is that this debate is not easily resolved, especially when nondegreed officers may perceive their advancement potential to be threatened. Buckley (1991) found that officers who possessed a four-year degree believed that education enhanced their performance, and those without college suggested that "instincts," common sense, and experience were more important. A college environment challenges the student to seek and answer questions and to develop a proclivity to inquiry. Conversely, training is oftentimes developed around solutions that can be quickly implemented through a one-way dispersal of procedures, skills training, and presentation of facts.

This discussion is not to suggest that college is the answer to all of the challenges associated with policing or a replacement for valuable academy training. Education must complement both field experience and the technical training necessary to carry out law enforcement activities. Some states have adopted tailored education models that incorporate both aspects. In Texas, for example, the Texas Commission on Law Enforcement Officer Standards and Education (TCLEOSE) adopted a program designed to encourage the hiring of college-degreed police officers. The Criminal Justice Center at Sam Houston State University was the first four-year institution to put such an approach into practice (Blair, 1988). The curriculum provides students with a sequence of college classroom courses (in addition to the many university-designated degree requirements) recognized by The Texas Higher Education Coordinating Board. These courses meet more than one-third of the 230+ performance objectives of TCLEOSE's Basic Peace Officer Licensing Course. "Hands-on" training is conducted and coordinated within the traditional academy setting and is offered on a schedule that coincides with most

Texas college and university summer semesters. On the student's graduation from the university, this program results in a college-educated *and* academy-trained individual prepared for police service.

The importance of a college education for police officers should not be confined to criminal justice programs. In fact, research demonstrating the benefits of a college education on policing finds little distinction in one's major course of study. Although there may be some advantages in programs geared toward criminal justice, those officers with degrees in psychology, sociology, public administration, accounting, government, etc. also benefit. Research suggests that the college experience, coupled with the required courses that colleges and universities demand, combine to form a more well-rounded and better-prepared officer. Worden (1990) found that higher-educated police officers (regardless of major) tended to be less rigid, had better discretionary judgment, exhibited more positive attitudes toward policing's legal challenges, and held a broader perspective of the police role. Clearly, the college experience can provide the future officer with a well-rounded background and a level of performance beyond a high school diploma or a GED.

Now Is the Time for Change

Many of the educational recommendations for police officers proposed by presidential commissions, task forces, and other groups have never fully been realized. At the time the recommendations were made, several impediments were present, including inadequate salaries to compete for college-educated individuals, a cultural bias among long-time officers opposed to requirements that might jeopardize their positions or promotability, insufficient college programs, and a fear of litigation against those departments considering raising their standards. However, some researchers contend that several events have converged, making this the time for change. Many of the impediments of a college educational requirement have been addressed and overcome. For example, the salaries in most major police agencies are commensurate with other occupations that require a college degree, and the organizational climate opposed to increased standards has changed. In fact, although few departments require a college degree, many find that their best candidates are those who have one. In many ways a degree has become a de facto requirement in departmental hiring and promoting (Sheehan & Cordner, 1995). Finally, the courts have consistently held that college educational requirements for police officers are a Bona Fide Occupational Qualification (BFOQ) (e.g., *Davis v. Dallas* 777 f.2d 205, 5th Cir. 1985; see also Scott, 1986), and these standards have not had an adverse effect on women or minority recruitment (Carter, Sapp, & Stephens, 1988; Carter & Sapp, 1990). In fact, Carter and Sapp (1990) found that among police officers "all minority racial/ethnic groups contained higher percentages of graduate degrees than did whites" (p. 67).

Requiring a College Education for Entry-Level Police Officers

There are sound arguments to be made in support of a college degree requirement for entry level police officers. These are discussed under three general headings and attempt to show how the benefits of a college education can positively impact organizational changes, societal changes, and technological changes.

Organizational Changes

Today's policing organizations are much different from those that existed when LEAA and LEEP were begun in the 1970s. More officers involved in police service have college degrees, and the bias of the police culture against "college cops" has abated significantly. In fact, Carter and Sapp (1990) found that 65.2 percent of officers had one year or more of college credits and 22.6 percent had attained a bachelor's degree. As a result of time and experience, more police managers and administrators are college-educated and are incorporating organizational changes that are commensurate with the needs of a college-educated force. The challenges of community policing require today's officers to exert more discretion in problem solving and decision making. Officers must be attuned to the cultural differences and sensitive to the community's needs and recognize and value the diversity that they encounter. Studies have suggested that a successful community policing approach is dependent on the quality of educated police officers an agency can attract.

Because of these organizational changes, today's officers are more highly educated than at any other time in history. Departments can now recruit college-educated officers and provide them with salaries commensurate to those of other entry-level occupations requiring degreed candidates. Furthermore, many police organizations offer incentives—in the form of increased educational pay, tuition assistance, or preferential semester scheduling—to those officers who continue their education or pursue a college degree.

Although few states require a college education as a minimum qualification for police service, more and more departments are moving in this direction. Many require at least some college, some require an associate's degree, and others mandate an entry-level bachelor's degree (Carter & Sapp, 1990). Agencies also may require entry-level officers to have sixty hours of college but stipulate that only those with baccalaureate degrees or higher are eligible for promotion. Again, although the number of agencies that mandate higher education are increasing, much more needs to be achieved.

Interestingly, although the qualifications posted by many agencies do not necessarily require a college degree, researchers have found that, in the hiring and promotional process, college is a clear advantage. Hooper's study (1988) indicated that four-year college graduates rated highest in police academy performance, and

Garner (1996) found that 97 percent of those graduating in the top 10 percent of a preservice regional police academy were college graduates. In some ways, a college education has become a de facto requirement, although not always formalized into policy. When police chiefs and administrators were surveyed, they overwhelmingly identified a college education as an essential requirement for those entering police service today.

An interesting corollary to the college debate is the decreased confidence of police administrators in those officers holding only a high school diploma. Once an indicator of a minimum skill and education, high school diplomas today may be awarded through social promotion rather than demonstrated competence. Many university professors contend that, as a group, the communication and analytic skills of incoming college freshmen are less developed than a decade ago. Again, this issue further supports the argument favoring a college education requirement for police officers.

Organizational policing challenges are greater than ever before. The move toward community, problem-solving, and solution-oriented policing requires officers to possess reasoning skills beyond those that were required in the past. Research has shown that officers with college degrees possess a greater sense of problem solving and analytic ability and a greater sensitivity to the community's diverse needs. The philosophical shift toward community policing has caused departments to realign their management and organizational goals. Line officers, for example, are given greater discretion and are encouraged to develop innovative ways to address their mission. According to Radelet and Carter (1994), "given the nature of this change, the issue of college education is even more critical. The knowledge and skills officers are being asked to exercise in community policing appears to be tailored to college preparation" (p. 156).

Societal Changes

Today's police organizations are encountering a more culturally and ethnically diverse population than previously known. Ethnic slurs that were once pervasive throughout many police organizations are no longer tolerated. Officers must be culturally sensitive and willing to value ethnic differences. Interestingly, most college degree programs emphasize courses in areas such as cultural diversity, ethics, and cross-cultural comparisons, and some even require a foreign language. These courses are invaluable to the repertoire of today's police professionals. Research has indicated that those officers who are exposed to such an educational experience fare far better when dealing with diverse community groups.

In addition to the need for officers who are better attuned to cultural and diversity issues, departments must recognize that members of the community are also becoming more educated. As this occurs, the citizen's expectations toward police services and activities will also increase. One would expect nothing less than to require police officers to raise their educational levels to represent the populations they serve. In a recent survey (Garner, 1997), 89 percent of citizens reported that a college education was an important requirement for police officers. Interestingly, most respondents were surprised that a college degree was not already required.

Psychology, sociology, and human behavior courses all can contribute to a better understanding of the complex social world. The academy approach represents only one dimension of the knowledge continuum needed by the professional officer of today. The minimal amount of training hours devoted to "cultural diversity or human relations" is much less than the equivalent of an intense semester covering each topic.

Technological Changes

Today's police officer is faced with more modern technology than ever before. The regulation field notebook has been replaced with the laptop. Fingerprints and mug shots are now taken through photo digital transfer. The traditional teletype is practically a machine of the past, as more powerful and sophisticated computers can perform millions of calculations per second and speed information to police agencies in ways unimaginable only a few decades ago. Video retrieval systems, mobile digital computers, and computer-based dispatch and tracking are the policing technologies of the present. We have traded our ten-code for binary transfer protocols. In addition, the Internet, World Wide Web, and e-mail have expanded resources and data collection techniques, and the emphasis on solution-oriented policing has placed greater demands on crime analysis, problem solving, and computer sophistication.

As innovative ways to address crime and social disorder are developed, departments must have officers who are able to accurately measure the impact of these approaches with methodologically sound techniques. Again, this sophistication level was not a part of the "increased educational equation" during the time when the presidential commissions and others were emphasizing the importance of a college education—making it all the more important now. Fortunately, most college degree plans require courses that are beneficial in today's technologically rich environment (i.e., computer sciences, information systems, research methods, statistical analysis, etc.).

In sum, now is the time to increase the educational standards envisioned more than eighty years ago by August Vollmer. A baccalaureate degree should be the minimal requirement for entry into police service. The societal, technological, and organizational sophistication of policing requires this minimum criterion. If policing is ever to be viewed as a true profession, we must demand the types of educational standards commensurate with that designation. To reduce the potential difficulties that could be encountered by local and political influences, state Police Officer Standards and Training (POST) commissions should adopt and mandate the minimum baccalaureate standard. The American Police Association now lists among its goals to require at least a baccalaureate degree for all officers with law enforcement authority ("College-Educated Police Form APA," 1997).

Policing is an occupation that demands the education and skills of a teacher, lawyer, counselor, social worker, doctor, psychologist, and minister. Yet it is interesting to note that all of these professions long ago required a college degree—even before receiving their advanced training. Clearly, one could argue that the challenges of policing in today's society are equally or more demanding. Now is the time to provide our officers with the educational tools and professional acceptance that is needed in policing our rapidly changing environment.

REFERENCES

Blair, G. (1988). The 'compleat' law enforcement officer. *Texas Police Journal,* September, 5–7.
Buckley, L. (1991). Attitudes toward higher education among mid-career police officers. *Canadian Police College Journal, 15,* 257–274.
Buckley, L., McGinnis, J., & Petrunik, M. (1992). Police perceptions of education as an entitlement to promotion: An equity theory perspective. *American Journal of Police, 12* (2), 77–100.
Carte, G. (1973). August Vollmer and the origins of police professionalism. *Journal of Police Science and Administration, 1*(3), 274.
Carter, D., & Sapp, A. (1990). The evolution of higher education in law enforcement: Preliminary findings from a national study. *Journal of Criminal Justice Education, 1,* 59–85.
Carter, D., Sapp, A., & Stephens, D. (1988). Higher education as a bona fide occupational qualification (BFOQ) for police: A blueprint. *American Journal of Police, 7*(2), 16–18.
College-educated police form APA. (1997). *CJ Update: Anderson Newsletter for Criminal Justice Educators, 25*(2), 1.
Garner, R. (1996). College education and academy training: Performance comparisons. Manuscript submitted for publication.
Garner, R. (1997). Citizens views on police education. (Tech. Rep. No. 1). Huntsville, TX: Sam Houston State University, Criminal Justice Center.
Hooper, M. (1988). *The Relationship of College Education to Police Officer Job Performance.* Ph.D. dissertation, Claremont Graduate School. Ann Arbor, Mich.: University Microfilms International.
National Advisory Commission on Higher Education for Police Officers. (1979). *Proceedings of the National Symposium on Higher Education for Police Officers.* Washington, D.C.: Police Foundation.
President's Commission on Law Enforcement and Administration of Justice. (1967). *The Challenge of Crime in a Free Society.* Washington, DC: U.S. Government Printing Office.

Radelet, L., & Carter, D. (1994). *The police and the community* (5th ed.). New York: Macmillan.

Scott, W. (1986). College education requirements for police entry level and promotion: A case study. *Journal of Police and Criminal Psychology, 2*(1), 10–28.

Sheehan, R., & Cordner, G. (1995). *Police administration* (3rd ed.). Cincinnati: Anderson.

Walker, S. (1992). *The police in America: An introduction* (2nd ed.). New York: McGraw-Hill.

Worden, R. (1990). A badge and a baccalaureate: Policies, hypotheses, and further evidence. *Justice Quarterly, 7*(3), 565–592.

Rejoinder to Dr. Garner   R. Lynn

Dr. Garner offers a compelling treatise regarding the implementation of a college degree requirement for entry-level police officers. He makes sound arguments for the *potential* benefit that a college education may have, as one considers all of the organizational, societal, and technological changes that have occurred in the last two decades. Let me emphasize, I am not opposed to increased educational requirements—we just have to think it through. I agree with Dr. Garner that the more recent research on college-educated officers is promising, but this is still a long way from mandating that we should require a degree as a minimum standard. As Garner correctly states, few agencies have actually implemented such a proposal. Despite any discussion regarding a degree as a "de facto" requirement, police agencies have been hesitant to make it formal policy. We must ask ourselves why this might be and consider the implications involved.

On another level, many of my concerns are of a more practical nature—how will we fairly implement this proposal, how will we pay for it, and how will it impact our ability to attract dedicated personnel? It is easy to offer the suggestion; the devil is in the details, however. Garner and others cite reasons why a degree might advantageous in policing, but few offer recommendations on how to implement these ideas in a way that will not be disruptive to the organization. I can envision many potential conflicts between the degreed and nondegreed officers, especially in areas of pay, assignment, and promotion. Furthermore, smaller agencies may be unfairly burdened with the expense of competing for and retaining qualified applicants. How can small agencies expect to attract qualified applicants on limited budgets and meager resources?

Again, I support the need to provide our law enforcement officers with the education that they believe necessary to meet the demands of the profession. My reservations regarding many of the issues I have outlined in my segment of this debate, however, remain. Certainly the argument is not that a college degree is detrimental; in fact, many, if not most, may benefit from this educational experience.

The major question, however, is whether there is sufficient evidence to *mandate* this as a minimum requirement, thus excluding many potential applicants from the pool. In my judgment, the jury is still out on this issue.

NO

R. LYNN

There has been much debate about the value of a college education for police officers over the years. National Commissions (e.g., President's Commission on Law Enforcement and Administration of Justice), international police organizations (e.g., the International Association of Chiefs of Police), and others have argued that the road to the solidification of policing as a profession leads to America's colleges and universities. Despite these declarations, little evidence has been offered that this is truly the case.

Much of the discussion regarding upgrading the professional standards for policing originated after a period of social and civil upheaval in the late 1960s and early 1970s. This was a time in which the police were seeing growing social unrest coupled with an increase in judicial intervention into what was deemed to be acceptable police practices. Many celebrated Supreme Court cases placed significant restrictions on police enforcement and investigatory activities. Tales of alleged police indiscretions or abuse were met with a call for increased professionalism, stringent hiring requirements, and a substantial enhancement of educational standards.

The President's Commission on Law Enforcement and Administration of Justice (1967) called for increasing the minimum education for police officers to a bachelor's degree, suggesting that, by the mid-1980s, *all* individuals in police service should meet this standard. This sentiment was echoed by the Task Force Report: The Police (1967b), as well as other influential commissions, foundations, and research institutions. Unfortunately, in their zeal to suggest increased educational standards, the important issues of the *quality* of that education and the caliber of the curriculum were not addressed. It seems that the idea of having police officers with a college education was so enamoring that the concept of how that education would be achieved or delivered was lost. It was almost as though there was a notion that, by merely sending cops to college, many of the problems associated with the profession would be solved.

With the advent of the Law Enforcement Educational Program (LEEP), an offshoot of the Law Enforcement Assistance Administration, money began to flow to both officers and the colleges and universities who were to educate them. These educational institutions, however, were ill equipped to provide the type of generalized education suggested by the Commission. This seemed to be of little consequence to many of these institutions. As one politician put it, "if Uncle Sam is passing out the feed (read as 'easily obtainable money'), everybody will show up to the trough." The resulting "educational movement" was fraught with problems, incompetencies, and misdirection. The "quality" education offered by some institutions was little more than an upgraded academy class (e.g., Handcuffing 101) and bore no resemblance to the liberal educational ideals that had been suggested. To make their programs look successful and attract police students, some institutions offered "life experience" credit for one's time as an officer, hardly what the President's Commission had in mind. In fact, many colleges merely hired academy training staff as adjunct faculty to begin their program.

The Sherman Report (1979) (officially, the National Advisory Commission on Higher Education for Police Officers), which examined the state of higher education on police officers, was very critical of these practices and highlighted this misguided approach. Nearly a decade later, Southerland (1991) continued to find little consistency in criminal justice curriculum offered by institutions of higher learning.

Around the time of the Sherman Report, many researchers were beginning to examine the value of a college education for police officers. Griffin (1980) found no significant relationship between various education levels of police officers and their performance as patrol officers; although when combined with experience (months of service) the aggregate measure was related to performance. Smith and Ostrom (1974) found that increased education had a negative effect on performance ratings, and Gotlieb and Baker (1974) found no difference among officers with college versus those who had no college education. Fenster and Locke (1973) examined IQ scores among officers who had at least some college education and compared them with those with no college. They found only a slight (although statistically significant) difference between the two groups.

Still other studies have found that better-educated officers tend to have a greater level of dissatisfaction and may be more prone to leave a department after a short time (Burbeck & Furnham, 1985; Fielding & Fielding, 1987). Although this could be due to the unchanging organizational bureaucracy, it calls attention to the need to have a greater scrutiny of the educational requirements that have been proposed.

In fairness, much of the research examining the relationship between a college education and police performance involved sampling and other methodological flaws (see Hudzik, 1978; Southerland, 1984); however, these inconsistent findings should register as alarm bells that the complete picture on requiring a college degree is not present. Before we move to mandated college education as a minimum standard for policing, we should ensure that such a requirement would be advantageous to the officers, the departments, and our communities. If the empirical evidence reflects little consistency in the various educational programs and dubious quality in the curriculum, we should question any political or administrative movement to significantly alter the educational requirements for policing.

Certainly the argument here is not that a college education would be overtly detrimental to aspiring police officers. In fact, more recent research tends to show some positive trends (see Carter & Sapp, 1990). However, many officers who now have college degrees received them *after* they were already employed as law enforcement professionals. Given the suggestion of changing the minimum standard, how many quality individuals would we be *unable* to hire simply because they do not currently possess a college degree? Equally interesting to consider, how many excellent officers on the force today—some who now possess college degrees—would have been rejected had this new standard been in place?

No one would argue against the proposition that policing is becoming more complex as technology, society, and policing philosophies are changing. Nor would one suggest that increasing the education and training of police officers to meet these demands would be unwarranted. In fact, we must keep pace with the needs of our profession and the demand of our communities. The caution, however, is that we not move to uncritically implement the requirement of a college degree without fully assessing the impact this would have on policing through the United States. Many questions concerning this proposal remain unclear or unanswered; we must critically assess, for instance:

- How beneficial will a college degree really be to the officer on the beat?
- Do we need to require four-year degrees?
- Are there appreciable differences in officers who have four-year versus two-year degrees?
- Has the management of our police agencies kept pace with the times, providing a more accepting environment for the college-educated officer?
- What curriculum is appropriate? Will any degree do? Is a Liberal Arts degree equivalent to a Criminal Justice degree?
- Are we to hold law enforcement agencies of all sizes to the same educational standard? Should a department comprised of three officers meet the same minimum college degree requirement as a thousand-person force?
- Do we have the financial resources to attract, recruit, and retain college-educated officers?

In sum, only after these issues are more adequately addressed should we begin to set policy on what types of educational requirements are most advantageous to the law enforcement profession. Would we want to exclude otherwise qualified persons from law enforcement simply because they do not have a college degree? In our striving for increased professional status, we must not react with emotional decisions or politically correct platitudes. To do so may cause us to overlook the far-reaching impact that such a change in our minimum standards may present.

REFERENCES

Burbeck, E., & Furnham, A. (1985). Police officer selection: A critical review of the literature. *Journal of Police Science and Administration, 13,* 58–69.

Carter, D., & Sapp, A. (1990). The evolution of higher education in law enforcement: Preliminary findings from a national study. *Journal of Criminal Justice Education, 1*(1), 59–85.

Fenster, C., & Locke, B. (1973). The "dumb cop": Myth or reality? An examination of police intelligence. *Journal of Personality Assessment, 37*(3), 276–281.

Fielding, N., & Fielding, J. (1987). A study of resignation during British police training. *Journal of Police Science and Administration, 15,* 24–36.

Gotlieb, M., & Baker, C. (1974). Predicting police officer effectiveness. *Journal of Forensic Psychology, 12,* 35–46.

Griffin, G. (1980). *A study of relationships between level of college education and police patrolmen's performance.* Saratoga, CA: Century Twenty-One Publishing.

Hudzik, J. (1978). College education for police: Problems in measuring component and extraneous variables. *Journal of Criminal Justice, 6*(1), 69–81.

National Advisory Commission on Higher Education for Police Officers (1979). *Proceedings of the national symposium on higher education for police officers.* Washington, DC: Police Foundation.

President's Commission on Law Enforcement and Administration of Justice (1967a). *The challenge of crime in a free society.* Washington, DC: U.S. Government Printing Office.

President's Commission on Law Enforcement and Administration of Justice. (1967b). *Task force report: Police.* Washington, DC: U.S. Government Printing Office.

Radelet, L., & Carter, D. (1994). *The police and the community* (5th ed.). New York: Macmillan.

Smith, D., & Ostrom, E. (1974). The effects of training and education on police attitudes and performance: A preliminary analysis. In: H. Jacob (ed.). *The potential for reform in criminal justice.* Beverly Hills, CA: Sage Publications.

Southerland, M. (1991). Criminal justice curricula in the United States: An examination of baccalaureate programs, 1988–1989. *Journal of Criminal Justice Education, 2*(1), 45–68.

Rejoinder to R. Lynn

RANDALL L. GARNER

Professor Lynn's article shares many of the characterizations I discussed regarding the early attempts at enhancing police education. We both articulate many of the problems found when L.E.A.A. infused money into an unprepared educational system. Our point of departure, however, appears to revolve around the "absolute certainty" issue that I addressed. Although Lynn does not seem opposed to increased educational requirements, the tone of his article suggests that we must continue to wait for more evidence to verify the absolute nature of such an education. Unfortunately, this status quo thinking is exactly the problem.

Lynn acknowledges the increasing complexity of society and the associated difficulties of policing, yet would delay action that might address these needs. I can appreciate the cautious approach he offers; however, we cannot continue an intractable debate—we need to make progress. The policing environment is changing daily, and we cannot wait to ferret out every nuance of this issue. Recognizing and addressing the changing societal circumstances and their implications for the policing profession are what leadership is all about. The demand for "ultimate proof" is not a reasonable standard. The courts have regularly supported the position that educational requirements both are constitutional and represent a Bona Fide Occupational Qualification.

Additionally, many of the research references cited by Lynn to support his position are decades old and bear little resemblance to the information we have today. As I addressed in my own segment of this debate, the early equivocal findings concerning the impact of a college education on policing were not surprising given the newness of the movement (at that time) and the methodological complications. He fails to offer the more recent evidence that provides greater support for college-educated police personnel, although he does allude to this material in his text. A college degree certainly does not ensure complete competency in policing; however, as a recruitment tool, it can provide us with a more reasonable standard from which to select qualified applicants. As I previously suggested, the belief that there must be absolute certainty regarding the direct impact of a degree on policing before it can be instituted is not a position shared by other professions or the courts. We now have ample evidence regarding the benefit of a college education and should move forward to implement this standard.

Lynn also expresses concern regarding the application of the same educational standard to all departments, regardless of size. Although this is worthy of consideration, one must recall that the recommendations offered over the years have been from *national* organizations and commissions. These proposed standards were offered for *all* police officers with enforcement authority—regardless of the number of officers employed at any particular agency. To institute a system of varying standards based on personnel numbers would be to miss the point and create a class system within the law enforcement community, something that most would consider to be undesirable.

I agree with Professor Lynn that we should adequately assess any systematic changes we make in our police organizations, including enhancing police educational requirements. However, this assessment has been ongoing for more than twenty years, and the current evidence supports the implementation of the recommendations offered by the President's Commission on Law Enforcement thirty years ago. To protract the discussion further would be to ignore the important empirical, political, and social support for this proposition and leave our officers ill-equipped to deal with our rapidly changing world.

Police Executive Contracts: Are They a Foundation for Successful Tenure?

EDITOR'S NOTE: For most law enforcement officers, job protection takes many forms. Civil Service acts were an early method of protecting officers from unwarranted political interference. Contract efforts by police unions also clearly spelled out circumstances under which an officer could be disciplined or fired. When creative politicians and agency officials discovered ways to circumvent such laws or union power, police unions and associations successfully lobbied many state legislatures for a "police officer bill of rights," offering increased control over improper, and sometimes proper, administrative or criminal investigations. Yet, in most agencies, the individual afforded the least protection and involved in the most pronounced political environment is the appointed chief executive. With the high turnover rates traditionally associated with such positions, a major controversy becomes clear: how to protect an agency head from political interference with law enforcement operations *and* a community from an ineffective or incompetent chief.

Dr. Sutham Cheurprakobkit is Assistant Professor in the Department of Behavioral Sciences at the University of Texas of the Permian Basin. He received his bachelor's degree from the National Thai Police Cadet Academy, his master's degree in Criminal Justice from the University of Alabama at Birmingham, and his Ph.D. from Sam Houston State University. Before resigning from the Royal Thai Police as a police captain, Dr. Cheurprakobkit spent four years at a police station in Bangkok, Thailand, involved in traffic, patrol, and investigation work. He also spent one year serving as an instructor and advisor at the Thai Police Cadet Academy.

Most of his administrative experiences came from employment as a research assistant for two years at the Blackwood Law Enforcement Management Institute of Texas, Sam Houston State University.

William (Bill) E. Kirchhoff has over twenty-five years' experience as a city manager, managing cities ranging in size from 15,000 to 300,000. He has served on the National Commission on Accreditation for Law Enforcement Agencies and is a member of the U.S. Justice Department's Community Oriented Policing Services (COPS) Advisory Board. He is a standing lecturer for Northwestern University's Traffic Institute Executive Development Program and Sam Houston State University's Police Management Program. He is on the International Association of Chiefs of Police adjunct faculty and the author of numerous books, including *How Bright is Your Badge* and *Conflict Management: Lessons Learned from the Art of War.* Mr. Kirchhoff has successfully managed three police departments through the accreditation process. Two of the police departments he managed during the 1980s, Lakewood, Colorado, and Arlington, Texas, were selected by a panel of experts as being among the eight best suburban police departments in America. He was given the 1996 Award for Program Excellence in Public Safety from the International City/ County Management Association for his role in policing programs.

Dr. Gerald L. Williams is a principal associate with the Institute for Law and Justice in Alexandria, Virginia. Previously, he served as the executive director of the Blackwood Law Enforcement Management Institute of Texas (LEMIT) and, before that, as Director of the Law Enforcement Education and Research Project at North Carolina State University. He has served as police chief of Aurora, Colorado (population 230,000), and, earlier, as police chief in Arvada, Colorado (population 98,000), where he began his career as a police officer in 1969. Dr. Williams holds a bachelor's degree in sociology from Metropolitan State College and a master of criminal justice administration and D.P.A. from the University of Colorado. He has served as president of the Police Executive Research Forum (PERF), chair and commissioner of the Commission on Accreditation for Law Enforcement Agencies, and a member of the Executive Sessions on Policing at Harvard University's John F. Kennedy School of Government.

YES

GERALD L. WILLIAMS AND SUTHAM CHEURPRAKOBKIT

Police and politics have long been recognized as operating hand in hand. Unfortunately, this relationship is not entirely a healthy one. Despite occasional avowing by some police executives to keep politics out of the department, their postures do not yield much success and are often unrealistic. An independent police chief who enforces laws and departmental rules and regulations without regard for the political implications of his or her actions is difficult to find. Why? Because the police chief, although not directly elected, is politically selected, and "virtually everything the chief undertakes can have political implications" (Bouza, 1990, p. 42).

Considerable evidence indicates that police chiefs who lack protection from arbitrary and unjustified termination cannot objectively and independently fulfill their responsibilities. The average tenure of most police chiefs is three to six years. For their contracts (an extremely limited number of actually formal contractual cases exist) to be renewed at the end of the term, or their status as an at-will appointee to be continued, compromises of the chief's sense of responsibility may be necessary, especially if his or her decisions run counter to those of city officials. In a discussion of the lack of a reappointment agreement for Milwaukee's former Chief Philip Arreola, Mahtesian (1977) states,

> He wasn't exactly fired, but months before his scheduled reappointment for a second term, word simply filtered out of City Hall that Mayor John O. Norquist no longer saw eye to eye with the chief. It was not a matter of scandal or of incompetence, it was a case of political failure—too many constituencies, all with clear-cut agendas, and no way to satisfy all of them at once . . . It may seem curious for a city to can a respected police chief without any whiff of impropriety or misconduct, but in fact it is the norm these days, not the exception. The sacking of the police chief is part of the routine of the 1990s in urban America. (p. 19)

The advent of community policing as the evolving contemporary policing strategy emphasizes enhanced relations between the police and the public and demands that police chiefs possess new skills and attitudes and become effective visionary leaders. In other words, chiefs must not be reluctant to pioneer innovative programs geared toward community problem-solving policing goals. The inherent risks, however, are obvious, and failure of these high-profile public projects may jeopardize the chief's position.

For a moment, let's consider where police chiefs come from. Most top police executives today, as in the past, reach their position as police chief in the twilight of their policing careers. Charles Gain, former chief of the Oakland, California, Police Department, argued that police chiefs in this twilight period tend to resist organizational change because they fear the loss of the position for which they have so long waited, and, as they are in the final stages of their career, they engage in a "holding action" (Ruiz, 1997). Gain further comments that when chiefs make it to the top, they are not going to jeopardize their position by setting new goals and moving ahead (Ruiz, 1997).

Ruiz cites another example as demonstration of this bankrupt leadership style. Researchers of the Police Executive Development Project at Pennsylvania State University found that top police executives showed greater devotion for their personal moral standards than for the citizens they serve. Findings also indicated that top police executives showed greater submission to authority than does the general public. This subservient attitude has been formed as a result of working in a rigid organizational structure that demands and rewards obedience to authority (Ruiz, 1997). The results of the project indicated that the average police executive failed to possess initiative, self-reliance, and confidence, because of a lifelong habit of submission and social conformity. The study concluded that these findings correlate to some extent with the suggestion that police chiefs tend to treat their job as a sinecure and are incapable of innovation at this late stage in their police careers (Ruiz, 1997). Without some form of contract protection, it is difficult to expect any police chief to jeopardize his or her job by implementing a vision or a program that has any chance of failure.

This debate discusses politics in terms of the forces that may affect the chief's decisions and how the chief of police serves as a political actor, leading to a discussion of the importance of administrative freedom and contracts. We conclude with a discussion of how a written contract would benefit both the chief of police and the appointing authority.

Decisions to improve the agency and the quality of service the agency provides to the community will, to a large degree, always be tempered by consideration of the political realities of job survival. For a chief of police to be a fully effective leader, however, reasonable job security and independence is needed (Greenberg, 1992).

> Job security does not diminish accountability to elected or appointed officials nor does it eliminate the potential to remove a chief of police from office for cause. Rather, it provides a foundation on which an executive can build, experiment, innovate, and serve. (Greenberg, 1992, p. 7)

Why a Contract?

Many chiefs of police function effectively, commit to long-term efforts, surpass expectations, and assume professional leadership roles without written contracts or letters of agreement that provide job security. They rely almost solely on their relationship with the appointing authority as the basis for their tenure.

A contract provides specific benefits to the chief of police and to the city, county, or state's appointing authority. It clarifies the employer/employee relationship as well as the employee's scope of authority. It benefits the employer by establishing a structure for accountability and promoting responsiveness, and it benefits the employee by defining the nature of his or her responsibilities and clarifying the length of the appointment or term.

A chief of police with a contract may evolve into a different leader than an executive who functions without one. The police chief without a contract may focus on programs and make decisions that ensure job security rather than on those more relevant to the needs of the department or community. Some programs and decisions may be suppressed out of concern that they may jeopardize the chief's tenure. Crisis situations may be handled too conservatively. And, the chief of police may be less likely to commit to long-term projects since short-term efforts generally provide immediate results and, therefore, more rapidly demonstrate and reinforce the chief's impact and worth. Experimentation and innovation may take a back seat to maintaining the status quo, not because of logical choice or need but simply because it is safe. (Greenberg, 1992, pp. 7–8)

Defining Employment Agreements or Contracts

Although commonly used in business, industry, education, and public management, the concept of an executive contract for a police chief is relatively new. The Police Executive Research Forum (PERF) (1981) identified three elements as being crucial to a police chief's contract: (1) term of office, (2) severance pay, and (3) approaches to discipline and termination. Greenberg (1992) suggests that discussion on all three of these elements, as well as others, should occur only after the candidate has researched state and municipal law governing appointments, removal of appointees, and terms in office. For a detailed discussion of these three essential elements, we suggest Greenberg's text *On the Dotted Line*.

Other components of a police employment contract are (1) nature of duties, (2) compensation, (3) automobile and automobile allowance, (4) hours of work, (5) professional development, (6) performance evaluation, (7) insurance, (8) retirement, (9) residency, (10) benefits package, (11) indemnification for professional liability, and (12) a concluding section generally referred to as General Provisions. Again, these sections, as well as the initial three essential areas of a contract, are detailed in *On the Dotted Line* (Greenberg, 1992).

Politics and the Police Chief

Police departments operate within larger governmental systems. Both administrative and policy decisions made by police agencies are influenced by the agency's structure and procedures and other parts of the governmental system (Hunt & Magenau, 1993), as well as by some organized societal interest groups (Gamson, 1968). Hunt and Magenau (1993) identified a number of potentially influential parties that can prevent the police chief from having the final decision in particular cases. These influential parties include quasi-public ones (e.g., police unions, police review commissions), interorganizational agencies, other police departments, the public, institutional partners (i.e., mayors, city managers, and council members), and other parties (e.g., the media or university professors). Even though a police chief strives to attain the organization's goals, these partisan groups can create con-fusion for and pressures on the chief and make it difficult to promote the agency's goals. Overall, these influential parties, especially the institutional partners, have turned police departments into "political milieus."

The institutional partners play major roles not only in controlling the police agency's budgets but also in appointing and dismissing the chief of police. Al-though the police chief must be able to present budgets and negotiate changes, most of the police department's financial resources can be at the institutional part-ners' mercy, regardless of how promising the proposed policies are. However, the issue that concerns many police chiefs may not be a budgetary one but that of the mayor's influence on the chief's position. According to Bouza (1990), mayors are the most important people in law enforcement because they hold the purse and ap-pointment power, as well as the power of dismissal. Therefore, it is not surprising that the political environment that develops from the mayor–chief relationship is local and sometimes adversarial (to a large degree the city manager–chief relation-ship is consistent with the observations made regarding mayors and police chiefs). The police chief, who is usually recognized as a social or public worker, thus can be pressured to play the role of a political actor (Hunt & Magenau, 1993).

Being a chief of police is difficult enough in a normal situation in which both internal and external factors often make it hard for the police chief to discern the public interest. However, it is tolerable only if time and effort are needed to solve a problem. Some situations and conflicts, however, are outside the chief's control, yet their occurrence may cost the police chief his or her job. Mintzberg (1983) refers to these conflicts as "political arenas" and divides them into four types based on their duration, intensity, and pervasiveness.

The first political arena type is "confrontation." In this most common type, the situational conflict is intense but brief and confined. An obvious example may be the Rodney King incident, which put an end to the contract of Daryl Gates as the Los Angeles Chief of Police. The second political arena is a "shaky alliance," in which conflict is less intense but still pervasive. A shaky alliance may be a se-quel to a confrontational situation. Chief Willie Williams, Daryl Gates's successor and the first outsider appointed as chief in over forty years, had to deal with both external (i.e., the impact of the King incident on the public) and internal pressures (i.e., resentful feelings from his own police officers). This was a shaky alliance, and at the end of his term in 1996, Williams's contract was not renewed. The third type of political arena, a "politicized organization," features pervasive but muted conflict that is tolerable for a time. This kind of conflict is commonplace in Amer-ican policing, and the agency's police chief's survival depends on external support. Examples include riots against police brutality such as those in 1996 in St. Peters-burg, Florida, or the protracted JonBenet Ramsey homicide investigation in Boul-der, Colorado. The "complete" political arena is the final situation in which the conflict is pervasive, intense, brief, and out of control. Fortunately, police chiefs seldom face this type of conflict. However, when it does occur, termination is the only alternative. Because of the "common occurrence" of the third type, the politi-cized organization arena, several expanded cases are offered.

In the St. Petersburg "politicized organization" example, riots began on Thursday night, October 25, 1996, after a white police officer shot and killed a black man driving a stolen car. Recognizing that Police Chief Darrel Stephens is considered by most to be an enlightened visionary leader, the *St. Petersburg Times,* in a front-page story on October 30, reflected Stephens' philosophy:

> I've always believed that we would be able to keep something like this from happening. Personally, you look at what's happening and you have lots of questions about what more we could have done in this situation to keep it from developing ... In many respects, his [Stephens] actions at the scene reflect a policing philosophy and management style that have brought national attention to the St. Petersburg force, but have frustrated officers who prefer a tougher approach to crime or see the department as understaffed and over-worked. Stephens now finds himself facing new scrutiny. Last Thursday's violence has been his administration's biggest crisis since he was hired in December 1992 to restore morale in a department troubled by racial friction and political factions.

An editorial entitled "Help Stephens Succeed" in the *St. Petersburg Times,* on October 31, reported that,

> One casualty of the riot in south St. Petersburg could be the city's common sense approach to law enforcement—community policing. That would be a shame and a setback for citizens, both black and white. In the aftermath of the fatal shooting ... by a police officer and the ensuing chaos, some people are criticizing Police Chief Darrel Stephens' approach to law enforcement and his tempered reaction to rioters. Emotion rules such arguments and ignores history. Stephens was hired four years ago to return stability and respect to the police department after the firing of combative Chief Ernest "Curt" Curtsinger. An expert on community policing, Stephens took some officers out of their patrol cars and put them in neighborhoods to help residents solve their problems ... Community policing cannot be expected to resolve the broader problems in St. Petersburg's poor black neighborhoods: unemployment, broken families and the hopelessness of poverty. Those who hold the police responsible for such breaches in the nation's social fabric are misguided. Instead, St. Petersburg residents—both black and white—should be asking how they can help Stephens succeed. Black residents can invite police officers into their communities and offer their help. White residents can support measures that strengthen Stephens' work. We should not let the emotion of the moment stop progress toward a police force that serves all citizens.

It is interesting that in the third arena of politicized support, not only did Stephens have the support of the *St. Petersburg Times* editorial staff, he also had the mayor's continued political support. On reelection to a second term, the mayor asked Stephens to become the city administrator for St. Petersburg in June 1997. The mayor and newly promoted city administrator quickly named a new police chief from within the ranks of the department. This all occurred within the span of several days during June.

In the JonBenet Ramsey murder investigation in Boulder, Colorado, Police Chief Tom Koby, the Boulder Police Department, and the entire city of Boulder have been under intense national media scrutiny since the murder of the six-year-old JonBenet Ramsey on December 26, 1996. Both of Denver's major newspapers, the *Denver Post* and the *Rocky Mountain News,* have been openly critical of the investigation and of Chief Koby. On June 8, 1997, an article in the *Rocky Mountain News* was titled "Ramsey Case a Tragedy of Errors." Similarly, the *Denver Post* printed the following headlines: "Cops Grumpy with Koby," "DA Brushes Off Koby Problems," "Is the Trail Too Cold?," "Mute Leaders," "Cops' Vote on Koby Negative," and "It's Ludicrous." As a yet unproductive, as this debate was finalized, investigation in a city in which murder cases are rare, and an unsolved murder case unheard of, it would appear that the case has polarized the department as well as city politicians. As a May 30, 1997, column in the *Denver Post* noted:

> Here is a glimpse into the inner workings of the city of Boulder: The troops, by a vote of 2 to 1, say they have lost confidence in Police Chief Tom Koby. Spense Havlik, deputy mayor of Boulder, was 'quite surprised' by the vote. Havlik must have spent most of April and May on Comet Hale-Bopp. Havlik's incredulous statement underscores a mystery as mystifying as Jon-Benet Ramsey's murder itself—where is the political and moral leadership in Boulder? Just like Chief Koby and District Attorney Alex Hunter—the two men supervising the investigation of the murder—Havlik doesn't have a clue. While the rank-and-file cops have no confidence in Koby, Councilman Havlik and most other political officers in the city are heartily endorsing the city's beleaguered police chief. Leading the parade for Koby are Mayor Leslie Durgin and City Manager Tim Honey, two people who also were surprised by the rank-and-file vote on Koby.

On May 29, members of Boulder's police union voted 78 to 31 that they had no confidence in Chief Tom Koby's leadership. The vote came amidst rumblings that Boulder's elected officials were displeased with Koby's boss, City Manager Tim Honey (*Denver Post,* 30 May 1997). On June 8, 1997, the *Rocky Mountain News* reported "the night that Boulder City Manager Tim Honey tendered his forced resignation to the city council, he said, 'this investigation is going to lead to an arrest.'"

As for Chief Koby? Although he announced that he would retire at the end of 1998, his tenure as chief of police ended on June 28, 1998, when he was forced to step down by an acting city manager. He was terminated because of a combination of factors, including little or no support from the media, crumbling or divided political support within the city council, and support from less than 40 percent of the department's rank and file.

Without support from the mayor and the media, could Stephens initially have been promoted to city administrator or, even worse, would he, without that support, have been in a situation similar to that Koby experienced? Conversely, had Koby received positive editorials and strong political and rank and file support, would his situation have turned out differently?

There are several cases in which police chiefs either were terminated or their contracts were not renewed despite the lack of valid grounds. For example, Cleveland, Ohio's mayor ousted three police chiefs in a four-year period for political reasons. In 1992, Police Chief Elizabeth Watson was terminated by the newly elected mayor in Houston, Texas, because her advocacy of community-oriented policing was criticized for reducing the effectiveness of the police as crime fighters. As already noted, in 1996, Police Chief Philip Arreola of Milwaukee, Wisconsin, was forced to resign because of failure to satisfy all of the constituencies. Police Commissioner William Bratton of New York was forced to resign after only twenty-seven months in the position, despite the fact that during his administration the city experienced the largest two-year decline of crime in its history. The most recent termination involved Los Angeles Police Chief Willie Williams, whose contract was not renewed in 1997.

Being chiefs of police in the 1990s is very difficult, as they can be terminated or forced to resign either because they do things too progressively or quickly (as in the cases of Chiefs Watson and Arreola) or because they are perceived as doing things too slowly (as in the case of Chief Williams). Chiefs also can be forced to resign because they do what they are supposed to, as in the case of Commissioner Bratton (Mahtesian, 1997).

Should police chiefs be allowed to keep their positions if there is no evidence that they are incompetent, unethical, or involved in illegal activities? Should chiefs be terminated for cause and not personal or political reasons? Unfortunately, terminating police chiefs has become the norm in the 1990s. A recent Los Angeles City charter change guaranteed that no one will ever again hold the position as long as Gates did. In other cities where chiefs serve at the mayor's pleasure, they are virtually assured of a brief stay. All of this is occurring at a time when big-city police chiefs as a group are more educated, more skilled at public relations, and better trained in management than ever before. Furthermore, even the most adroit police chief tends to run into political conflicts, and, whether by his or her own choice or by the mayor or city manager's command, the chief is frequently terminated within a few years of a much-publicized arrival (Mahtesian, 1997).

One might argue that as long as there are available talented replacements, why take any action? Organizationally, replacing chiefs every two years can leave a department in a seemingly never-ending spiral of change, as each new chief strives to remedy the problems he or she was hired to solve and to create a loyal and cohesive command staff. Worse is the possibility that meaningful progress is not attempted because the rank and file believe that it is futile to begin a project that will never be finished. Just as progress is begun, there very likely will be another change.

Throughout the United States, those individuals for whom police chiefs work have some form of contract. For example, mayors have a set term in office, and city managers, for the most part, have contracts that stipulate the terms of their employment. The city manager is also financially protected if he or she is terminated without reasonable grounds. It appears that a written contract could serve as a built-in financial consequence to the city if a police chief is terminated without just cause.

Because a police chief's job is clearly far more visible than that of a city manager, if a form of protection that is fair to both parties is not developed, the quality of police chief applicants could be negatively impacted. One of the reasons we believe that city managers have benefited in the area of contracts is based on their frequent movement from city to city. Over the years, the reality that city managers will most likely be fired has become the rule rather than the exception. For this reason, in our opinion, managers' employment contracts are justified. The similarities between city managers and police chiefs, especially in larger cities, is expressed best when considering former New York Commissioner William Bratton:

> The very fact that Bratton speaks in terms of his own media style and message makes a crucial point not only about him but also about the way the job itself is changing. With so many pressures from all sides, handling the media and cultivating political constituencies are becoming standard equipment for police chiefs, just as they now are for school superintendents and city managers, neither of whom used to worry much about publicity in the old days. Bratton did not last in New York, but the reputation he achieved, and the virtual celebrity status that he has acquired around the country since his departure, suggest a career path for future police chiefs very different from the old one: Strike for quick results, make sure they are publicized, and be prepared for a quick exit. (Mahtesian, 1997)

Unless a legal, balanced, and reliable method of protection against arbitrary dismissals is developed, it may become more difficult to attract the best-qualified individuals to accept the position of police chief.

Administrative Freedom and Contracts

A contract is vital to a police chief's administrative freedom. Politics are necessary to achieve police accountability in a democratic society; yet, inefficiency and corruption are, historically, often outcomes of political interference. Police professionalism requires a certain amount of independence from direct political interference so that decisions can be freely made without fear of negative consequences. Police chiefs' administrative managerial freedom is essential as police work requires changes, innovations, and calculated risk-taking in serving the public's needs and interests. Even though police chiefs in medium to large cities are better prepared today than ever before with effective leadership styles, if they have no contract, fear of being terminated can threaten their innovations. Therefore, administrative freedom and contracts are inseparable because the chiefs cannot freely make decisions if they fear losing their jobs.

A balance between the legitimate and illegitimate political aspects in policing can be achieved through the separation of policy and administrative decision making. Policy decisions should be made by elected officials, whereas administrative decisions should be made by police administrators (Andrews, 1985). Policy decisions include budgetary and the size of the police force issues, and administrative decisions involve implementation of agency programs and deployment of patrol officers.

The Benefits of a Contract

Generally, police chiefs are aware of the political implications of their decisions or programs because they have little protection from arbitrary and unjustified dismissal. Many chiefs commit to long-term efforts and assume their responsibilities without written documents for job security. The chiefs must rely on their relationship with the appointing officials for their survival. As a result, they tend to make decisions and initiate programs that ensure job security rather than focusing on those more relevant to the organization's or public's need (Greenberg, 1992).

A contract helps solve several important issues. It balances the relationship between the chiefs and their appointing authority and clarifies the authorities and responsibilities of each party. For a detailed analysis of the benefits of a contract to both the employee and the employer, see Greenberg (1992), *On the Dotted Line,* pages 8–11.

Conclusion

Despite the traditional belief that most police officers resist change, American policing for the past twenty-five years has undergone significant changes in terms of both police personnel and the role of the police. Overall, these changes require more effort and responsibility on the part of top law enforcement executives. Extensive police experience is no longer the single qualification for dealing with the selection of a police chief; a four-year college degree with a graduate degree (preferred) is generally required. The police mission that once was crime fighting and controling civil disorder now includes order maintenance, services, and employee and community relations. Police executives in the 1990s seek to attend training programs and seminars so that they are well equipped to deal with more sophisticated policing tasks.

Yet one concern remains: With all the effort police executives exert to accomplish the goals of the organization, what protection do they receive from being dismissed arbitrarily? Requiring more from police chiefs without providing them with some protection to ensure job security seems unfair and irrational.

Under the Peace Officers' Bill of Rights, Civil Service rules, and city personnel policies, just about everyone but the chief has a form of contract in most departments. It is arguable that the chief may need a contract the most when we recognize the role of the police chief as a decision maker rather than a police officer (O'Brien, 1979). Under the community policing umbrella, where police researchers are still searching for clear-cut guidelines for police chiefs to follow, the chiefs must be innovative and responsible for the results of their decisions. Any innovative decisions that may have political implications will most likely be avoided if fear of an arbitrary dismissal exists. Formal written contracts as outlined within this debate, we believe, will benefit both the chiefs and the appointing authority.

REFERENCES

Andrews, A. H. (1985). Structuring the political independence of the police chief. In: W. A. Geller (ed.). *Police leadership in America: Crisis and opportunity.* New York: Praeger.

Bouza, A. V. (1990). *The police mystique: An insider's look at cops, crime, and the criminal justice system.* New York: Plenum.

Gamson, W. A. (1968). *Power and discontent.* Homewood, IL: Dorsey.

Green, C. (1997). "Boulder leadership missing in action." *Denver Post,* May 30.

Greenberg, S. F. (1992). *On the dotted line: Police executive contracts.* Washington, DC: Police Executive Research Forum.

"Help Stephens succeed." (1996). *St. Petersburg Times,* October 31, editorial page.

Hunt, R. G., & Magenau, J. M. (1993). *Power and the police chief: An institutional and organizational analysis.* Newbury Park, CA: Sage.

International City Management Association (ICMA). (1984). *Employee agreements for managers: Guidelines for local government managers.* Washington, DC: ICMA.

Kirchhoff, W. (1989). *How bright is your badge?* Arlington, TX: Arlington Century Printing, Inc.

Mahtesian, C. (1997, January). Mission impossible. *Governing,* pp. 19–23.

Mintzberg, H. (1983). *Power in and around organizations.* Englewood Cliffs, NJ: Prentice-Hall.

O'Brien, J. T. (1979). Problems in police leadership. In: J. T. O'Brien and M. Marcus (eds.). *Crime and justice in America* (pp. 285–308). Elmsford, NY: Pergamon Press.

Roche, T. (1996). "Chief's policy thrust into debate." *St. Petersburg Times,* October 31, p. 1A.

Ruiz, J. (1997). *The return of the ultimate outsider: A civilian administrator as the top cop.* Unpublished paper.

Rejoinder to Drs. Williams and Cheurprakobkit

WILLIAM E. KIRCHHOFF

The position of Drs. Williams and Cheurprakobkit is a bit narrow for my democratic blood. Unlimited tenure, tenure that is too long, or tenure restricted by the ellusive, vaporous, and impossible term "for cause" can have deleterious effects. I concur with the need for tenure, but I will argue for a shorter variety of the species so that our democratic institutions of local government are not compromised.

Ultimately in our form of government, the *people,* through either their elected civilian leadership (the mayor) or their professional leadership (the manager), must have reasonable control over the actions and performance of their police chief.

To do this, the civilian boss must have the authority to hire and fire the police chief. Interestingly, if mayors and managers would do all the right things necessary to hire qualified police chiefs, then seldom would we have to worry about our ability to terminate them. But, of course, it does not happen that way in real life.

Members of the federal bench are not known for their predilection to cause change, nor does the institution move with speed. Like the halls of academia, unrestricted tenure may suffice, but not so in police work. Jumping out of the pages of law enforcement history as a reason for limiting long-term tenure is J. Edgar Hoover.

And what about the Golden Hill, Oregon, police chief who was fired for selling cosmetics out of her patrol cruiser? With tenure, could she have been fired just because all suspects got a dusting of Evening in Paris along with their Miranda rights? Probably not.

Conversely, I am a strong advocate of enough tenure so that a professional man or woman taking the difficult position of police chief has sufficient time to accomplish whatever it is that needs to be done as dictated by the community. And practically speaking, what needs to be done and how long it will take varies from city to city for a host of reasons—community politics, condition of the department, departmental philosophy and available leadership, the mayor or manager, and so on.

Having hired a number of qualified police chiefs away from good, solid law enforcement jobs, at a bare minimum I want to guarantee them enough time in the saddle to do three things: First, they ought to be able to recover the financial cost of relocating their families, which is not a significant task in itself. In most instances, this will take two years. But it could take a lot longer, depending on the circumstances of housing costs, special family needs, spousal occupation, and so forth.

Second, these executives should have some comfort that they will hold the job long enough for a legitimate career move. Anything less than three years will raise eyebrows. Mayors, managers, and their communities are not inclined to hire someone who is perceived as an up-the-ladder "careerist," no matter how strong their credentials are, how successful they have been, or how willing they are to take on a tough task.

Third, a new chief needs enough time to accomplish whatever it is the mayor or manager wants done. This may be the relatively simple task of maintaining stability in a small, quality police department. Or it may involve an ugly wrestle with a union-dominated department that is controlled by the local version of Tammany Hall.

Because my resistance is not tenure, but rather tenure that is too long, I'll advance the argument of a four-year term, renegotiable after the chief has served three years, rather than getting ourselves wrapped around the axle debating the merits of three versus five years, five versus ten years, or whatever.

Four years is long enough for a chief to recapture the financial costs of moving and eliminate the stigma of job jumping. More important, four years is enough time for a chief to either make the required departmental changes or at least make sufficient headway in the right direction. Only in an the army-like, recalcitrant, change-resistant police department, such as the LAPD or NYPD, is four years not sufficient. And even in these locations, four years should be enough time to at least begin a positive change of direction.

The model I will use is the Armed Forces Chief of Staff. The Chief of Staff is appointed to a four-year term by the president. Unless there is a clear dereliction of duty or an outright scandal, the chief of staff has what amounts to a four-year appointment. If successful, he can be reappointed for another four years. If major institutional changes can be made in the military while at the same time fighting a war or two in a four-year period, then one would logically conclude that a police chief should be able to accomplish his or her mission in four years or less.

My bottom line suggestion for a city wanting the services of quality police chiefs over the years is to go through the excruciating, but necessary, vetting process before selecting a chief. Then, once the search and selection process is completed, give the new chief a four-year contract, which amounts to four years of tenure. At that point the risks are few, probably only political, but the gains will be significant. The winners will be the community, the department, the chief, and the person who did the hiring—a function and responsibility far more important than that of firing.

NO

WILLIAM E. KIRCHHOFF

Make no mistake about it, the police chief position is one of exceptionally high risk. It's like walking on a high wire, hyped on adrenaline, with no safety net below. The chief balances precariously on the thin wire above the city, edging toward a vision with a recalcitrant department on his back, while many in the crowd below hope for the fall. It might be an ego-driven mayor, a bottom-line city manager, a militant union, Machiavellian police commanders, the gun lobby, or any other special interest group that views the chief as an obstructionist to their agenda.

America's police chiefs are generally solid people who know their business. Their personal and professional lives have been exposed to an excruciating vetting process. From the day they were given their shields, they have been under a level of scrutiny seldom given anyone other than a presidential appointee. Mayors and managers usually need not worry that the person they hire as chief has a closet full of skeletons. The doors to their closets have been opened many times over the years. It is the nature of the profession. One might argue that this sufficiently minimizes one problem associated with tenure, that of hiring an unworthy person on a permanent basis.

Conversely, most chiefs, if they are honest with themselves and listen to that anonymous voice inside, will privately admit that they ended up at the top of the heap because of a bucketful of luck. Because, like every other institution in America—churches, industry, the military, and especially city government—the people at the top of a police department are not necessarily the best and the brightest with the right stuff. Recognition of this alone erases the argument that the police chief should be protected by unqualified tenure.

Today's chiefs are usually the successful products of the paramilitary organizational model that created the nonpartisan law enforcement executive, surrounded by the almost impenetrable organizational culture that placed a high value on law and order. Police departments are still, for the most part, civil service organizations with all the attendant baggage of tedious process, excruciating rule making, and a snail-paced promotional process. Nevertheless, it is assumed that the bright stars who learned the system and carried no baggage would gravitate toward the top, some becoming chiefs. It was also assumed that once in office the chief would remain in office until he/she made the decision, not the mayor or manager, to turn over the reins. But that has changed dramatically. Now, incumbent police chiefs, sitting on the dynamite keg of their offices, are extremely vulnerable to shifting political winds.

Contemporary police chiefs face societal expectations that change with the speed of a laser and performance boundaries that wiggle like a steroid-driven amoeba. From one minute to the next, law enforcement professionals often do not know what is expected of them in the new order of local politics. The old standards of honesty, professionalism, technical competence, and operational efficiency are often left out of the politico's short-term view of how long the chief should remain in office. This, among other things, shortens the career span of even the best chiefs.

Conversely, caution must be exercised against reflexively pronouncing this as simply bad government. It must be understood that this is part of an evolution within our democratic system, ultimately willed and dictated by society. Those who mistake this as some sort of evil process requiring reform fail to grasp the dynamics of changing public policy. Society's expectations of what a police chief should do are causing the high wire to vibrate out of control. The police chief manual is certainly no longer a sure bet for solution. The agendas of many groups in the community, and the sometimes politically schizoid personalities of the chief's boss, dictate the chief's length of service far more than good solid police work.

Mayors and city managers *should* be able to wall off the nervousness that attacks their guts every time a police department hits the front pages of the local newspaper. They *should* understand the complexity of the everyday decisions that have to be made by overworked and often undersupervised patrol officers, investigators, booking clerks, jailers, supervisors, shift commanders, and range officers under the bright glare of the media and television crews. They *should* recognize the likelihood that a "get rid of the chief 'incident'" looms daily like a hungry pride of lions watching the gazelle. But it just does not always happen that way, and often the chief is asked to leave because of something over which he or she had no control.

If we hope to achieve quality law enforcement, then it is necessary to provide the police with job security and the financial peace of mind that goes with it. Yet there is clearly another dimension to this public policy issue that cannot be ignored no matter how strongly one feels about the security of a police chief. Our traditions and culture cause us to reject the iron-fisted, powerfully autonomous police chief. Our forms of local government are designed to protect us from such. The last thing we will tolerate is a morally corrupt police chief protected by the social and legal boundaries that blanketed certain postwar southern sheriffs and law enforcement personalities such as Frank Rizzo, J. Edgar Hoover, and Daryl Gates.

Unqualified tenure has been sufficiently experimented with in America to demonstrate its limitations. Colleges and universities are the best example of tenure's constipating effect. Well-intended as it may be, unqualified tenure for a police executive builds a defensive wall too thick to extract the performance initiatives necessary for good law enforcement. Tenure is not the answer, but neither is a handshake assurance. Perhaps the Performance Protection Contract is.

The Performance Protection Contract (PPC) is a legitimate alternative that balances reasonable job security for the police chief against the ability of the chief civilian executive to replace a poorly performing law enforcement executive. Although it is of utmost importance that a police chief be provided with a sufficient length of service to accomplish what has been mandated of him, it is much more important that the civilian CEO, mayor, or manager has the flexibility to replace the chief if his or her performance is not adequate.

Admittedly, the PPC is not perfect, but its very existence will cause four things to happen: First, the city willing to give a chief a legally binding contract is more likely to hire a competent professional. This alone solves many of the employment problems that face a not-so-competent chief. Second, the goal setting and evaluation process, often ignored in the public arena, is cast in concrete and must be done because it is part of the contract. Third, the cost of relieving a chief before his or her term expires, and having to pay him or her, causes everyone involved to think through the implications, especially the political ones. Finally, because of the renegotiation requirement, the chief will always have at least one year of financial security and the opportunity to look elsewhere for a new job.

The PPC concept is simple. Hire the new police chief for a specific term, say, three years, with a contractual guarantee that he or she will be paid for the length of the term even if he or she is discharged for anything other than a criminal act. An important provision of the PPC will require the civilian boss to review the chief's performance at the end of two years and then renegotiate a new contract, release the chief from service with pay, or advise him or her that at the end of the term (the remaining one year) his or her services will no longer be needed.

The effect is that the new chief enters the job with a guarantee of job security for a specific number of years (three years in this case) and will find out one year *before* his or her term is up whether he or she will still be employed. If the mayor or manager wants to break off the employment relationship, this process increases the chances for the termination to be handled in a more professional manner, without the harmful political posturing that often accompanies the firing of a police chief.

There is nothing sacred about a three-year term that would be renegotiated at the end of two years of service. It could just as easily be a five-year term—renegotiable after three years of service—or a two-year term that is renegotiated after one year of service. Generally, the tougher the job, the longer the fixed term should be. But no matter how long the original term is, the contract needs to be renegotiated at least one year before it expires.

The genesis of this concept is found in the world of public education. This type of contract is commonplace in city and county school systems across America. To hire quality school superintendents, shield them from politics, and protect the public's interest, the PPC has been used for many years.

Without question, the mayor or manager has to give up the ability to relieve the chief at any time, but so what? Cities provide city managers with employment agreements, trash haulers with long-term franchises, and the rank and file with multiyear labor contracts. Why can't cities do it with the police chief and other critical staff positions?

In a sense, the PPC is a "barrier contract" designed to prevent the midnight firing of the police chief by the mayor or manager who has been hammered by some special interest group. Just as important, it is a performance-driven contract, requiring the chief to accomplish certain goals and objectives that have been established in writing by the mayor or manager.

Subscribing to the PPC concept is one thing. Making it work is another. Making it work obligates the mayor or manager to do three specific things: First, a qualified chief must be selected. Second, a jointly agreed-on performance plan with clear-cut objectives needs to be established in writing as part of the contract.

Last, an objective evaluation must be rendered at least one year *before* the contractual term ends so that the renegotiations can commence.

But even if the boss hires a qualified chief, establishes workable performance objectives, and then does a reasonable job evaluating the results, the modern-day police chief does not have enough security to do the job society hands him or her. There are too many land mines in the field that must be crossed each day to deliver effective police services. The solution is the legally binding financial guarantee in the PPC that requires the chief to be paid through the end of his contractual term of service.

For those who buy into the PPC concept, the length of the contract will probably be the central argument. Obviously, more than one factor will come into play with respect to how long the city will commit to a contract—reputation of the new chief, size of the department, internal problems, state law and municipal ordinances, sophistication of the mayor or manager, and so forth.

The fundamental flaw in a fixed-term contract without a renegotiating requirement preceding the end of the term is that it promotes unnecessary political and emotional tension. When the city of Los Angeles hired Willie Williams, he received what amounted to a guarantee of five years of employment. At first blush that seems like a long time. But five years is a blink of the eye and not nearly enough time to change an entrenched police department culture, as was the task assigned to Chief Williams. Every day, his fixed-term contract wound down to the date of expiration like a slow-spinning top, and everybody knew it. A contract without the renegotiating feature invites unnecessary political, organizational, and personal trauma.

Rejoinder to Mr. Kirchhoff Gerald L. Williams

As always, Mr. Kirchhoff's persuasive writing causes one to examine stated positions. His tenure as city manager of five cities and his experiences with chiefs of police—both inherited from previous administrations and appointed by him—lend valued perspective to the police chiefs' tenure or contract issue. In arguing against unqualified tenure, Mr. Kirchhoff does not disappoint the reader.

I found the analogy of the police chief as a "high-wire walker" particularly apt, and his recognition of the political pressures in modern policing refreshing. One can imagine a number of police executives longing for a city manager with the understanding and empathy with which Mr. Kirchhoff writes. I am, therefore, puzzled by Mr. Kirchhoff's statement in his rejoinder that, if mayors and city managers did "all the right things necessary to hire qualified police chiefs, then seldom would we have to worry about our ability to terminate them." While this speaks to the fallible nature of city managers, mayors, and police chiefs, it ignores the outside forces that play such a dramatic role in their performance as well as the perceptions of performance that were the focus of both articles.

Perhaps this is Mr. Kirchhoff's way of stating the obvious, that the people about whom we speak are, above all, imperfect human beings. In a flawless world, the perfect city manager, anticipating the future political, economic and social changes, would hire the perfect police chief, equipped with the requisite intelligence, intuition, and character to lead his or her department, and tenure or contracts would be superfluous. However, the city government's reality gives us recalcitrant chiefs, fearful of innovation, mayors looking to the next election, and the hot issues they anticipate will swing voter blocks, and city managers who are all too aware that the "get rid of the chief issue" looming on the horizon may become a "get rid of the manager issue" in a heartbeat. People act out of self-interest, and the proposed performance contracts are viable alternatives to either at-will employment or unqualified tenure.

In a contemporary classic, *The New Blue Line,* Skolnick and Bayley (1986) contemplate the possibility of policing innovation. They cite five impediments: first, the powerful pull of tradition; second, resistance to change on the part of the public; third, intransigent police unions; fourth, possible costly transition periods; and finally, a lack of vision on the part of police executives. "[T]here are chiefs who, though possessing vision and wanting to introduce experiments in their departments, lack either the courage of their convictions or the management savvy to overcome internal obstacles" (Skolnick and Bayley, 1986, p. 226). Their observations regarding the chief as an impediment seem to be consistent with those of former chief Charles Gain (Oakland, California), when he described the twilight phenomenon as a holding action where organizational change is resisted because the chief fears the loss of the position for which he or she has so long worked (Ruiz, 1997). The courage to act on one's convictions is often influenced in some measure, I believe, by job protection. Whether the type of limited tenure suggested by the preceding pages would empower police executives to take necessary risks or simply provide unwarranted protection to ineffective leadership is unknown.

Kirchhoff suggests a Performance Protection Contract (PPC) as a legitimate alternative to unqualified tenure. I agree not only with his remarks regarding the limitations of unqualified tenure, but also on the PPC's conceptual framework. Kirchhoff enumerates four major points of the PPC: a contract leads to (1) a greater likelihood of hiring a competent professional; (2) the impact of goal-setting and evaluation on both parties; (3) the implications, both financial and political, of relieving a chief; and (4) the financial security created by the renegotiation requirement, all of which are components of the model offered in our side of this debate. It appears that, although coming from different sides of the issue, we have arrived at the same place.

Cheruprakobkit and I did not discuss in any detail the contract's term. Once again, I tend to agree with Kirchhoff's remarks that the contract's length may turn out to be of central concern during negotiations. Based on the variables raised, one would believe that a minimum of three and a maximum of five years would represent a good span within which to work.

Nothing contained in either side of this debate will change the basic high-wire nature of the police executive's daily walk. What Kirchhoff advocates in the PPC would, I believe, replace the wire with a platform providing a stable footing for job performance. Concurrently, the spectators and other actors (internal and external special interest groups and the mayor or city manager) would have the opportunity to establish the chief's expectations and ground rules. The net outcome might provide less entertainment for those anticipating the fall, while providing a higher performance level in this critical position.

REFERENCES

Ruiz, J. (1997). *The return of the ultimate outsider: A civilian administrator as the top cop.* Unpublished paper.

Skolnick, J. H., & Bayley, D. H. (1986). *The new blue line.* New York: The Free Press.

Are Ethical Problems in Policing a Function of Poor Organizational Communications?

EDITOR'S NOTE: The issue of professional and personal integrity of both public officials and public employees is one of the most critical facing our society. Nowhere is the issue more profound than in law enforcement, where incidents of brutality, corruption, and dishonesty can shake a citizen's faith in the criminal justice system and the foundation of our democracy. In confronting the issue of ethics and integrity within the profession and specific departments, a natural controversy appears: the role of a department in defining acceptable behavior and the responsibility of the individual officer in behaving acceptably.

Dr. Susan Braunstein is Associate Professor of Communications at Barry University, Miami, Florida. She writes and lectures extensively on ethics and organizational communication. She is a researcher and evaluator for National Institute of Justice grants to police departments and sheriffs' offices and provides consulting services to law enforcement agencies and major organizations, including Federal Express and Pratt Whitney Aircraft. Her writing credits include books, journal articles, films, and videotapes. Dr. Braunstein spent seven years as a columnist and feature writer for the *Miami Herald.* She has served on the editorial advisory board of Collegiate Press and has been a judge for the Ohio State University Awards for Achievement in Broadcasting. In 1996 she won a Best in State Award for Radio Commentary from the Associated Press.

Mitchell L. Tyre is Chief of Police for the Town of Juno Beach, Florida. Before accepting the chief's position in 1986, he worked for the Stuart, Florida, Police Department from 1974 as sergeant in command of the Special Services Unit.

He received his Master's of Business Administration degree in 1987 from Florida Institute of Technology and is a graduate of the FBI National Academy. He serves as Adjunct Faculty for Barry University, Indian River Community College, Palm Beach Community College, and Nova University. He has published numerous articles in professional journals and has served as a consultant for departments across the United States.

YES

SUSAN BRAUNSTEIN

Citizen complaints about unethical policing most often focus on transgressions by individual officers. However, as horrifying as are cases of personal abuse of power, dereliction of duty, or other individual unethical behaviors that cause those complaints, widespread organizational corruption is far more dangerous. The worst problem in policing is not bad police; it is bad police departments. The white-hot glare of truly massive media coverage is reserved for large-scale corruption. When it appears that an agency has created a climate in which unethical acts are tolerated, public outrage mounts, and the resultant scandal brings in its wake an attempt to "clean up" the agency. Usually reforms ensue. However, as public attention to specific organizational problems inevitably wanes, other ethical issues arise, giving rise in some communities to apparently endless cycles of corruption and reform.

In the mid-1990s, the Rodney King and O. J. Simpson trials made clear on a national level what some knowledgeable criminal justice practitioners and sociologists have long suspected: there are people who—by virtue of their own experience or cultural affiliation—believe that the police are corrupt and that this corruption is endemic, in fact, a cultural pattern in law enforcement organizations.

Organizational Culture

Organizational culture—an organization's past and present influences, beliefs, myths, and patterns of behavior—is powerful in shaping member behavior and is itself open to being shaped by its members and by its leaders. Because leaders have formal power to shape the working environment, including sanctions and rewards for behavior, they have disproportionate power for their numbers. When police leaders and administrators tolerate unethical organizational culture, they are derelict in their duties and responsible for the unethical action of their troops.

Paine's comments on corporate America are as apt for the chief's office as they are for the boardroom:

> ...Ethics has everything to do with management. Rarely do the character flaws of a lone actor fully explain corporate misconduct. More typically, un-

ethical business practice involves the tacit, if not explicit, cooperation of others and reflects the values, attitudes, beliefs, language and behavioral patterns that define an organization's operating culture. Ethics, then, is as much an organizational as a personal issue. Managers who fail to provide proper leadership and to institute systems that facilitate ethical conduct share responsibility with those who conceive, execute, and knowingly benefit from corporate misdeeds. (Paine, 1994, p. 106)

In any organization, public or private, law enforcement or profit making,

coexisting with the formal organization are informal systems for communication, status, and responsibility. A supplementary set of peer pressures also guides individual behavior, establishing work and social norms. Peer groups promote both compliance with and disregard for organizational policies. To achieve honesty and ethical behavior as an organizational norm, administrators must deal with a complex range of formal and informal pressures. (Kornblum, 1976)

Organizational Communications

This range of formal and informal pressures is part of organizational culture, and the vehicle for organizational culture is organizational communications, or all the written, spoken, and electronic communication in an organization. Traditionally, organizational communication is spoken of as having two audiences: internal and external, and three directions: up, down, and sideways.

External Communications

External communications both comes into the agency and leaves the agency. Many law enforcement agencies employ a public information officer (PIO), who is frequently a well-trained, highly skilled individual knowledgeable about working with the media and the public. In many agencies, the us-against-them organizational culture discourages any interaction between the agency and the public. In such agencies, the culture is sufficiently internalized that officers may view the PIO with distrust because he or she "consorts with the enemy." When departments develop bunker mentalities or lose sight of the necessity of keeping the public properly informed, they do a disservice both to the public they serve and to the agency.

It Is a Fundamental Right That the Public Be Informed Accurately and in a Timely Manner.

Perception is a crucial part of the communication process. If the police agency acts responsibly and ethically, but the public perceives that it is deceptive or unethical, then the agency has failed in its mission because part of that mission is to earn and keep public trust. Good organizational communications are critical if the agency is to succeed in keeping the public trust.

Under the auspices of community policing, many departments have undertaken increased efforts to expand their external communications so they enhance their public trust and more effectively provide their services. In getting their information out to the public, some departments have instituted such innovations as agency or area newsletters and call-in telephone lines so citizens can hear crime reports for their districts or neighborhoods. Most often the innovations are clearly efforts at one-way communication.

Citizens' academies and neighborhood watch groups are also often one-way efforts, although they would be most valuable to policing if they served as sources for genuine two-way communication. When citizen groups are encouraged to give input on their perceptions of police performance, policies, and procedures, and when this input is recognized as valuable information by managers, law enforcement becomes both more effective and more ethical.

Another effort to interact with the community is based on current business practice. Just as businesses nationwide take surveys to measure the satisfaction of their customers, many law enforcement agencies design avenues for customer response. Some agencies use follow-up telephone calls for those individuals who use law enforcement services. Many departments distribute questionnaires. With thoughtful design, distribution, analysis, synthesis, and implementation, these surveys can serve an important purpose by providing insight into civilian perceptions and guidance on areas to consider for change. All too often, however, the surveys are merely public relations ploys.

In true community policing, the police have to trust the community to provide honest perceptions, and the police must act honorably on those perceptions. Law enforcement needs incoming external communications to do its job effectively and ethically. When the police pervert the process, limiting public input or substituting their visions for the public's, the police are acting unethically.

Perhaps the most dreaded of all incoming external communication is the civilian complaint. It is recognized that "civilian complaints are one form of communication from the public. . . . Except for a comprehensive proactive plan . . . , a complaint registered against an officer is the most significant indicator of untoward conduct, both for individual officers and for the department as a whole." (U.S. DOJ, 1989)

Although civilian complaints are a form of communication crucial to the task of maintaining an ethical environment, many law enforcement agencies make it difficult for unhappy civilians to file complaints. For example, some agencies require civilians who wish to file a complaint to go to a police station. If that civilian believes that the agency is generally corrupt, or if he or she is intimidated by a specific officer or by officers in general, there may be an inhibiting factor on filing the complaint.

Once a civilian files a complaint, many types of organizational communications should occur. Internal communication should go up, down, and sideways about the case. For the complaint process to be useful in maintaining the ethical standards of the agency, the department must act in a timely manner and must act fairly, and be *seen* to be acting fairly, by all employees. In addition, external communication is critical in complaint cases, and the greater the sensitivity of a particular case, the greater is the need for communication with the external audience.

Citizens are rarely aware of the rigors of the internal affairs process. The public perception is that cops cannot or will not clean their own houses. In times and communities where many people view police with suspicion, and in the aftermath of volatile cases such as the shooting of a juvenile or a minority civilian, citizens and media often clamor for civilian review boards. Such demands are a signal that the public—or a segment of it—believes that it does not have sufficient voice in law enforcement. The public demands two-way external communication with law enforcement, and it wants its opinions given more than cursory attention.

During this process, the PIO or designated departmental spokesperson must continue to provide information—recognizing, of course, the rights of all parties, including officers. It should be the goal of the agency to think long-term. The agency must act responsibly both to its employees and to any accused individuals. The agency must not stonewall. Sealing off communications rarely serves a long-term purpose, and ethical conduct emphasizes long-term thinking. In fact, according to a report by the U.S. Department of Justice, earlier and more comprehensive public communication from the agency about complaints will best serve the long-term interests of the department: "A police department that regularly furnishes to the media a list of officers charged with misconduct, subsequent results of the investigation, and resultant punitive measures will help to develop and sustain public trust." (U.S. DOJ, 1989)

Internal Communications

It is because law enforcement agencies recognize that communication with their external audiences is important that so many of them have a job slot or a whole section of the agency devoted to the accomplishment of that role. Communicating with their own employees is equally important, but most police managers believe the task is so obvious and so natural that they require no special training or job description. Nonetheless, internal communications are rarely as effective as they might be in police organizations and are often a major source of conflict.

Effective organizations recognize that to function with peak performance, internal communication must go up, down, and horizontally. However, law enforcement agencies traditionally stress downward communication. Most police agencies recognize and reward effective and efficient downward communication because this is the channel through which policies, procedures, practices, indoctrination, and instruction are all formally transmitted.

Because downward communication is not merely the preferred, but often the near-to-exclusive mode of communication, police managers who legitimately attempt to implement change in existing agency norms may think that change has taken place because the chief has decreed it. However, the larger the agency, the older the agency, and the more ranks there are within the agency, the less is the likelihood that the change will be implemented at the lowest level of the organization, patrol officers dealing with the public. The usual consequence is top-down statement of ethical codes that do not work.

Another ethical problem may lay in downward communication. In many large agencies and some small ones, the chief becomes a distant figure. Troops may rarely see the chief or receive communication from command staff. In such agencies, where there is no personal interaction with the chief and where upper-level, top-down communication is rare, poor communication and misconceptions can run rife, and distance can breed contempt.

Delattre (1991) specifically cites organizational communication as one of the areas that "matters profoundly" in combating corruption and brutality. He asks "What kinds of procedures does the department have for the *real* upward and downward flow of information among personnel?" Later, Delattre says "senior police, regardless of rank, carry moral authority by virtue of office." It is self-evident that law enforcement leaders must behave morally. Unfortunately, however, "the *perception* of proper conduct at top levels of management is as important and powerful as a policy which demands proper conduct of police department employees. Management cannot expect proper conduct from officers if they [the officers] perceive improper conduct at the top. If conduct is not actively perceived as proper, it will be perceived as improper" (U.S. DOJ, 1989).

If failings are great in downward communications, they are even greater in other modes. Stressing their "paramilitary" nature, many law enforcement agencies give little attention to effective upward communication. In a culture that rewards troops for taking orders, crucial messages that are most often conveyed through upward communication may not be sought or may be actively discouraged. Consequently, managers may receive little or no direct, honest feedback on how effectively management policies and decisions are being implemented. Promulgating mission and value statements about ethical policing and service to the community is a meaningless management activity if command staff does not routinely check implementation. The most effective check on implementation is routine, honest upward communication. In a "shoot the messenger" climate, message delivery ceases.

In addition, and vitally important in the creation and continuation of ethical police agencies, the most reliable source for information on the prevention and diagnosis of problem situations and people is upward communication from the ranks. When the organizational structure and climate do not actively encourage upward communication by building policies, procedure, and trust between management and troops, management limits its ability to manage effectively.

Horizontal or lateral communication between people of equal power or rank most often poses ethical problems in police agencies in its informal manifestations. Locker room conversations, jokes, and organizational myths that appear to condone unethical behavior including racism, bias, and excessive force can, through repetition and apparent acceptance, take on respectability and turn into practices diametrically opposed to the stated goals of the agency.

To provide checks and balances in the use of power and promote wise decision making, both formal and informal reporting relationships should go up, down, and sideways. Police administrators wise in the ways of buttressing ethical behavior encourage assignments that bring together members from various specializations and disciplines. Such efforts also lead to decreased organizational fragmentation because the informal and formal relationships can lead to greater coordination and cooperation between and among various groups.

A Good Example

Some communications efforts cross all boundaries: internal and external, up, down, and sideways. The Kansas City, Missouri, Early Warning System, colloquially known as "Bad Boys School," recognized that communication was the medium for change both in identifying at-risk officers and in enhancing their skills to reduce complaints against them. The department identified poor communication as the root of most civilian complaints and recognized that improving the communications skills of officers would reduce those complaints. Internal communication changes were the first steps in the change process. The department had long had the raw data on citizen complaints and use of force incidents. A breakthrough of the Early Warning System is that data are assembled from the relevant sources, reviewed, and communicated to appropriate internal parties in a timely manner so the department can take appropriate action. Second, the department specifically identified the method to reduce complaints as improving communication skills. Their techniques include internal communication in top-down commitment to the new program, line supervisors' instruction, and carefully planned training. The external aspect of communications comes from both the original complaint and the training that prepares officers to communicate successfully with the public in stressful situations.

A Bad Example

For many years, the Los Angeles Police Department was viewed as one of the best in the nation. Then came the Rodney King case and the subsequent worldwide media coverage of the Los Angeles Police Department. The original videotape, its impact enhanced through repeated airings, radio and press coverage of the beating incident, the LAPD response to criticism, long trials and their simultaneous media coverage, civil disturbances linked to the case and their media coverage, and a blue-ribbon, nationwide commission report on the LAPD all focused unprecedented, intense, long-term, international scrutiny on the organizational culture of a major law enforcement agency.

It is important to note that the failure in the LAPD was not in the stated or formal policies of the organization. Department policies explicitly opposed excessive force, corruption, racism, and bias. However, the organization created a climate that rewarded the very behavior it condemned. Both formal structures, such as promotions, and informal structures, such as recorded radio conversations between subordinates and supervisors, failed to discipline and, in fact, often rewarded officers for behavior that went against departmental policy.

The Christopher Commission (1991) found that "The failure to control ...officers is a management issue that is at the heart of the problem." The report concluded that in the LAPD officers are encouraged "to confront, not to communicate" (Christopher, 1991).

Conclusion

The importance of effective organizational communication in ethical policing cannot be overemphasized. Individuals in an organization may not agree with the values formally expressed by the organization. Nevertheless, the organization has the right *and* responsibility to ensure that the employees are informed of—and act and behave in accordance with—those values. Usually, it is the organization's ability to inculcate formal values as informal values that measures the success of its leaders.

Many studies indicate that officers' perceptions of what activities constitute unethical behavior depends on demographic and departmental characteristics. We know that some types of unethical behavioral are tolerated in some agencies and not in others (Martin, 1994).

"Philosophers argue that professionals' commitment to privilege one value over another can be traced to their perception of their roles" (Bebeau, 1994). It is the mission of the ethical department to communicate a perception that the role of the police officer is circumscribed by fixed ethical boundaries and that officers in that department will behave in accordance with the expected standards.

The individual police department has not only the right but also the responsibility to ensure that its employees are informed of the values of that organizational culture and that they comply with those values precisely because different departments can and do inculcate different values and norms. When a police department is structured with all the privileges and sanctions of the organization supporting ethical behavior, and when all forms of organizational communications are used responsibly and effectively to promote an ethical environment, officers are likely to act ethically.

Using organizational communications to create an ethical environment is no guarantee that all people within the environment will behave ethically, but it is evident that ethical problems in policing are, at least in part, a function of poor organizational communications and that good communications can increase the likelihood of ethical policing.

REFERENCES

Bebeau, M. J. (1994). Can ethics be taught? *Today's FDA Scientific, 6* (9), 1C–4C.

Christopher, W. (1991). *Report of the Independent Commission on the Los Angeles Police Department.* Los Angeles.

Delattre, E. J. (1991). *Against brutality and corruption: Integrity, wisdom and professionalism.* Tallahassee, FL: Florida Criminal Justice Executive Institute.

Kornblum, A. N. (1976). *The moral hazards: Police strategies for honesty and ethical behavior.* Lexington, MA: Lexington Books.

Martin, C. (1994). *Illinois municipal officers' perception of police ethics.* Chicago, IL: Statistical Analysis Center.

Paine, L. S. (1994). Managing for Organizational Integrity. *Harvard Business Review, 72*(2), 106–108.

U.S. Department of Justice. (1989). *Building integrity and reducing drug corruption in police departments.* Arlington, VA: International Association of Chiefs of Police.

Rejoinder to Dr. Braunstein   MITCHELL L. TYRE

My colleague has made some interesting points in her proposition supportive of a causative link between ethics and organizational communications. However, despite the importance of leadership and communication, one simply cannot talk about bad departments without talking about bad cops.

In the aftermath of the Rodney King beating, the Christopher Commission detailed abuse after abuse of both power and people. The report seemed to paint a picture of a department gone mad and out of control; a closer examination of the report actually showed that most of the abuses so dramatically displayed for the media actually centered on the actions of fewer than fifty officers. Of the thousands of men and women in the Los Angeles Police Department, about four dozen were responsible for the overwhelming majority of the problems cited in the Christopher Commission report. The fact that the public believes that corruption and brutality are endemic does not make it so. And those of us in positions to do so are obligated to provide reality checks for those that fall victim to exploitive reporting.

There is no question that police leadership is important, but policing is still an autonomous calling. As critical as corporate culture is, one cannot lose sight of the fact that individuals comprise organizations and thus create the culture of those organizations. Good leadership allows good cops to get better, and bad cops sometimes simply figure out better ways of hiding. Of course, once corrupt or brutal acts are discovered, police management should move as quickly and decisively as possible to eliminate those officers. This, however, is a function of management, not leadership. Leaders provide direction and a compass heading for the organization. Managers deal with how to achieve the goals set by management. So although leadership cannot be given short shrift, it still cannot be viewed as a panacea to inept or ethically bankrupt police organizations.

My colleague also draws a link between perception and the effectiveness of the communication of the agency, internally and externally. Although public trust does make the job of the officers easier, the more important link is between the media and the department, not between the various units within the department. Good cops will do their jobs as well as they can regardless of public perception, and the media does far more to shape public opinion than does the department's communication strategies. For instance, internal affairs investigations often play a pivotal role in shaping public trust. The public wants information. Sometimes they want genuine information on which to base decisions, and sometimes they just want facts to match their already distorted view of police agencies. The media, in their zeal to sell, will sometimes report that the chief or sheriff refused comment on any part of an internal investigation. In many states, however, such information is statutorily privileged and cannot be released without violating state laws. Instead of reporting that the constitutional protections and guarantees of fairness for the officers involved prevent comment, sometimes the media simply report that, while the chief refused comment, "our investigative reporters have uncovered...", leading the unwary to the erroneous conclusion that without the watchdog efforts of our local paper or television station, the jackbooted thugs of the local police will run roughshod over life, liberty, and democracy. What chance does even the best communicator have of trying to counter such one-sided reporting?

In fact, my colleague's position even makes my point more clearly than I have. She reports that the IACP says that departments that furnish results of investigations with the public will build trust. I believe that to be true, but only because such a report connects names and faces with illegal or abusive acts and does not allow the entire department to be tainted.

Communication is important, as is leadership and a host of other characteristics of good police departments. But the best departments are made up of the best people, and the most important role that leadership and organizational communications play is in attracting the type of personnel that will do good, ethical jobs without being told to. Those individual officers will then spread the reputation of the department, and it will subsequently attract like-minded officers as attrition dictates new hires.

One cannot dispute that organizational communications play a role in the development of an ethically sound department, but that role pales in comparison with the importance of the individual men and women doing the job every day. Such men and women know the difference between right and wrong and breathe life into those values every day in every call they handle without having to refer to a policy manual.

NO

MITCHELL L. TYRE

Police departments and police officers are and always will be in a constant state of turmoil because of the organizational tug-of-war that is a necessary part of policing. Police departments demand that officers adhere strictly to rules, regulations, and procedures and, at the same time, insist that they be autonomous, authoritative, and authoritarian. Police officers are told "this is *your* city/street/zone/whatever," and then departments pretend to be surprised when officers do whatever they need to do to get the job done as they perceive it needs to be done. *This statement of fact should not be taken as an endorsement of officer misdeeds.* Unfortunately, some cops step outside the bounds of departmental, constitutional, and statutory guidelines when on the job. They do it for different reasons: some because they are brutal, some because they believe that "alley justice" is a better solution than the judicial process, and some because they are just bad people who have managed to slip through the screening net. Some are officers who just make an mistake, and others are nothing more than crooks with badges.

But whatever the reason or rationale, the common denominator is that individuals, not departments, are making these decisions. To be sure, departmental communication and culture matter, but the fact remains that individuals within the departments constitute the culture of a department.

To say that the ethical timbre of a police department hinges on organizational communication patterns is simplistic at best. Organizational communication is important and is a critical element in the successful management scheme of a department, but if the individual officers in a department are corrupt or inefficient, then that department will be corrupt or inefficient.

The ethical department begins and ends with its personnel. The men and women of an agency determine the culture and influence the kind of person recruited into the organization. Peer pressure among cops is far more powerful than formalistic, corporate America slogans about cross-communication. As Howard Cohen explained in *Overstepping Police Authority,* "Police operate in a world that is not nicely packaged and clearly labeled. They regularly step into situations in which neither their objectives nor their functions are particularly obvious" (1983). In those situations, officers are much more likely to make decisions based on their upbringing and beliefs about right and wrong, rather than what the policy manual may say. Because of the role police officers play in our society and the wide discretion necessarily given them, individual traits, training, and education are critical factors in the wise use of this discretion.

Good, ethical cops do not need a rule to tell them not to steal, be brutal, or plant evidence. They will not anyway. And if they are predisposed to do these things, they will, regardless of what the "book" says, because they—like criminals on the street—often do not believe they will get caught.

The key to a good, ethically sound department lies more in recruiting and selecting the right person. As Delattre (1989) explained:

> The more students grasp the connections between good habits and reason, the more they can do for themselves. They may be trusted with discretion, according to their ability to apply reason to novel situation, and, in that way, become good police officers. Good professionals understand the standards of their profession, sustain those standards by habit, and know how to use reason to make necessary decisions. (p. 146)

This is the crux of a good department—recruiting and selecting those people who can function in the absence of strong organizational communication. Police officers rarely operate under direct supervision. In fact, most of their decisions are made while they are by themselves, not in the presence of other officers or supervisors. Reports generated will reflect the version of the incident the officer wishes to reflect, not necessarily what happened as viewed through the eyes of an independent observer.

Although some research indicates that ethics training for police officers can change behavior, several authorities still hold to the notion that values, morals, and the things that make up ethical behavior are formed by the time a child is four or five years old. To be sure, a person can be encouraged to grow and develop professionally and personally through education and training, but that person has to be "programmed" to accept what the training offers. Even if a person is willing to accept the benefits of intellectual growth, topics such as ethics are not usually taught in a manner conducive to long-term benefit. Often, departments schedule ethics training after a crisis of confidence has occurred. In many departments, only patrol officers and sergeants are required to attend. No executive officers, no midlevel supervisors, and no civilian personnel participate, which sends a message to those forced to attend that the department is not really serious anyway.

The other glaring problem with this Band-Aid approach is that, because the training is not reinforced through integration with everything else the department does and says, the officers have the impression that such training is something that, once endured, can be put on a shelf. Ethical training in isolation will not and cannot have the influence needed to change a person's view of the world and, consequently, how he or she interacts with that world.

Some ethics trainers view departmental ethics training the same way police officers view locks on doors: they are there to keep honest people honest. Ethics training helps keep ethical cops ethical by reinforcing what they already believe to be true. Officers who are corrupt and have been corrupt for years are unlikely to change their behavior or pattern of beliefs based on information received during a four- or eight-hour session on ethics.

However, departments offering only four hours of training in ethics should not be dismissed as obviously deficient. Historically, ethics training has been given short shrift. For instance, in Florida, recruits are required to attend at least 520 hours of basic law enforcement training before being eligible to take the state certification examination. Of that, *one hour* is set aside for ethics training. If the new recruit is a blank canvas on which we paint the rudimentary knowledge necessary to learn how to be a cop, one tiny stroke is unlikely to affect the finished product. Armed with this knowledge, it is even more incumbent on chiefs and sheriffs to hire officers most likely to choose the right and ethical course of action in the absence of direct supervision or threat of prosecution for misdeeds.

The growing popularity of community-oriented policing provides another example of the importance of individual accountability as opposed to a focus on the organization. Community policing, in whatever form, usually involves closer ties with the community. Officers are encouraged to listen to and take their action cues from the community. No longer are officers robots in metal cages, but rather real people dealing with real people. Because of the individualistic nature of community policing responses, the public has a greater propensity to lean on "their" officer. If the officer commits malfeasance (a wrong act), nonfeasance (an omission to act), or misfeasance (a legal duty performed in a wrong manner), then the harm committed by the officer has a name and a face and is not just another anonymous bureaucrat. The anger, hostility, and disappointment become personal in nature. This personal bitterness will be sure to fuel discontent in at-risk neighborhoods, because now the disenchanted citizen has a focus.

Of course, if the officer is faced with a situation in which one or the other party will be unhappy with his or her actions, officers with low ethical thresholds are more likely to choose a course of action based on whom they personally like or their own personal gain, rather than what is legally and morally correct.

As policing becomes more decentralized and the shadow of immediate supervision loses its impact, so does the impact of policies. Community policing is fraught with peril, as is every opportunity or innovation. But what makes community policing work is not an organizational mission statement—it is the men and women on the street who believe they are doing something good for their communities.

Organizational communication, mission statements, rules, regulations, and policies have a place in all professional agencies, but they do not take the place of honest, hard-working police officers. The backbone of a uniformed police agency is the Patrol or Corrections Division, typically the largest divisions in the department. Almost every real and potential crisis and lawsuit was either started by the actions of a patrol officer or corrections officer or stopped in its tracks by those officers. The large majority of decisions in a police department are made by patrol officers and are based on a personal notion of what right is, tempered by education and training. But the standard by which an officer gauges a response is an internal gauge, not what the dusty policy manual bouncing around in the trunk of the car or lying forgotten in the bottom of a locker says.

A poignant example of the power of individual actions occurred in Iowa City, Iowa, in August 1996. Around midnight on August 29, a three-year veteran

Iowa City police officer entered the open door of a studio in an area recently plagued by burglaries. He found a thirty-one-year-old man sitting at a desk, talking to a friend on the telephone. With no warning or words exchanged between the two men, the police officer shot and killed the man, who was later identified as the owner of the studio. The county prosecutor decided that the shooting was a mere "error in judgment" not meriting prosecution of any sort.

When it is midnight, and you are a police officer, and you fear the presence of people who might try to kill you, the least determining factor in your actions or omissions is the communication patterns of your police department. Internal beliefs will win out every time over external control mechanisms in such a situation.

The challenge for police executives is in finding those people who do not need the organizational communication or policies to guide their actions and thinking, but rather use those guidelines to simply enhance and assure them that are already on the right track. Recruitment, selection, and field training are crucial in making sure the right people are in the right positions. Once so assured, policies and regulations will help keep honest cops honest.

REFERENCES

Cohen, H. (1983). Teaching Police Ethics. *Teaching Philosophy, 6*(3), 231–243.
Delattre, E. J. (1989). *Character and cops: Ethics in policing.* Washington, DC: American Enterprises Institute for Public Policy Research.

Rejoinder to Chief Tyre
Susan Braunstein

Chief Tyre says "good, ethical cops do not need a rule to tell them not to steal, be brutal, or plant evidence. They will not anyway." He says "police officers rarely operate under direct supervision. In fact, most of their decisions are made while they are by themselves.... [And] reports generated will reflect the version of the incident the officer wishes to reflect...." He says, "internal beliefs will win out every time over external control mechanisms." The gist of his argument is that "the standard by which an officer gauges a response is an internal gauge" and that organizational communications have little impact on individual behavior. He implies that organizational communications are confined to the "dusty policy manual bouncing around the trunk of the car or lying forgotten in the bottom of a locker."

Nonsense!

Of course individual cops will make individual decisions, and some of those inevitably will be poor decisions. However, good departments do everything they can to help cops make good decisions. From careful selection processes to competent training, good departments seek ways to bolster an organizational climate of ethical behavior. Organizational communication is more than the medium for the message of ethics. It is a powerful means of influencing the behavior of all the members of the department. Good departments employ all the avenues of organizational communications to send a coherent message that their employees must act ethically.

Chief Tyre is right when he says "peer pressure among cops is far more powerful than in formalistic, corporate America . . ." and it is precisely that point that makes organizational communications so important in law enforcement. In departments and agencies where all the structures are in place to support ethical behavior, more ethical decisions will be made. It is not true that "internal beliefs win out every time." With the proper external support through management and communications processes, good police officers will overcome internal or even instinctive beliefs. Despite the adrenaline rush of a high-speed pursuit, they will refrain from kicking handcuffed suspects. Despite personal beliefs about cultural diversity, they will treat all suspects with respect. Despite provocation, they will use the minimum force necessary to accomplish their lawful objectives. They will do so because they took an oath to do so. They will do so because all their training and habits incline them to do so. They will do so because their peers expect and require them to do so.

When policy demands particular actions, and accepted practice in the department violates those policies and contraindicates those actions, officers quickly decipher the mixed message to mean "It's OK to do what we do, just don't get caught." Effective organizational management and organizational communications reduce that ambiguity. When policy and organizational communications practices are in sync, officers derive support from a consistent system. The written policy, the words and actions of their leaders, and the words and actions of their peers help officers act in a way that brings credit to themselves and their agency.

It is the responsibility of the department to develop policies and to practice procedures that ensure that those policies are the guiding force of actions taken under color of the badge. Individual notions of ethics must be subordinated to departmental policy precisely because the individual may believe he or she is just or fair or right when he or she is, in fact, acting in a way that contradicts departmental policy. When officers abuse certain types of suspects, they may claim or even believe that they are justified in doing so. However, officers are the official agents of government and, as such in this nation, must act in accordance with policy, law, and the judicial system. An individual's actions, no matter how sincere his or her beliefs to the contrary, must conform with departmental policy.

Organizational communications are more than a dusty manual or a mission statement. Both the manual and the mission statement are a part of the organizational communications of a law enforcement agency, but they are often among the least influential communication tools. Organization communications include all the written, spoken, and electronic communications, both formal and informal, that are part of the department's life. The cops, the civilians, and the customers they serve all are influenced by the organizational communications employed.

Communication in organizations goes up, down, and sideways. Orders come down. Information should go up, down, and sideways. Information flows into the agency and out to others. Organizational communications are as formal as a letter of reprimand and as informal as a cartoon on a briefing room bulletin board. Often the informal are a more powerful tool for shaping behavior than the formal, especially when there is incongruity between the two.

When police leaders determine that a one-hour course on ethics is sufficient attention in an academy, when they decry racism and let racist comments go unpunished, and when they refuse to prosecute bad cops, they employ organizational communications. Each of these actions is bad in itself. Each is worse as part of a pattern that sends a clear message that ethics are something to talk about, not something to practice.

Of course, recruitment, selection, and training are significant factors in ethical organizational behavior, as are mission, vision, supervision, discipline, and myriad other organizational factors. All are factors in organizational moral health. None of these is, however, a more significant contributor to ethical behavior than organizational communications. To reach their potential, police departments must employ organizational communications that clearly and unambiguously support an ethical organizational climate.

Is It Time to Change Law Enforcement's Paramilitary Structure?

Editor's Note: Since its formal beginnings in 1829 England, policing has been conceptualized as a paramilitary organization. In the United States, this has been manifested in an organization that is extremely hierarchical and characterized by the use of a rank structure that is military in both nomenclature and emblem. Yet, in recent years, the American business organization has flattened, and its workforce has come to expect fewer orders from above and more involvement in decisions affecting their work life. The dilemma America law enforcement now faces is a critical reexamination of the very structure that has allowed it to perform its mission for over 150 years.

Sheldon F. Greenberg, Ph.D., is Chair of the Department of Interdisciplinary Programs, Division of Business and Management, Johns Hopkins University, and serves as Director of the Johns Hopkins University's Police Executive Leadership Program. Before joining Johns Hopkins University, he served as Associate Director of the Police Executive Research Forum (PERF) in Washington, DC. Dr. Greenberg began his career as an officer in the Howard County, Maryland, Police Department, where he served as criminal investigator, public information officer, supervisor of the records and information division, supervisor of the youth unit, director of the police academy, director of research and planning, assistant to the chief of police, and commander of the administrative services bureau. He is the author of several books, including *Stress and the Helping Professions, Stress and the Teaching Profession,* and *On The Dotted Line,* a comprehensive guide on police executive selection and contracts, and numerous articles.

Lieutenant Carol E. Rasor, Ph.D., is a 17-year veteran with the Pinellas County Sheriff's Office in Florida. She serves as commander of the Community

Services Division, including the Central District Community Policing Unit, the Crime Prevention Section, and the Field Training Section. She holds bachelor's and master's degrees in Criminal Justice and a Ph.D. in Education from the University of South Florida. She is a graduate of the Senior Management Institute of Police, Police Executive Research Forum. She has commanded the Law Enforcement Training Section and has also had assignments in the Economic Crimes Unit, Crimes Against Children Unit, and the Patrol Operations Bureau. For the past ten years, she has taught in academic, academy, advanced, and in-service programs. Her area of instructional expertise is management training.

YES

CAROL E. RASOR

Police agencies are experiencing turbulent times as the result of social, cultural, economic, and political changes in the external environment. Chiefs and sheriffs are being asked to do more with less resources and to customize the delivery of services to a diverse client population. Constituents demand from police agencies flexibility and sensitivity in handling and resolving problems in their communities. Community policing is being hailed as the preferred philosophical and operational strategy to cure the social ills and criminal behavior found across the nation. Yet, the internal structure of the policy agency refuses to offer to its own constituents flexibility, autonomy, and empowerment to successfully participate in a partnership with the community. It is time to reinvent the bureaucratic structure existing in police agencies.

The Limitations of the Bureaucratic Model

Throughout history, police organizations have experienced numerous evolutions as the result of advances in civilizations. The responsibility for dealing with unacceptable behavior shifted from the family, to a ruler, to the military, to a volunteer civilian police force, and, finally, to a paid police force. Today's police organizations are designed in accordance to Max Weber's bureaucratic model. Weber, the German sociologist, conceptualized the bureaucratic model at the turn of the century and visualized his model as both an answer to the subjective managerial practices found during the early days of the Industrial Revolution and a means to ensure a predictable process for labor. Mintzberg (1983) noted the basic structural elements characterizing the bureaucratic organization:

> Highly specialized routine operating tasks; very formalized procedures in the operation core; a proliferation of rules, regulations, and formalized communication throughout the organization; large-size units at the operating level; re-

liance on the functional basis for grouping tasks; relatively centralized power for decision making; and an elaborate administrative structure with a sharp distinction between line and staff. (p. 164)

Police agencies use this bureaucratic model to create a multilayered pyramid designed to promote uniformity in personnel and procedures. The model creates standard rules and operating procedures in which behavior can be predicted, a centralized authority approves the actions taken by its employees, and an impersonal philosophy offers consistent treatment of all employees. Perrow (1986) pointed out that the bureaucratic model strives to create a fine-tuned machine capable of optimum efficiency, accountable control, technical expertise, impartiality of personnel, and cost-effectiveness. These characteristics have made the bureaucratic model attractive to administrators. However, administrators must recognize the deficiencies of the same bureaucratic model.

In the bureaucratic organization, the focal point for control rests on the creation of a hierarchy. Rules and procedures are created, but the emphasis for control is placed on the hierarchy. Perrow (1986) noted the following negative effects of such a hierarchy:

The hierarchy promotes delays and sluggishness; everything must be kicked upstairs for a decision either because the boss insists or because the subordinate does not want to risk making a poor decision. All this indecision exists at the same time that superiors are being authoritarian, dictatorial, and rigid, making snap judgements that they refuse to reconsider, implementing on-the-spot decisions without consulting their subordinates, and generally stifling any independence or creativity at the subordinate level. (p. 29)

The benefits of a bureaucratic structure are maximized for simple, routine tasks that occur in a stable environment. Osborne and Plastrik (1997), critics of the bureaucratic structure, describe these organizations "as systems designed by a genius to be run by idiots" (p.17). When tasks are nonroutine and complex within an environment in a state of change, bureaucratic organizations are less adaptive.

Today's police agencies face challenges similar to those that occur in both public and private organizations. Technology is rapidly advancing, requiring continuous upgrades and training. Needs of the communities vary from neighborhood to neighborhood. Changes in the workplace include greater diversity with less military experience and increased education. There is a greater demand for problem solving and innovation at the lowest level in the organizational pyramid and an increased need for horizontal and lateral communication to ensure efficiency.

Because of these challenges in both the internal and external environments, the bureaucratic model can only offer stagnation in police organizations and heighten the barriers for leaders who try to implement changes in a system that is inflexible and unresponsive to innovations. Bureaucracies may no longer provide police organizations with the efficiency and effectiveness once offered at the infancy of modern policing. To survive in a world in which private entities espouse that they can provide quality service at reduced costs, police organizations must consider restructuring. This restructuring effort may include either a change in the managerial philosophy, a reconfiguration of the pyramid, or both.

Rethinking the Multilayered Structure

Police agencies that have implemented community policing, whether on a small scale, such as designating an individual officer as the "community officer," or a large scale to include all bureaus within the agency, have wrestled with the difficulties of trying to fit a flexible and customized delivery system into a rigid, uniform structure. The backbone of this rigid structure is a multilayered system of ranks created to ensure efficiency and accountability. Yet, when the motives for creating a rank within the structure are examined, it becomes apparent that, in many cases, these layers were created as a reward system for the members and not for the efficiency of the operation of the agency. The chief's or sheriff's well-intended method of rewarding officers results in creating his own barricaded environment. Sparrow (1988) described the effect of this multilayer system:

> Certainly such a deep rank structure provides a very effective natural barrier, insulating the chief officer from his patrol force. It makes it possible for the police chief to believe that all his officers are busily implementing the ideas which, last month, he asked his deputy to ask his assistants to implement—while, in fact, the sergeant is telling his officers that the latest missive from those cookies at headquarters 'who have forgotten what this job is all about' shouldn't actually affect them at all. (p. 5)

Therefore, to implement a change in the managerial philosophy or a reconfiguration of the pyramid, organizations must begin by rejecting a reward system that results in the proliferation of a multilayered system. As Sparrow (1988) pointed out, in the United States large metropolitan police agencies have nine to thirteen ranks, depending on the size of the agency. Yet, the Roman Catholic Church with over 600 million members functions with only five layers.

With the combination of exemplary leadership and competent staff, reducing the number of ranks within an agency will lead to greater efficiency in terms of getting the most results with the available resources. Community policing requires a decentralized command structure to enable problem solving, decision making, and accountability to be the responsibility of all levels in the hierarchy. Moore and Stephens (1991) noted that decentralization of problem solving enables officers to be more effective and creative because decisions are based on firsthand knowledge of the facts. "Patrol officers will experience greater job satisfaction as they accept higher levels of responsibility and accountability" (Community Policing Consortium, 1994, p. 5). A competent staff trained in problem solving can enable a manager to supervise a larger span of control. The higher-level managers also benefit from decentralization, enabling them to spend more time formulating strategies to improve the performance of the entire organization. The paramilitary structure does not and cannot offer the flexibility to decentralize decision making and will hinder an organization's challenge to ensure optimum efficiency. Eliminating the paramilitary structure may be too drastic for most agencies; however, the number of ranks should be minimized to enhance communication, problem solving, and decision making.

Promoting a Culture Based on Values

The philosophy of the paramilitary structure needs to be retooled to focus on teaching its members the importance of organizational values in making decisions. Today's paramilitary structure uses policies and procedures to direct supervisors in their decision making. Policies and procedures are also used to reduce the agency's liability by detailing appropriate action to be taken in a situation. However, policies and procedures cannot identify the correct response in every situation. The philosophy of community policing supports an officer's use of creative thinking to resolve problems. A system that relies on policies and procedures will stifle the officer's initiative to step "outside of the box" for problem solving and lead to the officer being cynical that the true purpose of the policies and procedures is primarily for disciplinary purposes. Sparrow, Moore, and Kennedy (1990) summarized the limitations of relying on policies and procedures to guide an officer's actions:

> For all the considerable merits of tried and codified operating procedures, high standards, and strict accountability, getting them via a centralized, paramilitary style has important liabilities for police departments. The emphasis on procedure and discipline blunts the initiative and adaptability of officers in the field. The system encourages officers to think in terms of avoiding blame rather than taking any unusual action, and it places heavy emphasis on treating all cases as though they were similar even when there are circumstances that make them seem different to the officers on the scene. As a result, the department does less work, and less particularly adapted work, than it would if the officers were given freer reign. (p. 120)

Perhaps reducing the number of ranks in an agency is a far easier task for a chief or sheriff than the challenge of teaching his subordinates the importance of values. A chief or sheriff who espouses the importance of values and models the value-laden behavior ingrains in his managers and members the deepest bond of commitment. As Colonel Donnithorne (1993), at the U.S. Military Academy at West Point, pointed out, "Leaders make clear to subordinates, early in the relationship, their commitment to the highest values of the military profession. Leaders abide by those values and encourage subordinates to do the same" (p.158). Nair (1994) presented a concept originated by Gandhi to support the benefits of values-centered leadership: "Incorporating moral values and strategy motivates people at every level in every type of organization—business, political, and academic—because of its appeal to what is basic in all of us: our desire to do what we know is right" (p. 124).

Police agencies are ripe grounds for teaching value-centered leadership because the individuals who choose this profession have a deep desire to do the right thing for our society. Yet, values must be incorporated into in-service training to enable the organization to be as proficient in value-laden decision making as a "shoot–don't shoot" situation. For the troops to be committed to organizational values, they must also witness these values being consistently practiced by the chief or sheriff down through their managerial staff. For it is only through the combination of training in and the modeling of these values that an organization will be able to move itself from a philosophy based on policies to action based on values.

Conclusion

Is it time to change the police paramilitary organization? The philosophy and operational strategy of community policing have caused an awakening in managers that the current structure of a police agency may no longer fit the mission. The paramilitary–bureaucratic structure has outlived its usefulness in providing optimum organizational effectiveness and efficiency. A police agency still needs order, yet the number of links in the chain of command can and should be significantly reduced.

Front-line personnel need to be given the latitude to make decisions and solve problems creatively without asking the chain-of-command to approve all decisions. Policies and procedures should not be the exclusive guiding force for decision making. Values should be the impetus behind all decisions made by each member of the organization. With an increase in the educational level of police officers and the existence of values-driven organizational culture, police officers can be trusted to choose the appropriate course of action and be held accountable for their decisions. The challenge of the millennium for police executives will be to accept the need for change and lead the organization through the transformation from bureaucracy to innovation.

REFERENCES

Community Policing Consortium. (1994). Assessing the progress of community policing. In: *Understanding community policing: A framework for action* [On-line]. Available: cpa@communitypolicing.org.

Donnithorne, L. (1993). *The West Point way of leadership: From learning principled leadership to practicing it.* New York: Doubleday.

Mitzberg, H. (1983). *Structuring in fives.* Englewood Cliffs, NJ: Prentice-Hall.

Moore, M., & Stephens, D. (1991). *Beyond command and control: The strategic management of police departments.* Washington, DC: Police Executive Research Forum.

Nair, K. (1994). *A higher standard of leadership: Lessons from the life of Gandhi.* San Francisco: Berrett-Koehler Publishers.

Osborne, D., & Plastrik, P. (1997). *Banishing bureaucracy: The five strategies for reinventing government.* Reading, MA: Addison-Wesley.

Perrow, C. (1986). *Complex organizations: A critical essay.* New York: Random House.

Sparrow, M. (1988). Implementing community policing. *Perspectives on Policing,* 9, 1–12.

Sparrow, M., Moore, M., & Kennedy, D. (1990). *Beyond 911: A new era of policing.* New York: HarperCollins Publishers, Inc.

Rejoinder to Dr. Rasor   SHELDON F. GREENBERG

In stating that it is time to change the paramilitary structure in police agencies, Dr. Rasor focuses on almost every conceivable weakness in organizational behavior and management. She implies that changing the paramilitary structure will reduce or eliminate stagnation and barriers to change. She calls the paramilitary structure rigid and implies that it is responsible for an array of ills that plague American policing. Attacking the paramilitary structure is safe and easy. It avoids having to criticize police leaders.

The successes of modern policing (response to thousands of calls for service daily, the movement to embrace community policing, new crime control and accountability models in urban areas, experimentation with 311 to unburden 911, and more), all of which have occurred within agencies that retain the traditional hierarchical structure, go unmentioned.

Dr. Rasor fails to put forth an important question: Has the paramilitary structure created weak leaders or have weak leaders misused and abused the paramilitary structure? I believe strongly that the police profession suffers from leaders who have misused and abused the structure.

Despite the criticism Dr. Rasor lodges, the paramilitary model is not the cause of all failings of modern police service. There is nothing within the paramilitary model that inhibits a police agency from implementing quality training, promoting qualified individuals, rotating supervisors and administrators to give them a well-rounded work experience, or flattening the internal structure. Nothing in the paramilitary model prevents a police agency from developing its leaders over time, using and engaging in research, collaborating with other agencies, embracing crime analysis, or forecasting and problem solving to address community needs.

Nothing in the model prevents an agency from holding its commander accountable. The crime control model developed in New York and now prevalent in major cities throughout the country is based as much on accountability as it is on data analysis. (In fact, the NYPD accountability model was established in one of the most cumbersome hierarchical structures in the nation!) Nothing in the paramilitary model prevents a police agency from doing a better job of assessing its future or changing organizational structure and behavior. And, nothing in the model prevents quality internal and external communication.

Departments such as those in San Diego, Baltimore County, Seattle, St. Petersburg, Lakewood, Madison, and others have implemented new programs, taken risks, and embraced community policing while maintaining a traditional paramilitary structure. Each of these agencies focused on developing leaders, adhering to values, making service delivery a high priority, minimizing political interference, hiring and promoting skilled individuals, motivating personnel, and more. Some of these and other agencies, such as in Baltimore, have flattened their rank structure and did so without condemning or abandoning the paramilitary model.

Blaming the ills of policing on the paramilitary model is scapegoating. Too few people, including Dr. Rasor, are willing to state directly that one of the problems is weak leaders who do not know or are not willing to tailor the paramilitary model to suit the needs of their community.

The paramilitary structure can be made to work and work well. It requires an understanding of organizational behavior and a willingness to change. Dr. Rasor needs to focus on these areas rather than condemn the paramilitary model.

NO

SHELDON F. GREENBERG

No police agency remains static and no police agency can be established or reorganized in final form.
—William H. Parker, Chief of Police, Los Angeles, September, 1954

American policing, while among the world's finest and least-corrupt systems of public service, is not without its problems:

- There is poor leadership in many agencies.
- Policing in most states is highly fragmented, with minimal interaction among city, county, state, and township agencies.
- In some metropolitan areas, there are jurisdictional turf wars for qualified recruits.
- Many law enforcement agencies are poorly organized.

- Many agencies continue to measure achievement by simple statistics.
- Few agencies focus on productivity.
- Police officers' successes are rarely touted.
- There are conflict and debate over philosophy and approach, from community policing to the New York crime control model.
- There continue to be political interference and micromanaging of police agencies by elected officials.

In speeches and articles, critics have blamed these and other concerns, all or in part, on the paramilitary structure. This paramilitary model or structure is well rooted in law enforcement history and the police culture. Historically, in many parts of the world, civilian police operations grew from militia groups and military organizations (Brewer, Adrian, Hume, Moxen-Browne, & Wilford, 1988). For generations, police officers have taken pride in achieving rank. In the eyes of the public, military rank is as much a part of policing as badges and marked police cars. Through popular media, the public learned to associate rank with authority and leadership in police and sheriffs' departments.

The paramilitary structure is one of several viable models of organization. Drucker (1996) cites the traditional hierarchical structure as one of three basic models through which leaders may be empowered and given opportunities. He discusses its limitations, as he does with other models of organization, but does not deny its value (Drucker, 1996). In discussing this issue, I must emphasize that a problem arises with *any* structure when leaders fail to implement change and progress based on the needs of the organizations and its clientele (Connor, 1992).

In recent years, the paramilitary rank structure used by most police departments has fallen under criticism. It has been blamed for interfering with accountability, inhibiting progress, constraining community policing, obstructing communication, and contributing to inefficiency in use of resources. And, it has been blamed for proliferating highly centralized, inefficient bureaucracies.

Critics of the paramilitary structure find it an easy target. The paramilitary structure is inanimate. Few people are offended when the rank structure is taken to task. It is far more difficult to criticize police executives for failing to lead, develop, and assess employees; prepare supervisors; define and commit to agency values; discipline wrongdoers quickly and effectively; and reward successful performance. A cumbersome or failed paramilitary structure is not necessarily the cause but, rather, the effect of these and other weaknesses.

Critics cite the "what," but often neglect the "who." An alternative model, whatever it may be, will result in little positive change if weak leaders (an oxymoron) are at the helm of the organization.

The paramilitary model is condemned inappropriately for the ills of organizations. It is not the cause of employees being prepared inadequately for supervision. Clearly, executives have the ability, with input from employees, to change the way they select and train new supervisors. The model is not responsible for poor communication among units. Systems to foster quality internal communication can be established. The paramilitary model is not the cause of poor discipline. Values can be implemented, integrity can be enhanced, early warning systems can be implemented, and discipline can be treated as a tool to improve the organization rather than "club" disfavored employees. And the organizational hierarchy is not the cause of ineffective top-down management or excessive bureaucratic process. These, too, can be corrected. The paramilitary model does not inhibit change.

At times, rhetoric and faultfinding by politicians have been aimed at the police paramilitary structure. Speaking at a public hearing on the police department's budget, a city council member (also a declared candidate for mayor) in a large urban jurisdiction criticized the police department's rank structure for "causing serious problems." He cited a rise in homicides and property crimes and complaints about response time as problems and attributed the department's failure to deal with them as the fault of "the bureaucracy." He called for the elimination of the "bureaucratic and militaristic system of police management." Instead of addressing weaknesses in the department's leadership or the chief's failure to communicate effectively with the council, he focused on the rank structure and called for the department to explore alternatives. As with many critics, his rhetoric focused on the structure rather than the people.

In progressive police agencies, the paramilitary structure is changing. Its purpose is to provide a clear hierarchy or chain of authority to support employees and their efforts to accomplish the goals of the organization. Consideration is given to eliminating unnecessary ranks and lines of communication are opened, both of which are conducive to community policing (Goldstein, 1993). In departments such as in San Diego and Portland, obstacles to communication and progress traditionally associated with the paramilitary hierarchy—top-down management, rule-oriented conduct, high degree of specialization—have been overcome, resulting in agency-wide commitment to community policing and problem solving and the elimination of unnecessary ranks (Zhao, 1996). Progressive agencies, while maintaining traditional ranks within the hierarchy, have expanded the span of control and modified the traditional notion of "unity of command" (Schermerhorn, Hunt, & Osborn, 1994).

In nonprogressive agencies, there is little review of or willingness to modify the structure based on resource allocation or other analyses. Resistance to change is the norm. When modifications to the hierarchical structure are made, they are often based on knee-jerk reaction to the internal crisis-of-the-month rather than careful study. This weakness rests with leadership or lack thereof and not the paramilitary model itself.

Some problems associated with the paramilitary structure—excessive ranks, too many people in some ranks, and ill-defined tasks for the various ranks—are the result of executives' inability or unwillingness to negotiate with or confront labor organizations. New and increased ranks are authorized to pacify union leaders, often at the insistence of politicians. Increased ranks are also created to provide salary increases to officers when raises are otherwise restricted or when employees have "topped out" in their pay grade. Ranks are also created to meet mandates of consent decrees.

In one metropolitan agency, after considerable study, the rank of corporal was eliminated to flatten the structure. After union leaders complained to politicians, the rank was restored—it was an election year.

Other problems rest at the doorstep of executives who misuse the system. In a state police department, there was a long-standing tradition of bestowing promotion on command officers who were nearing the end of the career—regardless of qualifications—simply to increase retirement benefits. This was not the fault of the structure but, rather, a system that had gone unchecked, the appointment of weak leaders from within the agency who fostered questionable traditions, and a failure by state authorities to take them to task.

Additionally, there is disparity in how the paramilitary model is applied. Small agencies with five or ten officers may have an excessive number of ranks, and some large agencies have flattened the number of ranks to a minimum. Little research compares the traditional paramilitary structure between police agencies or with alternative systems.

There are few examples of agencies that have pursued alternatives. The medium-sized Boulder, Colorado, Police Department, for example, implemented an alternative structure, reducing its ranks to four levels—officer, supervisor, manager, and chief of police. Other medium-sized agencies have flattened the structure to five ranks—officer, sergeant, lieutenant, captain, and chief of police.

Large departments have had success in strengthening the organization and improving internal communication without abandoning the paramilitary rank structure. Three years ago, the Baltimore Police Department, with over 3400 employees, flattened its structure to six positions—officer, sergeant, lieutenant, major, colonel, and commissioner. The ranks of captain, lieutenant colonel, and deputy commissioner were eliminated, with little outcry from employees or the labor organization. Only four ranks, officer to major, are present in the city's nine district stations. According to Commissioner Thomas Frazier, this flattened structure significantly enhanced communication and served the department in its efforts to implement community policing, violence abatement, and CRIMESTAT (crime control model).

Teaming and Employee Involvement

The paramilitary model does not preclude teaming, employee involvement, or empowerment as means for accomplishing tasks. It does not inhibit commitment to or involvement in community policing and partnerships. It does not preclude gaining employee commitment to agency values. Employee commitment and participation are fostered by leaders who believe in their importance, regardless of titles used to define the hierarchy of the organization.

Teaming and employee participation evolve when leaders make them happen. In large departments—San Diego, St. Petersburg, Baltimore County, Portland, El Paso—great strides have been made in internal communication, employee involvement, community policing, employee accountability, and more without radically changing the paramilitary structure. Agencies that foster and reward employee initiative and problem solving—Arlington, Texas, Madison, and Lakewood—maintain the paramilitary structure.

In contrast to progressive police agencies that continue to use the paramilitary model, some businesses and industries with flat organizational structures and nontraditional titles have closed the door on openness and employee participation, turning to an authoritarian style of leadership.

> In the corridors and lunchrooms of corporate America, people have begun to whisper about a secret nobody wants to face. It's something that academic researchers have known for some time, but most people in the business world were too busy—or too self-invested—to find out.
>
> The secret is this: Teamwork is out, authoritarian leadership is in.
>
> To the chagrin of some managers and the relief of others, evidence is accumulating that an awful lot of those quality circles, 'high-performance teams' and autonomous work groups aren't living up to expectations. Although researchers in academia have suspected this for at least 10 years, only recently has word begun to filter out to the popular press. (Smither, 1991, p. 41)

While there are also businesses with cumbersome hierarchies—Chrysler, McDonald's, Disney—they inspire decision making, involvement, and accountability throughout the organization.

Conclusion

The paramilitary model is viable and can support a modern, progressive, values-based police agency committed to community policing. No model is perfect, and no model can withstand the ravages of weak leaders. Weak leaders, themselves, are fast to blame the structure for the ills of the agency. They tend to reorganize to gain a quick fix to the problem at hand.

The paramilitary model does not inhibit participative management, employee empowerment, or effective internal and external communication. It certainly does not inhibit implementing values or maintaining integrity. This has been demonstrated by police agencies in all regions of the nation.

The paramilitary model is not static. It is dynamic and flexible and should be viewed as ever-changing. The obstacles to change within the paramilitary model—

union agreements, political pressure, weak leadership—will be obstacles to change regardless of the type of hierarchy or structure within the organization.

Critics of the paramilitary model rarely offer alternatives. Rather, they refer to the need to flatten the structure, create an environment based on trust, and empower and recognize the capability of employees. Each of these needs, and more, can be met by the paramilitary model.

REFERENCES

Brewer, J. D., Adrian, G., Hume, I., Moxen-Browne, E., & Wilford, R. (1988). *The police, public order and the state.* New York: St. Martin's Press.

Connor, D. R. (1992). *Managing at the speed of change.* New York: Villard Books.

Drucker, P. F. (1996). *The leader of the future.* San Francisco: Jossey-Bass Publishers.

Goldstein, H. (1993). *The new policing: Confronting complexity.* National Institute of Justice Research in Brief. Washington, DC: NIJ.

Schermerhorn, J. R., Hunt, J., & Osborn, R. (1994). *Managing organizational behavior.* New York: John Wiley and Sons.

Smither, R. D. (1991). The return of the authoritarian manager. *Training, 28*(11), 40–44.

Zhao, J. (1996). *Why police organizations change: A study of community-oriented policing.* Washington, DC: Police Executive Research Forum.

Rejoinder to Dr. Greenberg
CAROL E. RASOR

I am in agreement with Dr. Greenberg's point that weaknesses exist in the leadership of police agencies. However, the paramilitary structure must not be excused, for it is a significant factor contributing to weak leadership. The paramilitary structure places great emphasis on tenure to achieve rank. In some cases, tenure is valued more than what one has contributed to advancing the mission of the police agency and enhancing the work environment and culture. The selection pool becomes smaller as the rank becomes higher in the organization. This limits the police executive's available selection of individuals truly qualified for high-ranking leadership positions because the paramilitary structure values selecting from an internal pool.

As Dr. Greenberg pointed out, executives have also misused the system by promoting command officers who were at the end of their careers as a means to increase their retirement benefits, without consideration of their qualifications. It is true that this is an example of poor leadership, yet the paramilitary structure is designed to facilitate these misuses. Dr. Greenberg is also correct in pointing out that pressure can be imposed by labor unions not to flatten the organizational structure. The problem is that a paramilitary structure rewards an individual's successful performance primarily by promotion. Dr. Greenberg also pointed out that histori-cally police officers have taken great pride in achieving rank. Eliminating unneces-sary ranks is needed for the operational and financial success of the organization, but an organization that bases an individual's success on attaining rank contradicts itself.

In a descriptive analogy, Wilson (1963) compared the police organization to the human hand, which has remarkable dexterity and flexibility of the fingers to work in unison to perform a task. Perhaps the structure of the police organization has caused the hand to take the form of a street fighter's clenched fist. The street fight-er's fingers work in unison, but after numerous fights, the closed fist becomes subject to fractures. Maybe police organizations do represent the clenched fist—a closed system that offers little flexibility.

In examining the literature on the structure of police organizations, Dr. Greenberg asserts that there is little research comparing the paramilitary model to alternative systems. However, the impetus for change that drives the need for re-search simply may not exist. Human nature may be deterring the leaders in the profession of policing to accept and embrace the need for change. Strecher (1997) explains this resistance:

> Even when new methods, techniques, or goals offer a promise of effective results, resistance to changes works to keep the priority default active. The status quo is easier—it is easier to defend (people know it; they're more comfortable with a predictable, known quantity) and it is less risky. Just like the default settings on a computer, the "bases are covered" without having to exert any effort. (p. 12)

There also may exist a subliminal resistance by police executives to change the paramilitary structure because it has been the vehicle for their own professional success.

Police executives should take an active role in working with universities and other police research organizations to empirically address the structure and leader-ship issues plaguing the successful performance of police agencies. Police agencies must evolve from a closed system and culture to an open system that welcomes scrutiny.

Dr. Greenberg states that some progressive agencies use the paramilitary structure to enable empowerment, team building, and employee participation, cit-ing several agencies, including St. Petersburg's. Yet, the paramilitary structure in-herently lends itself to an authoritative management style. Former Madison police Chief David Couper points out the incredible relationship policing has with the au-thoritarian structure; it exists because it is a lazy person's approach to leadership (Couper and Lobitz, 1991). The paramilitary structure also facilitates a paralysis of the chain of command. When a lack of leadership exists at the chief's or sheriff's level and a crisis occurs, the chain of command can become deadlocked. The handling of the riots by the Los Angeles and the St. Petersburg Police Departments are prime examples of inaction that may be attributed to leadership paralysis.

Critics of the paramilitary–bureaucratic organization are skeptical of the simultaneous existence of rank structure and the empowerment of all members in the organization. Osborne and Plastrik (1997) believe that the structure of an organization must change to enable empowerment throughout the organization and suggest:

> The best solution to this problem is to institutionalize administrative decentralization and work teams—to permanently change your bureaucratic structures. If you strip the central controllers of their authority and then greatly thin their ranks, it will be difficult for anyone to reimpose centralization. And if you reorganize work around permanent teams of collaborative, cross-function employees, it will be hard for managers to micromanage. (p. 228–229)

In conclusion, perhaps Dr. Greenberg and I have reached a common ground, that the paramilitary–bureaucratic structure of police agencies is changing. Progressive police agencies have eliminated unnecessary ranks and expanded the span of control. For example, Dr. Greenberg cites the accomplishments of the Boulder Police Department, which has reduced its rank structure to four levels—officer, supervisor, manager, and chief of police. The Boulder Police Department has also eliminated the paramilitary nomenclature of the titles representing the ranks. *Is it time to change the paramilitary structure?* may no longer be the appropriate question to debate. Perhaps, the central question is, *when is a paramilitary structure in a police agency no longer a paramilitary structure?*

REFERENCES

Couper, D. C., & Lobitz, S. H. (1991). *Quality policing: The Madison experience.* Washington, DC: Police Executive Research Forum.

Osborne, D., & Plastrik, P. (1997). *Banishing bureaucracy: The five strategies for reinventing government.* Reading, MA: Addison-Wesley.

Strecher, V. G. (1997). *Planning community policing: Goal specific cases and exercises.* Prospect Heights, IL: Waveland Press, Inc.

Wilson, O. W. (1963). *Police administration.* New York: McGraw-Hill Book Company.

Is There a Distinct Subculture in American Policing?

Editor's Note: Especially since the early 1950s, students of law enforcement—whether academic researchers, police professionals, or true graduates and undergraduates—have tried to understand the profession and the intellectual, behavioral, emotional, and social makeup of those attracted to it. Perhaps more than in any other profession or, depending on one's point of view, occupation, theorists and researchers have attempted to unlock the world of the police officer and open it to scrutiny and understanding. In particular, Westley, Bittner, Wilson, and others have attempted to define a subculture of policing and the attributes generally seen in its members. In light of their research, the controversy becomes clear: Does a police subculture *really* exist?

James S. Albritton is currently Professor and Associate Director of the Criminology and Law Studies Program at Marquette University in Milwaukee, Wisconsin. He has taught and done research in the field of criminal justice for over twenty years and has devoted considerable attention to research and writing on police matters. A former police officer, he attempts to bring that experience and perspective to bear on all aspects of his research, teaching, and writing about contemporary policing.

Susan L. Sayles received her doctorate in Criminology from The Florida State University in 1991, a Master's in Business Administration from Nova Southeastern University in 1985, and an undergraduate degree from Florida State University in Criminology in 1973. Before obtaining her doctorate, Dr. Sayles was employed for thirteen years as a criminal investigator for the Palm Beach

County, Florida, State Attorney's Office and wrote and coordinated the Florida Attorney General's Task Force on Crime and the Elderly in 1989. Dr. Sayles taught at The Florida State University, the University of North Carolina at Wilmington, and Ball State University. She is currently writing a book to assist women who are entering or are already practicing within the criminal justice arena.

YES

SUSAN L. SAYLES

The term *police subculture* has its roots in sociological studies from the 1950s through the early 1980s (Westley, 1951; Niederhoffer, 1967; Manning, 1977, 1972; Manning and Van Maanen, 1978; Reuss-Ianni, 1983). More recent research acknowledges a police *culture* but has altered the previous nomenclature. The current literature refers to police behaviors, values, beliefs, attitudes, socialization, or personalities. These new categories may tend to alleviate some pathological implications previously suggested by the term *subculture.* For example, Skolnick (1994) examines the collective occupational outlook within the police profession. He does not suggest that all police are alike in their working personality, only that some very distinct cognitive tendencies become evident when studied as a collective whole. When subjected to the same scrutiny, all professions demonstrate distinctive cognitive and behavioral responses that tend to become institutionalized. These traits may be due to in-house training or occur because of the innate attitudes, abilities, and personalities of the individuals who gravitate toward such employment. The presence of danger, authority, and efficiency within the police domain creates a unique blend of elements that sets it apart from other occupational workforces.

Some studies have indicated that police, although unique, may even share some of the same occupational problems with other professions. There is a striking similarity between schoolteachers and police with respect to problems with authority. The dangerousness of the profession may be likened to military personnel. Industrial workers also share the need to prove themselves efficient (Skolnick, 1994). Police have been compared with public defenders in regard to social dominance theory (Sidanius, Liu, Shaw, & Pratto, 1994), and mental health workers face similar stress reactions in dealing with child sexual-assault victims (Follette, Polusny, & Milbeck, 1994).

What makes the police subculture different from other professions is the potential for the misuse of power—both individually and collectively. Discretion, an individual police officer's ability to interpret and enact sanctions on a case-by-case basis, is necessary for fair and smooth operation of justice. Police officers decide who gets arrested and which cases are pursued. It is that very essential nature of police work that can manifest the greatest potential violations of public trust.

At the heart of the mission statement promulgated by professional police organizations from the rank and file to the elite is *to fight crime in a professional and impartial way* (Sparrow, Moore, & Kennedy, 1990). It is the face that police proudly present to the public. Just like individuals who face the mirror each morning, there is a gap between a person's professional face and the real person behind the facade. Within each organization lie the overt statements of fact and the covert reality. To say that because each profession has its own *subculture* in no way detracts from a full investigation between what police say and what they actually do. Recruits are quickly socialized into the realities of daily police work. A secret code handed down from one generation of seasoned officers is perpetuated through each succeeding generation. Underlying these transmissions are several powerful beliefs.

The police believe themselves to be the only real crime fighters. There are other agencies, either public or private (e.g., prosecutors, courts, probation, crime watch programs), which the police view as merely ancillary. Only the police are the real guardians of justice—everybody else is just playing at it (Sparrow et al., 1994). Although law enforcement is designed as a paramilitary organization, the class distinctions are missing. Although someone with a college degree can enlist in the military as a lieutenant, there is no such recognition in police departments. All new employees have to start at the bottom of the hierarchy—either walking a beat or riding in a patrol unit. Lateral transfers between agencies are essentially nonexistent. Thus, all cops share a common background (Skolnick, 1994).

During this apprentice stage, the police officer's personality is being developed. A crucial element of the officer's job entails danger and, as such, rookies learn to become attentive to suspicious signs. Each person encountered is judged as to a possible propensity to violence or illicit activities. It does not take long for each officer to develop a profile of a symbolically dangerous character and contrast that with the conventional citizenry. Soon the rookie sees behind the facade of many people's alleged respectability. Through their work officers learn the dirty secrets of the person or persons whom they had admired: a minister is charged with molesting his stepdaughter, a county commissioner is busted for possession of cocaine, a neighbor confesses to embezzlement. Gone are the personal heroes. The recruit learns that everybody has something to hide.

With this cognitive development of suspicion and cynicism evolves social isolation. Officers come to believe no one really understands what real police work is all about. People believe they have a good concept of the role cops play within the criminal justice system, but much of their personal information is gleaned from television, movies, and the media. This distrust of people's knowledge base prevents open dialogue with the public. It also serves to discourage the adoption of any reform suggestions that come from outside the precinct walls. In a study of the Westville police, Skolnick (1994) notes that primary complaints are the lack of respect for the police, lack of cooperation in enforcement of the law, and the public's failure to adequately understand the rigorous requirements of police work.

Another cause for social isolation among police officers is the element of authority. The primary contact most citizenry have with the police involves traffic citations. Neither the citizen nor the officer enjoys these transactions. So too are officers called on to regulate public morality. These duties might entail the curtailment of gambling, prostitution enterprises, or public drunkenness, or patrolling lovers' lanes. Although officers may intercede without making an arrest, they are seen as admonitions necessary to protect the public order. This often leads to charges by the public of hypocrisy, as they are not always known to strictly adhere to moral norms themselves. Any profession, including teachers, ministers, and political leaders, whose employment is entrusted to the maintenance of discipline and ethics faces these same charges. The public has entrusted them with a greater responsibility to act above and beyond criticism as an essential nature of their employment. The combination of danger and authority causes an officer to be called on to act in what is often considered masculine ways. Like military personnel they must maintain a higher degree of physical fitness, agility, and emotional and physical strength. Persons with these personality traits are not always predisposed to being prudish when it comes to pasttimes dealing with sex, drinking, and gambling. An off-duty officer caught driving while intoxicated faces not only the court penalties, but internal disciplinary proscriptions as well. As a public figure, a derelict officer faces at least two times the punishment of an ordinary citizen.

Police tend to be conservative in their emotional and political outlooks. Their role as the ascribed guardians of the rules automatically implies that they affirm them. To do otherwise causes a state of conflicting cognitions (i.e., cognitive dissonance), a mindset that is extremely uncomfortable if not painful. Skolnick (1994) hedges on labeling the police as having an *authoritarian personality,* because too many questions could be raised about this negatively intermediated concept. He chooses instead to use the less value-laden attribute of a *conventional personality.* For good reason, the police are reluctant to be anything but impartial with regard to politics. They are often forbidden to publicly campaign for political candidates. Sudden changes via the election of a new head of an agency can spell disaster for an officer who had chosen the wrong side and lost.

Another correlate to social isolation brought on by perceived public hostility is the strong loyalty that police develop with other officers. This is brought about by a *bunker mentality,* a feeling that it is *us against them.* Professional courtesy (e.g., not writing traffic tickets to other officers) or collegialities are especially high in policing. Teamwork is strongly emphasized. Partners vow to protect each other when confronted with dangerous situations. Powerful feelings of empathy and cooperation develop during the daily routine. With these beliefs comes the Machiavellian attitude that the end justifies the means. The perceived need to bend the rules undermines the sanctity of the law. Once done, the door is opened to malpractice, and the door is kept ajar by avid loyalty to fellow officers (Skolnick, 1994; Sparrow et al., 1990).

Loyalty that is engendered because of shared experiences binds officers together. Mutual trust is a necessary lubricant to conducting business as usual. It is necessary and honorable, but it can lead to the greatest barrier in effectively fighting corruption—*the code of silence*—the unwritten commandment that dictates an officer shall never give incriminating information against any fellow officer (Gold-stein, 1977). Even officers who are otherwise honest refuse to break rank lest they face severe consequences. This comes in the form of ostracism and harassment, formal complaints, and personal threats. The biggest fear of all is that no one will come to their aid when they are faced with peril during an assignment. Supervisors also protect their subordinates from the hint of scandal. Often the most serious problems within departments develop from the narcotics trade. Police officers assigned to this duty have ample opportunities for stealing money, drugs, and other people's property from offenders who are not likely to complain (Winters, 1995).

Whether one buys into the existence of an actual subculture has little to do with public perception and media hype. Several high-profile cases have recently permeated the airways. The Rodney King incident caught police in a frenzied assault of gratuitous violence against a man already in custody. Crank and Langworthy (1992) suggest that the public's reaction to such a crisis of legitimization is a ritualistic and public admonishment and firing of the administration, as was done in the case of Los Angeles Police Chief Daryl F. Gates.

Mark Fuhrman gained national notoriety during the O. J. Simpson case, being perceived by the public as a perjuring bigot. The investigation into the JonBenet Ramsey child homicide made the Boulder Police Department look like a bad imitation of the Keystone Kops. Law enforcement has received devastating blows to its credibility, precipitating a crisis of legitimacy. The public, while thirsting for crime-related tidbits, has become nearly as cynical over police practices as the police are of them.

Internal police corruption investigations have typically ignored the problems surrounding police violence. Winters (1995) notes that an officer's propensity toward violence also may indicate an inclination toward corruption. Thus, the distinction usually devised between corruption and brutality no longer applies. Officers confess that their first encounter with breaking the rules generally begins with committing acts of brutality. A willingness to abuse offenders in custody can prove to other officers that you are a tough cop who can be trusted (Reiss, 1971). Some officers use violence to demonstrate dominance, toughness, and authority to the citizenry that they patrol. Others may use violence as extralegal, vigilante justice to punish those who might otherwise escape the formal proscriptions of the courts (Walker, 1983; Wilson, 1968). Some officers simply enjoy the power and thrills they receive as a result of their behavior.

It is not uncommon among those officers who do not participate in acts of violence and corruption to join their colleagues in lying and falsifying departmental records. Officers justify these actions as necessary and often are employed in covering up an illegal search or unlawful arrest that might be thrown out in court. The most glaring example of this type of behavior occurred during the O. J. Simpson investigation and was supported by the courts and the prosecutors. The primary rule drummed into all officers during training is the need for obtaining a warrant to search a premises if there is time to obtain one. The detectives at Simpson's house jumped the gate of his property, claiming exigent circumstances. Their reasoning was that Simpson's Ford Bronco was parked erratically and blood was found on his vehicle, and they feared that Simpson might also be injured or dead. The Bronco turned out to be parked no differently than most, the blood was the size of a dime and very faint, and Simpson was not even on the premises. Once the detectives ascertained that no party was in danger, they should have sealed off the property and called in for a warrant. Los Angeles County provides for a search warrant to be obtained by a phone call to a judge, so to not do so was unacceptable, especially in what logically would become a high-profile case. It is this author's opinion that the failure to obtain a timely warrant, and manufacturing weak arguments as to why they jumped the fence in the first place, tainted the entire subsequent investigation. The bloody glove obtained by Fuhrman should have been thrown out as fruit of the poisonous tree. The public's trust in the officers' statements was certainly eroded, as was indicated by not-guilty verdict.

Recent Study

Crank, Payn, and Jackson (1993) examine the relationship between police belief systems and attitudes toward police practices. The authors define *craftsmanship* as a mixture of both traditional and commonsense beliefs. Manning (1989) defines this concept of craftsmanship as an occupational culture that contains what members take for granted. It also includes the general rationales and beliefs that connect cognition with behavior. The authors focused on police attitudes in relation to street justice, apathy toward due process, and the code of secrecy defined as the *impenetrability of the police subculture to outside observers.*

Although the study validated some of the subcultural attitudes, the findings were somewhat contrary to expectations, especially in regard to tenure in office. The greater the length of time an officer had within the department, the less likely he or she was to support attitudes of street justice, be antagonistic toward due process concerns, and favor subcultural impenetrability. Older officers may be more likely to have a rich family life and would have less need for the traditional subcultural practices sometimes known as *choir practice* in the popular media. Also not supported by the study was the expectation that police professionalism or higher education provided an internal measure of accountability. This study is limited in that attitudes—not actual behaviors—are measured. According to the authors, recent studies indicate there are intervening variables that modify the influence of attitudes on subsequent behaviors (Worden, 1989).

Conclusion

Police are no different from other professions in that they have an underlying, unifying set of beliefs and practices. The term *subculture* has largely disappeared from the research literature, but is still a valid concept for discussion. Future research is needed to establish whether these subjective attitudes and beliefs continue to manifest themselves in overtly negative behaviors. Policing is a bureaucratic institution, and changes come slowly. This author believes that the infusion of women into the ranks of the sworn officers beginning in the early 1970s may be changing the mode of acceptable behaviors.

Recently this author conducted a snowball sampling of over twenty Indiana policewomen who had risen to the rank of lieutenant or above. They were questioned as to why they believed they had successfully made it through the ranks to positions of power and prestige. Almost without exception, they emphasized the importance of separating their personal lives from their professional lives and found no difficulty in having friends and interests outside of policing. They had made a conscious decision to not participate in the male drinking escapades, one woman noting they were not asked to participate, anyway. All these women had powerful people skills. They had learned how to open a suspect's door with verbal agility, not by flexing their muscles and busting in. The sample was split evenly as to being married or single. Perhaps the Crank and colleagues (1993) study relates to the fact that these women had been in police work an average of fifteen years and tended to view the criminal justice due process procedures favorably. Perhaps some of the alleged subcultural belief systems are breaking down.

REFERENCES

Crank, J. P., Payn, B., & Jackson, S. (1993). The relationship between police belief systems and attitudes toward police practices. *Criminal Justice and Behavior, 20* (2), 199–221.

Crank, J. P., & Langworthy, R. (1992). An institutional perspective of policing. *The Journal of Criminal Law and Criminology, 83* (2), 338–363.

Follette, V. M., Polusny, M. M., & Milbeck, K. (1994). Mental health and law enforcement professionals: Trauma history, psychological symptoms, and impact of providing services to child sexual abuse survivors. *Professional Psychology, Research and Practice, 24* (3), 275–283.

Goldstein, H. (1977). *Policing a free society.* Cambridge, MA: Harvard University Press.

Manning, P. K. (1989). Occupational culture. In: W. Bayley (Ed.). *The encyclopedia of police science.* New York: Garfield.

Manning, P. K. (1977). *Police work: The social organization of policing.* Cambridge, MA: MIT Press.

Manning, P. K. (1972). Observing the police: Deviants, respectables and the law. In: J. D. Douglas (Ed.). *Research on deviance.* New York. Random House.

Manning, P. K., & Van Maanen, J. (Eds.). (1978). *Policing: A view from the street.* Santa Monica, CA: Goodyear Publishing Co.

Niederhoffer, A. (1967). *Behind the shield.* New York: Doubleday.

Reiss, A. (1971). *The police and the public.* New Haven, CT: Yale University Press.

Reuss-Ianni, E. (1983). *Two cultures of policing: Street cops and management cops.* New Brunswick: Transaction Books.

Sidanius, J., Liu, J. H., Shaw, J. S., & Pratto, F. (1994). Social dominance orientation, hierarchy attenuators and hierarchy enhancers: Social dominance theory and the criminal justice system. *Journal of Applied Psychology, 24* (4).

Skolnick, J. (1994). *Justice without trial* (3rd ed.). New York, NY: MacMillan College Publishing Company, Inc.

Sparrow, M. K., Moore, M. H., & Kennedy, D. M. (1990). *Beyond 911: A new era for policing.* New York: Basic Books, Inc.

Walker, S. (1983). *The police in America.* New York: McGraw-Hill.

Westley, W. A. (1951). The police: A sociological study of law, custom, and morality. Ph.D. Dissertation: University of Chicago.

Wilson, J. Q. (1968). *Varieties of police behavior: The management of law and order in eight communities.* Cambridge, MA: Harvard University Press.

Winters, P., ed. (1995). *At issue: Policing the police.* San Diego: Greenhaven Press, Inc.

Worden, R. (1989). Situational and attitudinal explanations of police behavior: A theoretical reappraisal and empirical assessment. *Law and Society Review, 23,* 667–711.

Rejoinder to Dr. Sayles

James S. Albritton

Dr. Sayles presents a very lucid, insightful, and informed discussion of the evolution of the subcultural conception of policing. Her discussion is grounded in a solid understanding of the subcultural literature on policing, and the insights and analysis she provides are among the best I have seen on the topic in recent years. Thus, I do not have any major arguments with her evaluation of the subcultural approach.

I do, however, have some difficulty with the conclusions Dr. Sayles draws from her analysis at two levels. First, I am not as sanguine as she that "the term *subculture* has largely disappeared from the research literature." Admittedly, authors are increasingly hard put to justify or operationalize subcultural terminology in their research, or they employ surrogate concepts to focus attention on more dissect aspects of policing, as Dr. Sayles suggests. But every discussion I have read or heard in recent years regarding the "organizational culture" of policing makes abundant use of the subcultural apparatus or its controversy about police behavior, the immediate response seems to be, unfortunately, to resort to subcultural explanations of the event; the Rodney King and Mark Fuhrman "incidents" are cases in point. Moreover, I agree basically with Dr. Sayles that the influx of women into the ranks of policing has had an attenuating effect on the traditional occupational environment of policing. But there are *many* other factors whose influence has had a transforming effect on the working environment of policing as well. As I have argued elsewhere, I do not believe we can understand *anything* about policing without placing it in the broader context of the technological society in which we live. That is why I object to "subcultural" conceptions of police officers and do not find them particularly useful in understanding police work in either general or specific terms.

Second, Dr. Sayles responds to my discussion by stating that "a subculture by any other name is still a subculture." I am sorry to say that Dr. Sayles falls into the same trap of circuitous reading as the subculturists in uttering such a statement. And I feel the urge to respond with a tried and true Southern epigram: "If the shoe don't fit, don't wear it!" In any case, I agree that the subcultural approach has become "politically outmoded, outdated, value-laden, and no longer serves the purpose for which it was created." That was precisely one of my major arguments in my contribution to this volume. The subcultural paradigm has *always* been politically and ideologically motivated, either consciously or subconsciously, and it has no place in legitimate scientific research for those reasons. There is still much to be said and written about the nature of policing and how it fits into the context of contemporary society. The subcultural approach, however, leads only to a "closed system" of understanding in which stereotypical reductionist explanations abound. It is now time to move beyond this impasse.

NO

JAMES S. ALBRITTON

No conception of American urban policing has enjoyed wider acceptance, greater longevity, more intense study, and fewer criticisms than that of the "police subculture." Moreover, the assumptions on which this approach is based now constitute one of the dominant paradigms in contemporary police studies. The contours of the subcultural concept were forged progressively in a series of studies that span the decades from the 1950s through the 1970s, with very few modifications thereafter. Beginning with Westley's research (1951), however, only a handful of these studies have been employed as recurring frames of reference for subcultural research and analysis. These studies have consistently projected an overwhelmingly negative image of the manner in which American society has been policed over the decades.

In particular, the works of Skolnick (1966), Niederhoffer (1967), Manning (1977, 1972), Manning and Van Maanen (1978), and, more recently, Reuss-Ianni (1983) seem to have defined the "disciplinary matrix" through which all subcultural research must pass. Despite the reservations and subtleties built into the research of individual authors (e.g., Westley & Skolnick), what has emerged from these and similar studies is a global, implacable portrait of American policing as a subcultural cauldron of undesirable traits, attitudes, and behaviors. Indeed, the "police subculture" is most often depicted as an occupational and organizational environment that fosters highly questionable and singular codes of deviance, secrecy, silence, and cynicism, as well as such "pathological" personality dispositions as suspiciousness, insularity, brutality, authoritarianism, ultraconservatism, bigotry, and racism (Conser, 1980). Perceived by numerous authors as one of the most pervasive and durable vocational subcultures in the American workplace, the police subculture has been persistently analyzed and stigmatized as the most potent obstacle to progressive reform in policing, the effective source and cause of police abuses of power and authority, and the most salient characteristic of police organizations generally (e.g., Kappeler, Sluder, & Alpert, 1994).

That some contemporary police experts such as Walker (1992) have characterized much of the subcultural paradigm as "stereotypical," "ahistorical," and "impressionistic" has not yet deterred others from embracing it uncritically. To the contrary, the subcultural image continues to dominate the field and has had substantial effects on everything from policy formulations and reform movements to investigatory commissions and inquiries into alleged police misconduct over the last few decades (Walker, 1989). But what, precisely, are we talking about when the subcultural paradigm is invoked to explain such a vast array of police behaviors, organizations, and issues? Is there anything missing from the one-dimensional, global image of policing that this approach projects? Are there other ways of understanding the same phenomena portrayed in the subcultural paradigm, without denying the validity of some of its insights? I am firmly convinced that there are.

Based on my personal experience in both academics and policing, I have progressively understood the decisive importance of empathetic understanding in social scientific research. Without empathy, an essential part of the human element under study is lost to the observer, and the resultant research becomes nothing more than a projection of the researcher's assumptions, biases, or presuppositions about the object of study. Such has been the case, unfortunately, with the subcultural paradigm in police studies. This is why I am calling into question some of its most cherished assumptions about the nature of policing and the so-called police subculture. Three major concerns guide my critique. First, I raise some conceptual problems associated with subcultural research; second, I attempt to identify certain definitional inadequacies in the studies; and third, I argue that unstated political and ideological assumptions guide and distort this type of approach to understanding policing.

Conceptual Concerns

The subcultural concept is not unique to the field of police studies. Rather, it is almost entirely derivative of the fields of anthropology and sociology in which one of its recognized deficiencies is its inherent ambiguity (e.g., Fine & Kleinman, 1979). Because one of the major assumptions of the subcultural paradigm is the uniqueness of the police subculture in juxtaposition to the norms, values, beliefs, and attitudes that are presumed to exist in the larger society, it would be interesting to know with assurance whether the ethos of policing differs radically from what we find elsewhere. When this matter has been addressed seriously, most research indicates that police attitudes and values tend to mirror those found more generally in American society and that the relationship between police attitudes and on-the-job conduct is tenuous at best (e.g., Worden, 1989).

In other words, it is difficult to maintain that police officers as an occupational group develop a distinct "subculture" guided by a unique set of norms and values that set them apart from other social or occupational groups. For example, as Balch (1972) pointed out in his insightful review of these matters, "Authoritarianism, as a personality syndrome, is widespread in this country, and policemen may not be any more authoritarian than other people from similar socioeconomic backgrounds. Bigotry is hardly unusual in the United States. Nor is conservatism, cynicism, or any other authoritarian trait." Lefkowitz (1975) echoed many of Balch's findings and characterized most of the relevant literature as "mere opinion." In reviewing studies of the "cop personality," Tifft (1974) held that "the data indicate that the socialization processes and consequent attitude-personality development are much more complex than previously indicated. They are critically related to the task environment (danger, citizen attitudes, bureaucratic initiatives), to the nature of the work, to the relationships among the policemen and their superiors." Tifft further concluded that police officers generally developed an attitude of friendliness and helpfulness toward the public, and some suspicion, distrust, and cynicism emerged as "necessities."

The Tifft, Lefkowitz, and Balch reviews merit some reflection, as they are almost diametrically opposed to the dominant assumptions of the police subcultural literature (which apparently ignores or dismisses these kinds of critiques) and contain at least three essential nuances of empathetic understanding. First, the assumption of a "common personality structure" in policing that supports most of the "subcultural" traits identified by many authors does not withstand scrutiny. Police officers emerge from these reviews as reflective of the larger society from which they have been recruited and socialized; they are no more or less than a microcosm of cultural traits found generally in American society. In other words, police officers are actually products and reflections of the very society and culture from which they are purportedly "isolated" by the subcultural literature. Furthermore, police attitudes and values are not those of a subculture of "isolation" and "alienation;" rather, they mirror the mainstream—for good or ill. Perhaps it is precisely the unattractiveness of certain traits in American society and culture that motivates subculturists to confine them to their "subcultural" manifestations in policing. This has certainly been the case with the so-called subculture of violence thesis as applied to policing—as though police violence or brutality could somehow be better understood discretely and apart from the embarrassing history of violence and brutality in American society (e.g., Hofstadter & Wallace, 1970).

Second, both Balch and Tifft insist on the interactive nature of policing by showing that police norms and attitudes are products of the unique working environment of policing, rather than an ensemble of self-generated, esoteric, "deviant" predispositions. Could it be that in their "selective" contact with the American public, the police "see" certain "truths" about the citizenry and society that lead them inexorably to cynicism, insularity, prejudiced attitudes, and sporadic abuse of law and authority? Might there be some painful truths in what they see and reflect back to us, truths that we prefer not to acknowledge or admit about ourselves? Could it be, moreover, that the oft-mentioned transition of police officers from their initial idealism for the job to cynicism or disillusionment later on is due, at least in part, to the painful realities they witness and must confront as no one else in "the community"? Alas, this line of research has rarely, if ever, been pursued. And yet recognition of the validity of these dimensions of the police experience might produce a greater step forward in empathetic understanding between the police and the public than any of the accusatory and cynical assumptions now prevalent in subcultural literature.

Finally, Tifft's observation that most police attitudes toward the public derive from the "necessities" of the task environment of policing is far more profound conceptually than it might appear. Little concession has ever been accorded to the order of necessity that governs police work; yet the response to social necessity is as central to American policing as the use of coercive force and conformity to the requirements of democratic law. In fact, the latter are arguably byproducts and expressions of that same social necessity. When Tifft applies the term "necessity" to policing, he implies that the police must eventually adapt their beliefs and behavior, by whatever means necessary, to the prevailing social, political, legal, and cultural climate of the moment, regardless of how unreasonable, illogical, or unjust that climate may appear to them. Thus the police have been called on consistently and simultaneously to wage "wars" on crime and drugs, enforce unpopular laws, maintain the "quality of life" and social order of certain segments of society, and meet the often competing, ambiguous, or contradictory "community standards" that define their services. Police adaptations have led them historically to adopt and condone means that were either at the limits of legality, in violation of departmental policies and procedures, or overtly illegal. All of this has led to the formulation of the "impossible mandate" of policing (Manning, 1977) and the somewhat disingenuous concession of subculturists to a degree of "complexity" in the "task environment" of policing.

Although this brief discussion does not exhaust the topic, one can see that there has been a dearth of empathetic understanding displayed at the conceptual level of the subcultural paradigm. Instead, a systematically negative and deprecating image of policing pervades the subcultural paradigm. Moreover, this dearth of empathy has caused most subculturists to ignore essential ingredients in a comprehensive understanding of policing. This is equally true of the definitional difficulties that arise from what I have mentioned above.

Definitional Differences

Providing precise definitions of social phenomena is not just an enhancement to research, it is basic to serious scientific inquiry. Therefore, proceeding to an analysis of presumed "subcultural traits" in policing, without an attentive and constant reflection on the viability of the subcultural concept itself, is at best irresponsible. Conser (1980), in his extensive review of subcultural research, unfortunately demonstrates how most subcultural research proceeds willy-nilly. In characteristic fashion, Conser states that "an occupational subculture . . . refers to the distinctive beliefs, values, and behavior patterns of a particular group of workers." He then advances, not to a clarification of the legitimacy of the concept in police studies, but to an analysis of the "characteristics" of the police subculture in terms of alleged personality traits and occupational group norms. He concludes by asserting that "the problematic aspect of the police subculture is not whether it exists and what its characteristics are. The problem is its negative impact on policing which many claim to be very significant."

Conser's review demonstrates a persistent and pervasive paradox in all subcultural research: the tendency to proceed by exhortation rather than carefully defining and testing hypotheses. The fact that the subcultural approach always begins with the presupposition that the police subculture has a "negative impact" on whatever other topic is being discussed inexorably taints the analysis from the outset. Has nothing really changed in urban policing since the early formulations of the police subculture in the 1950s and 1960s? Do prevailing definitions of the police subculture contain any understanding or allowance for historical, social, and cultural changes in the occupation over the decades? What effects have several major reform movements, the "professionalization" process, the size of the department, accreditation, higher educational requirements, affirmative action recruitment of women and minorities, major policy and procedure revisions, civil and criminal litigation, unionization, civilianization, personnel attrition rates, and myriad other changes (see esp., Walker, 1992; 1989) had on the reliability and validity of the subcultural concept? Has the subcultural concept become a mere metaphor or label of convenience, a kind of shorthand used to depict the much more complex and demanding reality of policing? Or might there be some serious flaws in the way subculturists define that reality?

As Klockars (1983) notes perceptively, "almost nothing worth saying about police can be said without also saying something about something else. This is so because police are but a portion of the fabric of the society they work in and are no more understandable apart from its history, culture, and organization than they are from the history, culture, and organization of policing itself." The problem of placing policing in its proper social context is not, therefore, a trite matter.

In this regard, however, the only recent refinement in the subcultural literature in this direction is Reuss-Ianni's (1983) hypothesis about the "two cultures" of policing. She argues strongly that we must now take into consideration two distinct and antagonistic "cultures"—street cops and management cops—to better understand the subcultural dynamics of urban police organizations. Her research has the merit of attempting to define the "two cultures" much more extensively than in previous studies, but her insights have led to a veritable floodgate of "multi-subcultural" research that asserts that any subgrouping within policing deserves the subcultural title. This trend has mobilized legions of graduate students to the task, and we now see a proliferation of subcultural research on every aspect of policing, virtually all of which further empties the concept of any precise meaning whatsoever.

The tendency of subcultural theorists to reify their concepts has become a permanent fixture in the paradigm and has taken many forms. Skolnick's (1966) original and intelligent insights into the "working personality" of police officers is a case in point. Skolnick argued that the occupational exigencies of danger, authority, and efficiency (the latter being symptomatically omitted or ignored by subsequent researchers) produced "distinctive cognitive lenses and tendencies" in police behavior. He did not imply that all police officers were alike in their responses to the job, but that "as a result of the combined features of their social situation, [they] tend to develop ways of looking at the world distinctive of themselves." Had the idea of the "working personality" led to further concrete research, instead of becoming a centerpiece for the stereotypical and reductionist subcultural approach, it might have opened the avenue to an empathetic understanding of why police officers, of necessity, perceive the world somewhat differently from the average citizen. In light of the Balch, Lefkowitz, and Tifft analyses mentioned earlier, for example, it might have been better to argue that police officers develop a "working persona" to cope with the stresses and necessities of the job; that is, a persona that may not totally define them as human beings that accounts for the differences in their attitudes and behavior while on the job. The "working persona" is a far less deterministic and intransigent notion than the insistence on a one-dimensional "police subcultural personality" that totally defines and delineates the variety of individuals and attitudes found in policing. The same notion might also help to clarify some of the controversies surrounding Niederhoffer's (1967) "authoritarianism-cynicism" personality syndromes, which have also given rise to a great deal of misunderstanding about police attitudes and behavior.

Even Manning and Van Maanen (1978), both of whom are most often associated with the subcultural paradigm, seem to recognize the difficulties in defining the "police world" clearly. "The police world is partitioned into so many subworlds that it is quite difficult to see any unity of purpose or overall strategy behind police actions . . . police organizations represent a hodgepodge of cliques, cabals, and conspiracies." The ambiguity in such a statement lies in the fact that it can be interpreted in at least two ways; either it reinforces the "multi-subcultural" approach to policing without actually challenging the subcultural paradigm itself, or it supports the idea that there is a plurality of subgroups in police organizations that has not yet been accounted for in the existing subcultural research. Either way, subcultural research is extremely vulnerable to criticism at this level of ambiguity and at another, more substantial, level of concern.

Political and Ideological Assumptions

Political and ideological controversies permeate virtually all intellectual and scientific endeavors. But a serious problem arises when researchers' ideological commitments remain unstated and affect the very assumptions on which their scientific research is conducted and presented. Miller (1973) astutely and convincingly analyzed the "ideological" climate of criminal justice studies and defined "ideology" as "a set of general and abstract beliefs or assumptions about the correct or proper state of things, particularly with respect to the moral order and political arrangements, which serve to shape one's position on specific issues." For Miller, these beliefs and assumptions constitute the "permanent hidden agenda of criminal justice." Police studies certainly have not escaped this "hidden agenda," and subcultural research on policing seems to be one of the prime areas in which it has materialized. Because, for diverse reasons, policing generates a source of quasi-permanent controversy in a democratic society, and because entirely "disinterested" research on policing is a rarity, police studies have given rise to some of the most blatantly political and ideological research in the field of criminal justice.

In particular, subcultural researchers, to their credit, have never pretended to be entirely "value neutral" in their approach to policing. In the early studies of the mysterium tremendum of policing, subcultural researchers unlocked the mystery by borrowing generously from other areas of sociology, anthropology, and psychology, but especially from the sociology of deviant and delinquent behavior. The choice of this strategy was dictated in part by the assumptions of subcultural research, but also by political and ideological presuppositions about the nature of police work in American society. Police work was "dirty work," performed by unprofessional and undereducated blue collar "craftsmen," who often shocked the sensibilities of the more educated researchers. According to Grimshaw and Jefferson (1987), a diffuse form of "sociological liberal-idealism" dominates most of the critical studies of policing. Disenchanted by the perceived failure of formal police organizations to realize and implement their interpretation of "democratic ideals," many researchers turned their attention to the "informal organization" of policing, from which the dominant traits of the police subculture were derived. Manning (1972) articulates best, perhaps, the presuppositions of a generation of these researchers:

> The role seems to attract men who are apparently deeply ambivalent about the law, politically conservative, perhaps reactionary, and persons of lower- or lower-middle-class origins with a high school or less education. The police attributes suggested by the brief listing of the postulates of the police culture—suspiciousness, fear, low self-esteem, and distrust of others—are

almost diametrically opposed to the usual conception of the desirable democratic man. (p. 244)

Manning does not expound on what "the usual conception of the desirable democratic man" might be in actuality, but he does have the merit of stating explicitly what appears to be in the minds of most researchers who share the subcultural paradigm. It is obvious also that the uncompromising portrait he paints is not meant to flatter. Nor is it the sign of a "value-neutral" inquiry into the manners and customs of the police. Bittner (1970), however, in his seminal work on policing, seems to provide the perfect counterpoint when he states that "the constant reminder that officers should be wise, considerate, and just, without providing them with opportunities to exercise these virtues is little more than vacuous sermonizing." Thus the ideological battle lines were drawn early between opposing viewpoints about policing—primarily on the basis of conflicting political assumptions about the role and requirements of policing a democratic society. Those battle lines still exist today, yet neither viewpoint completely resolves the issue, because both situate themselves within the subcultural paradigm and do not offer any viable alternatives to it. Such is the state of police research to date.

Conclusion

I have attempted to argue in opposition to the idea that there is a distinct police subculture in American policing—not because I reject all the findings of subcultural research, but because I believe there are serious flaws and omissions in this approach. In other words, the subcultural approach is as deficient in what it ignores about policing as it is in its conclusions. A variety of conceptual, definitional, and ideological problems permeate this research and color its contentions about policing. As an alternative to the impasse created by this approach, I propose injecting a substantial dose of empathetic understanding into the fray, which I believe would provide a new and informative foundation for constructive dialogue about police matters. The stranglehold on research that the subcultural paradigm has enjoyed for decades must come to an end, and police studies must move beyond this paradigm if our research is to remain germane to a realistic and comprehensive assessment of contemporary developments and issues in policing.

REFERENCES

Albritton, J. S. (1991). Professor/policeman: Reflections on a practicum in policing. *Wisconsin Sociologist, 27* (1), 49–56.

Balch, R. (1972). The police personality: Fact or fiction? *Journal of Criminal Law, Criminology, and Police Science, 63* (1), 106–119.

Bittner, E. (1970). *The functions of the police in modern society.* Washington, DC: National Institute of Mental Health.

Cain, M. (1979). The trends in the sociology of police work. *International Journal of the Sociology of Law, 7,* 143–167.

Conser, J. A. (1980). A literary review of the police subculture: Its characteristics, impact and policy implications. *Police Studies, 2* (4), 46–54.

Fine, G. A., & Kleinman, S. (1979). Rethinking subculture: An interactionist analysis. *American Journal of Sociology, 85* (1), 1–20.

Grimshaw, R., & Jefferson, T. (1987). *Interpreting policework: Policy and practice in forms of beat policing.* London: Allen & Unwin.

Hofstadter, R., & Wallace, M. (1970). *American violence: A documentary history.* New York: Random House.

Kappeler, V. E., Sluder, R. D., & Alpert, G. P. (1994). *Forces of deviance: Understanding the dark side of policing.* Prospect Heights, IL: Waveland Press, Inc.

Klockars, C. B., ed. (1983). *Thinking about the police: Contemporary readings.* New York: McGraw-Hill.

Lefkowitz, J. (1975). Psychological attributes of policemen: A review of research and opinion. *Journal of Social Issues, 31* (1), 3–27.

Manning, P. K. (1977). *Police work: The social organization of policing.* Cambridge, MA: MIT Press.

Manning, P. K. (1972). Observing the police: Deviants, respectables and the law. In: J. D. Douglas (ed.), *Research on deviance.* New York: Random House.

Manning, P. K., & Van Maanen, J., eds. (1978). *Policing: A view from the street.* Santa Monica, CA: Goodyear Publishing.

Miller, W. B. (1973). Ideology and criminal justice police: Some current issues. In: A. S. Blumberg & E. Niederhoffer (eds.). (1985). *The ambivalent force: Perspectives on the police.* New York: Holt, Rinehart & Winston.

Niederhoffer, A. (1967). *Behind the shield.* New York: Doubleday.

Reuss-Ianni, E. (1983). *Two cultures of policing: Street cops and management cops.* New Brunswick: Transaction Books.

Skolnick, J. (1966). *Justice without trial.* New York: John Wiley & Sons.

Tifft, L. L. (1974). The 'cop personality' reconsidered. *Journal of Police Science and Administration, 2,* 266–278.

Walker, S. (1989). Conclusion: Paths to police reform—Reflections on 25 years of Change. In D. J. Kenney (ed.). (1989). *Police & policing: Contemporary issues.* New York: Praeger.

Walker, S. (1992). *The police in America: An introduction.* (2nd ed.). New York: McGraw-Hill.

Westley, W. A. (1951). *The police: A sociological study of law, custom, and morality.* Ph.D. Dissertation: University of Chicago.

Worden, R. E. (1989). Situational and attitudinal explanations of police behavior: A theoretical reappraisal and empirical assessment. *Law & Society Review, 23,* 667–711.

Rejoinder to Dr. Albritton
Susan L. Sayles

I have no argument with Dr. Albritton's assertion that the research involving police subculture is lacking in rigorous quantitative study. One major frustration in researching this topic was the absolute void of recent articles that addressed the subculture phenomenon by name. The result has been to break down each of the alleged behaviors and attitudes into newly created separate categories, which include police violence, corruption, cynicism, solidarity, and socialization. One of the reasons terminology is relegated to the backburner and new names are attached to old concepts is that the old term becomes politically outmoded, outdated, and value laden and no longer serves the purpose for which it was created. Having been in police work myself, I intuitively validate many of the assertions set forth in this paper. I concur with Dr. Albritton that empathetic understanding relative to the investigation of this phenomenon is needed, but a subculture by any other name is still a subculture.

Is It Time for Police Agencies to Eliminate Pursuits?

EDITOR'S NOTE: For many years, the pursuit was viewed as a necessary activity of law enforcement officers. No offender, regardless of the
seriousness of the transgression, was allowed to flee unchallenged, and
pity the officer who broke off a pursuit absent a true (and witnessed!) life-
threatening danger. Yet recent observations have caused us to reassess
this tactic. Many of those pursued are *not* serious offenders, and far too
many pursuits end in accident, injury, or fatality. An increasing number
of civil courts are finding against officers and agencies involved in pursuits, and, at the time of this writing, the United States Supreme Court is
considering whether to establish a nationwide legal standard for determining whether police chases violate constitutional protections. The dilemma becomes clear: Is it time for police agencies to eliminate—or, at
the very least, severely limit—police pursuits?

Sheldon F. Greenberg, Ph.D., is Chair of the Department of Interdisciplinary
Programs, Division of Business and Management, Johns Hopkins University, and
also serves as Director of the Johns Hopkins University's Police Executive Leadership Program. Before joining Johns Hopkins University, he served as Associate
Director of the Police Executive Research Forum (PERF) in Washington, DC. Dr.
Greenberg began his career as an officer in the Howard County, Maryland, Police
Department, where he served as a criminal investigator, public information officer,
supervisor of the records and information division, supervisor of the youth unit, director of the police academy, director of research and planning, assistant to the
chief of police, and commander of the administrative services bureau. He is the author of several books, including *Stress and the Helping Professions, Stress and the*

Teaching Profession, and *On The Dotted Line,* a comprehensive guide on police executive selection and contracts, and numerous articles.

Michael S. McCampbell is Project Director with Circle Solutions, Inc., a government contracting firm located in the Washington, DC, area. He currently manages several drug enforcement training and technical assistance programs funded by the Bureau of Justice Assistance. Mr. McCampbell, a retired law enforcement officer from the Arlington County (VA) Police Department, has coauthored several manuals and a Report to Congress on clandestine drug laboratory investigation and cleanup. During his law enforcement career, Mr. McCampbell was Visiting Fellow at the National Institute of Justice, the research branch of the U.S. Department of Justice. Mr. McCampbell has an M.S. in Special Studies from George Washington University and a B.S. in the Administration of Justice from American University. He has served as an adjunct faculty member and lecturer on law enforcement subjects at Northern Virginia Community College, George Mason University, University of North Florida, and Florida Atlantic University.

YES

Michael S. McCampbell

A police pursuit is defined as "an active attempt by a law enforcement officer operating a vehicle with emergency equipment to apprehend a suspected law violator in a motor vehicle, when the driver of the vehicle attempts to avoid apprehension" (Alpert & Dunham, 1992).

Police should not be allowed to engage in high-speed vehicle pursuits of suspected law violators. Pursuits are too dangerous for the officers, innocent bystanders, and even the fleeing lawbreaker, for police to continue this practice. Like the truncheon, the blackjack, and the call box, police pursuits have become outdated and need to be replaced with modern technology. The high-speed pursuit is an example of an outmoded police activity that is analogous to modern physicians using chloroform as an anesthetic. It can still be done, but given the advances in medicine over the past one hundred years, why would anyone consider using nineteenth-century technology in today's society?

Consider some recent examples gathered from newspaper articles by a police "trade newspaper" (*Law Enforcement News,* 1996) that illustrate the dangers of police pursuits:

- A twelve-year-old boy in Oregon led police on a high-speed chase at speeds in excess of 100 miles an hour, before rolling over several times and being involved in a head-on collision.
- A family in Indiana had their car windows shot out by state troopers who were firing at a bank robber attempting to escape by car.

- Five Philadelphia teenagers were killed during a police pursuit when the stolen car they were driving struck a utility pole at a high rate of speed.
- In Tacoma, Washington, a man was left partially paralyzed when his car was broadsided by a carload of gang members being chased by police.

These are horrendous examples, but they are not just isolated cases. Gruesome photographs in the newspapers and almost daily television news reports are constant reminders of the hazards of police pursuits. In most cases, pursuits create more danger than the benefits of apprehending the fleeing lawbreaker.

We need to apply the same standards to high-speed pursuits as those governing the use of deadly force. As a matter of practice and policy, police are not allowed to shoot at fleeing felons and should not be allowed to pursue lawbreakers *except* in cases where they know a violent felony has been committed. This practice would reduce the wide discretion given to police in deciding when to pursue. It would also save lives and reduce civil liability claims against police agencies. In the examples cited above, lives would have been spared had police not been chasing lawbreakers for property crimes and traffic offenses.

Research on Pursuits

Although there has been relatively little research into the issue, existing data show the danger involved in police vehicle pursuits. A group calling itself Solutions to Tragedies of Police Pursuits (STOPP) has gathered some frightening statistics:

- On average, about 300 people die each year from police pursuits.
- Up to 87 percent of all police pursuits are for minor traffic violations.
- One percent of all pursuits end in death, and 22 percent end in injuries (Campbell, 1997).

Even if these statistics are somewhat unreliable, other scholarly research has confirmed the seriousness of vehicle pursuits. A 1990 study (Alpert & Dunham, 1990) collected data on 952 pursuits from two major police agencies in Dade County, Florida (Miami Police Department and the Metro-Dade County Police Department). The study revealed that:

- Fifty-four percent of the pursuits were initiated for traffic offenses
- Thirty-three percent resulted in accidents
- Seventeen percent resulted in injuries
- Fewer than 1 percent resulted in deaths

Statistics collected by the New Jersey Attorney General's Office revealed that, in 1995, law enforcement agencies in that state engaged in 1237 chases, with 315 resulting in accidents that left eight people dead and 243 injured (*Law En-*

forcement News, 1996). Nationally, pursuit-related deaths rose from 347 in 1993 to 388 in 1994, according to information from the National Highway Traffic Safety Administration's Fatal Accident Reporting System.

Research findings support the idea of confining police pursuits to violent felonies. In a recently published report (Alpert, 1997), case records were reviewed from 1246 pursuits conducted by three agencies (Metro-Dade, Florida; Omaha, Nebraska; and Aiken, South Carolina) over a several-year period. Researchers found that pursuits in Metro-Dade were reduced 82 percent after the adoption of a "violent felony only" pursuit policy. Pursuits increased over 600 percent in Omaha when the department changed to a policy allowing pursuits for offenses that had been previously prohibited.

A national survey (Kenney & Alpert, 1997) of police pursuits found that many departments do not adequately train their officers to conduct pursuits. The average time devoted to pursuit driver training for entry-level officers is less than fourteen hours. Incredibly, only 60 percent of those agencies responding to the survey reported that they provided any training at all in this critical skill. Even more astounding was the finding that those agencies that provide training offer only about three hours of additional training to in-service personnel.

This study also found that just over 12 percent of the agencies disciplined officers at least once in 1993 for pursuit-related actions. Actual discipline ranged from oral reprimand or counseling to termination of two officers. The study's authors suggest that police should consider limiting pursuit to violent felons, and law enforcement agencies should pay close attention to these research findings.

Civil Liability Issues

Police pursuits have become one the most litigated areas in the criminal justice arena. A computerized search of Federal Courts of Appeals cases involving pursuits for the past three years revealed over 600 decisions!

Historically, the courts have applied similar standards to officer behavior in high-speed pursuits and the use of deadly force. The central focus in both issues is, *Do officers' actions under color of law violate injured parties' rights, privileges, or immunities guaranteed under the Constitution or laws of the United States?*

Until 1961, police officers, supervisors, and managers were immune from civil lawsuits. Then, in *Monroe v. Pape,* the Supreme Court held that individual line officers could be held liable for their actions under Title 42 U.S. Code, Section 1983, also known as the Civil Rights Act.

However, municipalities and other units of state and local governments were shielded under the concept of sovereign immunity from the negligent acts of police officers involved in high-speed pursuits and other acts. In 1978, in *Monell v. Department of Social Services of New York City,* the U.S. Supreme Court ruled that municipalities that violated constitutional rights under local custom, policy, or practice, could be sued. Then in 1980, the U.S. Supreme Court held in *Owen v.*

City of Independence that municipalities could not claim good-faith defenses to constitutional violations. This has resulted in a tremendous amount of litigation that has removed a lot of money from the "deep pockets" of jurisdictions. Individual officers may soon be paying out this money themselves.

Subsequent to this case law, the U.S. Supreme Court addressed the issue of police officer civil liability and immunity in pursuits in early 1998 (*County of Sacramento* and *Smith v. Lewis*). This civil rights lawsuit was brought against a Sacramento County (CA) deputy under Title 42 U.S. Code, Section 1983 and stems from the death of a teenager on a motorcycle during a pursuit. The deceased was a sixteen-year-old boy who was the passenger on a motorcycle being chased by police for traffic violations. He was killed when the officer pursuing the motorcycle skidded into him after a chase at speeds exceeding 100 miles per hour. Significantly, the Supreme Court held that "high-speed chases with no intent to harm suspects physically, or to worsen their legal plight, do not give rise to liability under the Fourteenth Amendment." Using its due process model in the decision, the Court maintained the standard previously adopted in *Rochin v. California* (1952) that, for liability to inure, the conduct precipitating the harm must be so egregious that it "shocks the conscience." With the responsibility assumed by the motorcycle driver in fleeing the police and with the reasonable actions of the police officers, this case did not rise to that level. It is clear that future cases, however, will be decided on an individual basis.

In the most recent study discussed earlier (Kenney & Alpert, 1997), 16 percent of the responding agencies reported that during 1993 they had been involved in litigation resulting from pursuits. Of those involved in litigation, 26 percent reported that they had either lost or settled actions against them. How many more lawsuits must be lost before the police wake up?

The response of local governments and agencies has been to reduce the discretion of officers who are considering engaging in a pursuit. In many agencies, pursuits are now subject to control by supervisory personnel who have the authority to terminate the pursuit. This is a positive step, but it does not go far enough. Several bodies of research have shown that involvement in a pursuit increases the participants'—both pursuer and pursued—adrenaline and excitement levels (Alpert et al., 1997). These two factors result in two or more 4000-pound weapons hurtling at unsafe speeds on public roadways, without regard for traffic density, laws, or good sense.

Technological Advances

Recent technological advances promise to provide the police with the tools to apprehend fleeing lawbreakers without resorting to high-speed pursuits. For years police agencies have been able to use helicopters and fixed-wing aircraft to monitor fleeing suspects and observe where they go. The spike belt, a recent invention, is a strip of spikes that can be placed across a roadway to slowly deflate a vehicle's tires, bringing it to a halt.

Other measures that were originally developed by the military are currently in various stages of reengineering for civilian police with funding provided by the National Institute of Justice, U.S. Department of Justice. For example, the U.S. Attorney's Office for the Southern District of California is conducting a field test of a device that enables police officers to send out an electromagnetic pulse that disables a vehicle's electronic system. This disruption shuts off the vehicle's engine, forcing it to coast to a stop.

Conclusion

High-speed pursuits must be strictly controlled. Localities can no longer afford to underwrite the cost of police chases that result in injuries, loss of lives, and increased civil liability. Taxpayers who must foot the bill for bad public policy deserve better and safer ways to apprehend lawbreakers without endangering innocent people. The courts continue to demand a strict accounting by localities for the actions of their employees and will soon require that individual police officers themselves pay for their actions.

REFERENCES

Alpert, G., & Dunham, R. (1992). *Policing in urban America* (2nd ed.). Prospect Heights, IL: Waveland.

Alpert, G., & Dunham, R. (1990). *Police pursuit driving: Controlling responses to emergency situations.* New York: Greenwood.

Alpert, G. (1997). Police pursuit: Policies and training. *NIJ Research in Brief.* Washington, D.C.: U.S. Department of Justice.

Alpert, G., Kenney, D., & Dunham, R. (1997). Police pursuits and the use of force: Recognizing and managing the 'pucker factor'—A research note. *Justice Quarterly, 14* (2), 371–385.

Campbell, P. (1997). To catch a thief. *Memphis Flyer,* February 6–12.

The constant quest for a technological edge. (1996, December 31). *Law Enforcement News.*

Kenney, D., & Alpert, G. (1997). A national survey of pursuits and the use of police force: Data from law enforcement agencies. *Journal of Criminal Justice, 25*(4), 315–324.

County of Sacramento and James E. Smith v. Lewis (1998). WL 259980.

Life, liberty, and pursuits. (1996, December 31). *Law Enforcement News.*

Monell v. Department of Social Services of New York City. (1978). 436 U.S. 690.

Owen v. City of Independence. (1990). 445 U.S. 622.

Rochin v. California (1952). 342 U.S. 165

Rejoinder to Mr. McCampbell   Sheldon F. Greenberg

Although I have tremendous respect and admiration for Michael McCampbell, I disagree with his statements about eliminating police pursuits. His opinion on police pursuits begins with the statement, "Police should not be allowed to engage in high-speed vehicle pursuits of suspected law violators." A few paragraphs later, he says, "I think we need to apply the same standards to high-speed pursuits as those governing the use of force."

Mr. McCampbell makes reference to police being allowed to shoot in cases in which they know a violent felony has been committed. In fact, restrictions on use of deadly force are far greater than he cited. The violent felon must give cause to believe that he or she may cause harm to others or self *before* police may act.

While speaking against pursuits and citing weaknesses such as insufficient training, Mr. McCampbell supports my opinion. By referencing research that supports more restrictive policies, he proposes that pursuits continue but with significant restriction. "Pursuits in Metro-Dade were reduced by 82 percent after the adoption of a 'violent felony only' pursuit policy." The reduction did not occur because the police department eliminated pursuits. Rather, it restricted, trained, and supervised, as I propose all departments should do.

Much of Mr. McCampbell's stand focuses on increased liability caused by police pursuits and the elimination of immunity for police departments. Although police agencies should seek to reduce liability caused by wrongdoing, they cannot allow potential lawsuits to dictate eliminating an important tool of the police profession. Lawsuits are commonplace when police apply lethal force. Over the past three decades, police agencies have continued to train and improve policy to better protect the public and reduce litigation resulting from use of force. Similar improvements are taking place regarding police pursuits. In many large agencies, positive change is occurring more rapidly than occurred with use of force.

In supporting his recommendation to disband police pursuits, Mr. McCampbell turns to technology. However, he states, "advances promise to provide the police with the tools to apprehend fleeing lawbreakers without resorting to high-speed pursuits." Unfortunately, that promise has not been realized. The use of "helicopters and fixed-wing aircraft to monitor fleeing suspects" exists only in large agencies and then only when the aircraft is in reasonable vicinity of the pursuit. Field testing of some equipment is taking place, but practical application, cost, and availability to large and small agencies remain questionable.

Mr. McCampbell begins his conclusion by stating, "High-speed pursuits must be strictly controlled." There is no counterpoint to this statement. He is absolutely correct. He goes on to add that the public deserves "better and safer ways to apprehend lawbreakers without endangering innocent people." Again there is no argument to be made.

The initial suggestion that pursuits be abandoned quickly changes to a suggestion that pursuits be restricted and better controlled through supervision, policy, training, and technology. In this regard, there is little difference in what both of us propose. Pursuit remains an important and viable means for effecting the arrest of criminal offenders and should not be eliminated.

NO

SHELDON F. GREENBERG

I would no more take pursuit away from police than take their firearms away. But you don't shoot every common criminal. And you don't chase every potential law violator.

> —Geoffrey Alpert, Ph.D.
> University of South Carolina

When you have a bad guy in your sights, it's so hard to let him go.... It goes against your grain.

> —Sheriff William Hackel
> Macomb County, Michigan

Most high-speed chase training is given from a textbook....

> —Assistant Chief Theodore Schoch
> Cincinnati

Police Pursuit: Policies and Training, a study of 737 law enforcement agencies conducted with support from the National Institute of Justice, cited that fewer than 5 percent of the states represented by the respondents mandate reporting on pursuits. When and where it occurs, postincident reporting of pursuits is generally informal, described by a supervisor or the pursuing officer in an incident report. The study showed that many police agencies acknowledged taking only limited steps to train officers in skills and procedures related to pursuits. Whereas 60 percent of the agencies reported providing entry-level recruits with pursuit-related training, the average time of the training was less than fourteen hours. This dropped to fewer than three hours per year for in-service officers. Most of the training focused on defensive driving, with some time spent on pursuit tactics. Training on terminating pursuits was reported to be minimal (1997).

Should police officers be prohibited from conducting vehicle pursuits? No. Should officers be allowed to pursue in every situation that lends itself to a vehicle pursuit? No. Should officers be provided with the authority, policy, support from dispatch, training, and supervision necessary to conduct pursuits effectively and ethically to minimize risk and effect an arrest? Yes.

Vehicle pursuit is an important tool available to police officers to resolve serious crimes and bring perpetrators to justice. In recent years, vehicle pursuits have been limited as a resource to be used only in critical situations, primarily those involving serious threat of harm to others. Most police officers acknowledge the need to limit the use of vehicle pursuits but few, if any, support eliminating them or overrestricting them. In a recent three-year study, over 80 percent of the 600 police agencies surveyed indicated that they had adopted policies that limited when and how officers conduct pursuits (1997).

Problems associated with police pursuits are well documented. Third-party injuries, injuries to police officers and suspects, deaths, and destruction of property result when police pursuits go bad. Cities, counties, states, and the federal government have had to outlay millions of dollars to settle lawsuits resulting from wrongful pursuits as well as proper pursuits that had a negative end.

Myth and Misperception

Many myths and misperceptions about police pursuits need to be put to rest if progress is to occur. Those who argue for the total or near-total restriction of an officer's discretion to pursue cling to these myths and too often convey them as fact. Among the most common myths about pursuits are:

- The vast majority of pursuits go bad.
- Prohibiting pursuits will send a signal to offenders to flee.
- Officers pursue out of anger or an adrenaline rush rather than a rational thought process or in accord with policy.
- Officers cannot or will not discontinue a pursuit.

A study conducted by the California Highway Patrol (1995) has received considerable attention for several reasons, including its shedding light on some of the misperception that exists about pursuits. In 1992, the California legislature mandated that information on *all* pursuits be collected, making it the first state to have a central database. The California Highway Patrol (CHP) established the Statewide Pursuit Information Database Resource (SPIDR). Data collected by SPIDR showed that only 1 percent of the drivers of the cars pursued by police were charged with only traffic violations. Two-thirds were charged with felony offenses other than eluding. And 73 percent of the pursuits resulted in one or more felony charges. The CHP data showed that the odds of a third party—someone other than the suspect or police officer—being killed was one in 3.9 million.

The National Highway Traffic Safety Administration tallied 3821 deaths resulting from police pursuits from 1981 to 1993. The highest number in a single year was 343. Although far too many, this is lower than the 2500 deaths put forth by some critics of police pursuit (Sweeney, 1997). Groups and organizations debating police pursuits put forth many unrelated arguments such as the probability of being involved in a pursuit being less than being struck by lightning or greater than being shot by a police officer. Arguments such as these cater to public emotion and media headlines but do little improve police policy and practice.

There is nothing improper or unethical about police pursuing a suspect who has committed a criminal act, provided the action taken—the decision to pursue and the extent of the pursuit—is reasonable, based on both the offense and the environment in which the pursuit takes place. There is something wrong with police pursuing carelessly or in violation of policy and procedure.

The public expects that the police will use whatever means are at their disposal, including pursuit, to apprehend criminals. The police see pursuit as a viable resource in attempting to bring crime to resolution. But both the public and the police expect pursuits to occur when appropriate to resolve serious offenses rather than for simple traffic violations.

Learn from Successes

For every pursuit that turns sour, countless pursuits end without harm. For every situation in which an officer pursues inappropriately or in violation of policy, countless pursuits are called off by supervisors. For every pursuit in which an excessive number of police cars are engaged, there are countless pursuits in which there is a single lead chase car and a single backup. For every pursuit that is conducted at speed that would impress an Indy 500 driver, countless pursuits take place at reasonable speed. Many pursuits end quickly and without incident.

One of the important issues that needs to be addressed is that most police agencies do not record successful pursuits in a database. Unless an officer or supervisor deems it important enough to include in the narrative of a report, there is no way to know that a pursuit took place. By contrast, pursuits that violate policy or turn sour become the incident, often gaining a separate incident report number.

There is little focus on successful pursuits. More research is needed, and questions need to be asked about police officers who pursue properly and how many police departments have gained compliance with pursuit policies.

In Irving, Texas, a city in the Dallas Metroplex, an officer called in a pursuit when a car he was following fled at excessive speed. It was evening rush hour. The officer gave the location, traffic conditions, and vehicle speed, which was 20 to 25 miles per hour over the speed limit. The pursuit began in an area of commercial centers and industrial parks. Shortly after calling in the tag, the dispatcher stated that the owner of the car was wanted on a narcotics warrant. Several officers radioed that they were in the area and would provide backup. A few seconds later, the patrol supervisor took control. He received updates from the officer that the speed was constant, traffic was moderate, and the suspect was headed toward the interstate highway. After checking on the location of units from the Texas Department of Public Safety, the supervisor called off all but one unit. As the suspect reached the highway, his speed increased dramatically, according to the pursuing officer. The supervisor recognized the increased risks and ordered an end to the pursuit; the chase officer acknowledged and complied. The supervisor made a point of getting on the air and stated simply that the officers had done a good job.

There have been many experiments and modifications to policies, procedures, and training designed to reduce injuries and the potential for injury resulting from police pursuits. For years in Omaha, legislation fixed liability on the police for *any* injuries resulting from a pursuit. The department was liable whether or not the officer pursued. The fact that the person fled was sufficient to establish police liability. The legislation has been modified. Over a decade ago in Baltimore, most marked police cars did not have sirens, to prevent officers from pursuing. Today, the city's police cars are fully equipped.

Inconsistency abounds. From agency to agency within the same region, there often is inconsistency in policy and procedures, training, and supervisory response. Such inconsistency needs to be reduced to minimize risks. In Connecticut, a bill passed by the state senate has established a statewide policy to reduce the inconsistency that exists among departments and, thereby, minimize some of the hazard associated with multijurisdictional pursuits (1997).

In 1993, the Illinois state senate adopted a resolution calling for a study of the training methods used to teach pursuit techniques to police officers and to bring some consistency to police training. This came about when elected officials learned that different pursuit procedures were being taught in the state's six police academies. The resolution established an interagency committee to support the Illinois Local Government Law Enforcement Officers Training Board in conducting the study and called for a standardized training model to be presented to the State Senate (Illinois Senate, Senate Resolution #143, May 4, 1993).

Inconsistency also abounds in the way in which officers who pursue are treated. Some receive awards for the same behavior for which others are disciplined. In many agencies, more emphasis is placed on outcome than on policy or process.

There is tremendous need for improved policy, procedure, training, supervision, and discipline if there is going to be improvement in the way in which police pursue. There is also need for improved legislation that recognizes the severity of the act of fleeing a police officer.

In New York, the state senate passed legislation making it a felony to flee a police officer. It also makes it a misdemeanor to fail to stop for a police officer in a reasonable amount of time, even if the motorist continues to obey all traffic laws (1997). Before this legislation, generally, traffic charges were placed against those who fled. Nationally, a bill introduced into Congress by Representative Byron Dorgan (N.D.) requires states to increase penalties against motorists who flee from the police; the legislation did not pass. Congressman Dorgan's mother was killed in 1986 as a result of a pursuit (1995).

In-service training in police pursuit practices should be given far greater priority than exists in most police agencies. In far too many departments, officers receive a brief initial practical experience in pursuit driving. If the department does not have a driving track, the recruit's sole experience in conducting a pursuit may include one or two technical exercises held on a shopping center parking, abandoned airfield, or other makeshift environment. In many departments, quality in-service training in pursuits is almost nonexistent. In a recent court case, a veteran officer testified that he had taken defensive driving but had no pursuit training during his fifteen-year career.

A major problem that needs to be addressed is the way in which "success" in pursuing a fleeing vehicle is recognized and rewarded. If a pursuit results in an arrest and no one is harmed, it is almost always viewed as successful. The end justifies the means when a pursuit is concluded safely. Pursuits that end without harm and with an arrest are rarely analyzed to ensure that policy and procedure were followed and that all players acted appropriately and in accord with training.

Taking away a police officer's discretionary authority to pursue is difficult and not necessarily in the best interest of the public. It goes against what most police officers and the public see as one of the agency's primary purposes—the capture of criminal offenders. In some jurisdictions in which pursuits have been nearly banned, officers have found ways to beat the system. In a recent pursuit situation in a jurisdiction that had severely restricted pursuits, a young officer radioed that he was "following the suspect vehicle to effect a better identification." Another officer in a pursuit situation radioed that she was engaged in a "rolling surveillance to identify the suspect's intended location."

Little is accomplished by restricting pursuits to the point where police lose a viable tool or offenders perceive that they can flee without consequence. Rather, police leaders must focus on correcting the bad operational habits and internal weaknesses that lead to improper pursuits. Some of the things that are needed include:

- **Clear policy**—Concise, well-written policies and procedures on which everyone is educated, particularly first-line supervisors and dispatchers.
- **Quality supervision**—Other than an officer's self-discipline and professionalism, there is no substitute for quality supervision in managing pursuits once they take place. What occurs in the field is a direct reflection of a supervisor's ability to lead his or her personnel.
- **Training**—Quality must be built into recruit training, field training officer programs, and in-service and supervisory training. Training should be provided using adult education techniques, which allow officers to engage in dialogue about the pursuit policy. Change will not be effected with traditional, one-shot, straight-lecture, short-term training programs.
- **Practical exercises**—Training should incorporate pursuit scenarios and practical exercises. These include situations in which officers are put under stress, supervisors call off pursuits, one- or two-car pursuits occur, and pursuits involve many cars from more than one jurisdiction result.
- **Pursuit Continuum or Matrix**—Departments should adopt a pursuit continuum and train officers in how it should be applied. It serves a similar purpose in guiding officers as a use of force continuum. (More details on the pursuit matrix are provided later.)

- **Debriefing**—Police departments need to learn from successful pursuits. Not all pursuits that end successfully are conducted in accord with policy and procedure. Careful assessment and debriefing should follow *all* pursuits, including those that that ended successfully and without injury.
- **Zero tolerance of inappropriate pursuit behaviors**—Regardless of outcome, police departments must hold officers and supervisors accountable for not following pursuit policy. Inappropriate behavior during a pursuit should be addressed quickly and consistently.

Pursuit Guideline Matrix (Pursuit Continuum)

The Baltimore County (Maryland) Police Department, among others, has adopted a pursuit matrix, paralleling the use of force matrix used in many agencies. Its purpose is to balance the need for apprehension against the risk created by the pursuit and to guide officers in using their discretion to initiate and discontinue a pursuit. It is also intended as a guide to supervisors who must monitor and evaluate pursuits.

The matrix (Table 11.1) is a simple, understandable document that is easily committed to memory. In addition to presenting the matrix to officers during in-service training, a copy is placed in all police vehicles and is posted near radios in all precinct buildings. In random discussions with officers in the Baltimore County Police Department, all were able to articulate the essential information put forth in the matrix. The department's commitment to policy and training was apparent.

The matrix lists four categories under "seriousness of offense," which are then compared with risk factors. There is no pursuit for traffic or civil offenses. As part of the matrix, the department provides a list of low-, medium-, and high-risk factors.

Call for Action

Few people would deny that police pursuits, particularly those undertaken against standing policy and practice, have resulted in death or injury to innocent people. These deaths and injuries, along with the liability police agencies have had to bear, spawned public criticism and a flurry of activity to cause police officers and their agencies to "clean up their act." They also caused some individuals to call for police officers to cease or severely curtail conducting pursuits.

How officers conduct pursuits is a by-product of the culture in which they work. Sound policy and practice supported by quality training, good supervisory response when pursuits ensue, debriefing and analysis, accountability, and discipline will minimize injuries and deaths. By contrast, executives who are not committed to these things will foster a culture in which officers pursue when and how they deem appropriate.

TABLE 11.1 **Baltimore County Pursuit Guideline Matrix**

	Risk Factor *		
Seriousness of Offense	**Low**	**Medium**	**High**
Any felony where an officer has knowledge that serious harm or death has been or will be inflicted if an apprehension is not made	May pursue	May pursue	May pursue but discontinue when risks exceed the known threat to public safety by the perpetrator if capture is delayed.
Any other incident where an officer has knowledge that serious harm or death may be or has been inflicted if an apprehension is not made	May pursue	May Pursue	
All other criminal acts	May pursue		
All other traffic/civil violations			

The risk factors provided with the matrix are as follows:

Low Risk	*Medium Risk*	*High Risk*
Clear weather	Medium traffic	Other jurisdiction pursuit
Dry roads	Reduced visibility	Pursuit entering other jurisdiction
Light traffic	and/or illumination	Heavy traffic density
Furtive actions	Furtive actions	Residential/school/commercial area
		Frequent intersections
		Curves
		Pedestrian traffic
		One-/two-lane roads
		Narrow roads
		Wet/slippery roads
		Poor weather
		Poor visibility and/or no illumination
		Furtive actions
		Traveling against the flow of traffic
		Excessive speeds

* The combination of risk factors may raise or lower the risk.

REFERENCES

Baltimore County (Maryland) Police Department. (1996). Motor Vehicle Pursuit Guidelines. *Special Order #1–96.*

California Highway Patrol. (1995). *The evaluation of risk: Initial causes vs. final outcome in police pursuits.*

Campaign targets high-speed police chases. (1995, September 3). *The Detroit News.*

Police call high speed chases important tactic. (1997, March 25). *Augusta Chronicle.*

Police pursuit: Policies and training. (1997). *NIJ Research in Brief.* Washington DC: U.S. Department of Justice, May.

Senate approves bill to set up statewide hot pursuit policy. (1997, May 31). *The News-Times,* Hartford, Connecticut.

Senate Bill S.4698. (1997). New York State Legislature, June.

Senate Resolution #143. (1996). Illinois State Senate, May.

Sweeney, E. M. (1997). Vehicular pursuit: Balancing the risk. *Police Chief, 64* (7), 14–15.

Rejoinder to Dr. Greenberg   MICHAEL S. MCCAMPBELL

Dr. Greenberg is correct in his "call for action" in addressing problems related to police pursuits. However, I disagree that the deaths and injuries resulting from pursuits have caused police officers and police agencies to "clean up their act." They have not. The research, quoted by both Dr. Greenberg and myself, is quite clear on this issue. Let me reiterate just a few of the findings.

First, the National Survey of Police Pursuits and the Use of Force (Kenney & Alpert, 1997) found that entry-level pursuit driver training among agencies averages less than fourteen hours, and only about three hours of additional training are provided to in-service personnel. Those same agencies require an average of more than eight hours a year of training in the use of force. This does not show much of a commitment to "clean up their act."

This same study reported that, in the past two years, half of the responding agencies had modified their pursuit policies to make them more restrictive. Yet, these modifications varied greatly—from permitting only marked vehicles to pursue, to allowing pursuits only in cases involving violent felonies. Most agencies placed responsibility on the supervisor to terminate a pursuit. These changes may be a step in the right direction, but they do not go far enough. Policies vary willy-nilly among agencies by size, type of agency, and geographic location, and show a wide range of pursuit practices (e.g., use of roadblocks; pursuits by unmarked vehicles) that I believe are unacceptable in today's society.

Dr. Greenberg spends considerable time discussing the Baltimore County (MD) Police Department's Pursuit Guideline Matrix that is intended to guide officers and supervisors in determining when to initiate and terminate a pursuit.

However, he did not indicate the amount or type of training that officers and supervisors are given on the policy. Are they given decision-making training on applying the policy while operating a vehicle in a simulated pursuit? What training do supervisors receive in applying the policy? Who has the ultimate responsibility for deciding when and where to pursue? These are important questions that need to be answered by every agency, even those such as the Baltimore County Police Department, who appear to have a logical, well-thought-out policy.

I applaud this agency for its policy of not allowing pursuits for traffic offenses, but many other law enforcement agencies are not as enlightened. The National Survey reported that nearly half of all police agencies allow pursuits for *any* offense (including traffic violations). How, then, can the police expect to reduce deaths, injuries, and civil liability when pursuit for a traffic offense is an acceptable practice? Dr. Greenberg quotes a study conducted by the California Highway Patrol (CHP) and published in August 1995 that reports on pursuits by police agencies in California over a three-year period. The study showed that 79 percent of all CHP and 52 percent of all other California police agency pursuits were initiated as a result of traffic violations. Unfortunately, the study does not address the number of fatalities and injuries that occurred as a direct result of these pursuits. The study dwells on the fact that the odds of a third party being killed in a pursuit is only one in 3.9 million, and the odds of being struck by lightning is one in 600,000. But the study provides no data on pursuit-related crashes in California. It would be helpful to know how many people were killed or injured by these pursuits and whether their deaths and injuries justified the pursuit. Perhaps we should ask these questions of the families and friends of those killed or injured rather than comparing pursuit-related statistics to lightning strike data.

Another area totally overlooked by previous studies is the impact of civil liability awards from lawsuits stemming from police pursuits. As I stated in my original segment of this debate, the Federal Courts of Appeals have rendered over 600 decisions (pro and con) in the past three years involving lawsuits from police pursuits. It is unknown how many other lawsuits are working their way through state and Federal judicial systems or have been settled out of court during this period.

What is known, however, is that police pursuits account for a tremendous number of lawsuits and high monetary awards against police agencies. These court cases should be examined to determine what commonalities exist among pursuits that ultimately result in findings of civil liability. In addition, we should review court decisions for indications of policy shortcomings; failure to supervise during pursuits; failure to properly train officers; and poor use of discretion. We should also look at the number of pursuits that were initiated as a result of traffic violations. A study of these and other issues found in court decisions would go a long way toward solving problems and improving practices related to police pursuits.

Another key area related to police pursuits should be addressed: the use of excessive force after the pursuit. In research conducted by Alpert, Kenney, and Dunham (1997), police admitted to using excessive force in 1 to 25 percent of pursuits that ended in arrest. These researchers found that officers and supervisors acknowledged that excessive force was used in many more instances than was reported in official pursuit report forms. Thus, it can be assumed that pursuits have resulted in many instances of excessive force during the arrest following the pursuit. The Rodney King incident comes to mind as a glaring example of this problem.

With all the problems surrounding police pursuits (deaths and injuries caused by poor policies, lack of training, excessive force, etc.), I return to my original statement that pursuits are too dangerous for the officers, innocent bystanders, and the fleeing lawbreakers to continue the practice. We must change our expectations and get away from the "apprehension at any cost" philosophy found in so many officers and law enforcement agencies. As has been the case with other police practices (for example, use of force, search and seizure), if the police do not "clean up their act" in pursuits, the courts will do it for them.

References

Albert, G., Kenney, D., and Dunham, R. (1997). Police pursuits and the use of force: Recognizing and managing the 'pucker factor'—A research note. *Justice Quarterly, 14* (2), 371–385.

Kenney, D., & Alpert, G. (1997). A national survey of pursuits and the use of police force: Data from law enforcement agencies. *Journal of Criminal Justice, 25* (4), 315–324.

Do We Need a War on Crime or Peace in the 'Hood?

EDITOR'S NOTE: American policing is in a state of transition: facing an open and honest effort to clearly define what it does, how it is organized, how it operates, and how it is composed. The questions are not merely internally driven; they are also externally generated. At the core of one of these issues is the proper police role: should police be, in the vernacular particularly of politicians, engaged in a war on crime or, instead, should they more directly attempt to ensure peace in the 'hood? *And,* are the two mutually exclusive?

William G. Doerner has been faculty member in the School of Criminology and Criminal Justice at Florida State University since 1977 and has served as Director of the Program in Criminal Justice. He is also in his eighteenth year as a part-time sworn law enforcement officer with the Tallahassee Police Department and works as a one-person patrol unit. In addition to numerous journal articles, he has written *Introduction to Law Enforcement: An Insider's View* and coauthored *Victimology.*

Dr. Gene Stephens has about a quarter of a century of experience as a teaching, writing, and consulting futurist. He began his career as a working journalist, specializing in political and investigative reporting. After earning graduate degrees, including a Ph.D. in public policy at Emory University (specializing in criminal justice), he joined the faculty of the University of South Carolina in 1976, where he is full professor and teaches courses including The Future of Criminal Justice. He has served on the faculties of several of the most prestigious criminal justice management and executive leadership programs in the country, including those in

California, Texas, and Florida. Currently, he is also editor of the *Police Futurist* and a contributing editor of *The Futurist.*

WAR ON CRIME

WILLIAM G. DOERNER

Policing is a luxury. Law enforcement is a necessity. The current focus on "*community* policing" is just another "feel good" approach. Most communities are not in a position to have their police departments embrace this motif. Diluting the law enforcement presence, particularly when agencies already have enough unfinished business, siphons away precious resources and misdirects attention. Instead, agencies should concentrate on upgrading "community *policing*." To explain my position, I have packaged my comments around six "C's": clearance rates, career criminals, college education, civilianization, cops on patrol, and crime prevention. By the time you finish this essay, I think you will agree that "*community* policing" is best left to talented, knowledgeable professionals who are trained in social work. Crime suppression—community *policing*—is best left to those who are trained in law enforcement.

Clearance Rates

One measure of police efficiency that appears in the FBI's annual Uniform Crime Reports (UCR) is the clearance rate. A *clearance rate* reflects how many crimes the police have solved. One way to clear a crime is to arrest the suspect responsible for the event. Another way to clear a crime is to amass enough evidence to implicate a suspect even though this person is not taken into custody.

There are a number of reasons the police may not be able to make a formal arrest in a case. Sometimes suspects flee the immediate jurisdiction. They may die. The victim may drop the charges. Or, the suspect may be arrested or imprisoned elsewhere and extradition is not feasible. In short, a clearance means the police have solved a criminal incident.

How successful are the police? In 1995, the clearance rate was 65 percent for criminal homicide, 56 percent for aggravated assault, 51 percent for forcible rape, 25 percent for robbery, 20 percent for larceny, 16 percent for arson, 14 percent for motor vehicle theft, and 13 percent for burglary (FBI, 1996). If one were to calculate a total clearance rate for the index offenses, that number would be 21 percent. In other words, the police solve one of every five known serious crimes. If one factored in less serious offenses, the clearance rate would dwindle into the single digits.

How many baseball, football, or basketball teams post a win–loss record of .210 and still get into the playoffs or other postseason contests? None. Why? Because such a record means this performance is a colossal failure. Why, then, distract or saddle law enforcement with additional responsibilities such as *"community policing"* when the focus ought to be on accountability and improving law enforcement performance?

Career Criminals

One criminological axiom is that a small number of criminals is responsible for an overwhelming amount of unlawful activity. Ordinary law-abiding people get up and go to work every day. Criminal busy bees, however, get up and go to crime. These predators are more than just mere recidivists. They are *chronic offenders* or *career criminals.*

Many law enforcement agencies have responded to this phenomenon by establishing special career criminal or repeat offender investigative units that target these offenders. The success of these special units, though, has been compromised by insatiable bureaucratic demands. It is not uncommon for members of these units to log a handful of felony arrests in the first part of the month. Knowing that pencil-pushing administrators want to see big numbers, investigators go into a frenzy at the end of the month trying to prop up their arrest statistics. Typically, they reach into the file cabinet, grab a handful of outstanding misdemeanor warrants from the backlog, race through telephone directories or public utility listings to get suspect addresses, and then round up all the recalcitrants they can locate.

Such salvage operations highlight a fundamental problem. The police lack sufficient resources to execute arrest warrants that are already in their possession and pick up known suspects. A sharper organizational vision would enhance the deterrence doctrine and ensure a better "quality of life," which, by the way, is the ostensible goal of "community policing."

College Education

The 1967 President's Commission on Law Enforcement and Administration of Justice strongly recommended that agencies upgrade the quality of their police departments by requiring officers to hold college degrees. Countless task forces and blue-ribbon commissions have reiterated this same refrain over and over again. So, where do we stand some thirty years later?

The Police Executive Research Forum (PERF) sponsored a national survey to look into the educational achievements of law enforcement officers (Carter, Sapp, & Stephens, 1989). It found that the minimum entrance requirement in 86 percent of local police agencies throughout the country is still a high school diploma or its equivalent (Carter et al., 1989). Fewer than a quarter of today's police officers have completed a four-year college program (Carter et al., 1989). The PERF report proclaims, "It is significant, indeed, that two decades ago only a handful of officers had stepped into the college classroom; today nearly 75 percent have" (Carter et al., 1989), and reveals an average educational attainment of 13.6 years of schooling (Carter et al., 1989). These figures are not anything to brag about. What these numbers really mean is that the average officer went off to college, performed dismally, and flunked out after the freshman year!

This picture is not outdated. Look at the following comments contained in an advertisement taken out by the American Police Association in the May 15, 1997, edition of *Law Enforcement News*. It optimistically states, "More than 100,000 of the 600,000 sworn officers in the fifty states possess four-year degrees. A critical mass now exists."

Take out a calculator and divide 100,000 by 600,000 and hit the percent key. What do you get? Cheapness. Most communities do not hire college graduates to work as law enforcement officers because degreed people command higher salaries.

In any event, it would seem that there is enough unfinished business here that should receive attention before embarking on another unproven reform effort.

Civilianization

A major trend in law enforcement is civilianization. *Civilianization* means hiring nonsworn personnel to free up sworn officers to do police work. Why tie up trained police officers to do secretarial or clerical work when they could be out on the streets performing law enforcement duties? In 1970, 12 percent of all police employees were civilians. Today, that figure is almost 28 percent (FBI, 1996). Yet, the push to do "community policing" defeats the logic behind civilianization. What it amounts to is deploying sworn personnel to do the job of social workers, a non-sworn function.

Cops on Patrol

The allocated police strength is a precious commodity. The average staffing figure is 2.4 police officers per 1,000 capita (FBI, 1996). In other words, if a city has 100,00 inhabitants, it should have 240 sworn officers. About half these officers are assigned to the highly visible uniformed patrol division. That would be 120 officers in our hypothetical case. Staffing requires almost five people to provide continuous coverage for a single slot (seven days a week multiplied by twenty-four hours per day divided by a forty-hour workweek). Without factoring in peak periods of activity, that number translates into an average of twenty-four officers assigned to the streets at any given moment. That is indeed a very thin blue line! Reallocating law enforcement officers to perform nonsworn social work tasks means stretching that thin blue line even further.

Crime Prevention

In addition to typical crime prevention efforts that emphasize target-hardening and neighborhood watch groups, there has been a push to provide school-based programs such as DARE (Drug Abuse Resistance Education). DARE programs have a specially trained officer deliver a curriculum over the span of a semester to children who are almost ready to enter middle or junior high school. The lessons are designed to help children build self-esteem, resist peer pressure, and learn about the risks associated with substance abuse.

What kind of advanced training do DARE officers receive? DARE officers in Florida must complete an eighty-hour training module at the police academy before entering the fifth-grade classroom. Think about that for a moment. Regular teachers have to graduate from college, complete all the requirements to become certified, and continue to earn graduate credit to renew their teaching licenses. In contrast, "kiddie kops" are not required to be college graduates; do not engage in semester-long internships as prospective teachers do before finishing their baccalaureate degrees; are not obliged to take any college classes in instructional techniques; and become instant subject area experts by completing perhaps the equivalent of one watered-down college course.

Go a step further. If a "kiddie kop" left police work today, he or she would be patently ineligible to teach kindergarten tomorrow. Switch gears for a moment. How would "kiddie kops" feel about a teacher sitting through a two-week course sponsored by the school board and then strapping on a gunbelt and heading out to patrol the streets?

Consider the DARE program itself. First, the curriculum addresses drug, alcohol, and tobacco use. These are health, not police, issues. How did indoctrinating children against cigarette smoking get transformed into police business? Second, go back to the earlier discussion of career criminals. A handful of people are responsible for an inordinate amount of criminal activity. Why, then, does DARE blanket everybody instead of focusing solely on at-risk children? Third, the evaluation literature finds very little, if any, support for program effectiveness.

Summary

The police belong in the crime-suppression business. They already have too many unfinished law enforcement tasks awaiting their attention without saddling them with the extra burden of a social agenda. Community policing is very labor intensive. In an effort to raise the quality of life, advocates would redeploy already scarce police resources and reallocate them to perform activities for which the police are not adequately trained.

The bottom line is very simple. If the goal is to mend the social fabric and make more social services available to less fortunate people, then hire social workers. If the priority is law enforcement, then equip police officers with the proper tools and let them do their jobs.

References

American police association marks first year. (1997, May 15). *Law Enforcement News, 23,* 5.

Carter, D. L., Sapp, A. D., & Stephens, D. W. (1989). *The state of police education: Policy direction for the 21st century.* Washington, DC: Police Executive Research Forum.

Federal Bureau of Investigation. (1996). *Uniform crime reports for the United States—1995.* Washington, DC: U.S. Government Printing Office.

Rejoinder to Dr. Doerner   GENE STEPHENS

It is interesting to read Professor Doerner's defense of traditional policing, as from the beginning, where he cites the dismal record of clearing by arrest or evidence only one of five major reported crimes. The essay seems to make my point—traditional policing has no chance of success in creating a safe, sane, relatively crime-free environment.

If only one in three major crimes is even reported to police and only one of five reported crimes leads to arrest (and far fewer to conviction), then doubling and even redoubling traditional policing efforts would not ameliorate the crime problem sufficiently, but would exact staggering costs to taxpayers.

As for the criminological axiom that a few chronic offenders or career criminals are responsible for the overwhelming amount of unlawful activity, this axiom simply has not held up under scrutiny by researchers. Indeed, the strongest evidence is that everyone or almost everyone commits crimes at sometime in his or her life, and everyone or almost everyone is a victim at sometime in life. *Victim today, offender tomorrow.* Longitudinal studies of high school seniors, for example, indicate that most admit to having committed at least one felony crime. Beyond this, career criminal programs focus on street crime only, not even considering the vastly larger white collar arena, where environmental and product safety offenders, among others, can kill and maim more people than all the violent street offenders combined.

Consider: If every street drug dealer in America were arrested in one gigantic coordinated multistate sweep today, what would happen tomorrow? Clearly, if demand for drugs remained, there would be a scramble among thousands of Americans to fill the vacuum and reap the rewards of the lucrative drug market. This example serves to dispel another criminological axiom: the myth that there is a major difference between criminals and noncriminals.

Dr. Doerner further argues that we need more police on the streets, and we probably won't be able to get more cops on the beat if we raise the standard from high school to college graduate to enter the field. He also argues that playing "kiddie kop" and other social work roles goes well beyond the scope of police training, education, and readiness. He concludes police belong in the crime suppression business.

On this final point, we agree, but we have vastly different philosophical and methodological beliefs about the proper and best way to suppress crime.

My esteemed colleague argues the thin blue line is simply overwhelmed, and thus relief from social work duties, assistance by civilians to handle service-related and clerical duties, and hiring and training more police would strengthen the force and allow sworn officers to get on with real police work.

Would "real" be the kind of racist, head-knocking by undereducated, untrained, underpaid crime fighters that has brought so many charges of corruption, brutality, and failure to curb crime? As a police chief from England declared after viewing American policing: "If it's not working, why would you think more of the same is what is needed to fix it?"

The fact is that numbers of police on the job do not correlate to less crime. In U.S. cities, the number of police per 10,000 citizens served differs greatly. At one point in the 1990s, Washington, D.C., had ninety-two officers per 10,000, compared with thirty-six in New York City and two in Los Angeles. Other big cities had similar widely varying ranges with no correlation to crime rates. It is not how many officers you have; it is how you use them. There may be a minimum critical mass, but some cities that would seem under forced have much lower rates than those with a thick blue line.

The cities with the lowest crime and fear rates use their officers in *proactive* rather than the traditional reactive roles. They place officers on walking beats or at least get them out of the patrol car into the communities, where they can talk to people, create trust, and finally gather information (and evidence) about crime, offenders, and criminal activity. Indeed, it is the only chance they have to achieve their mission of suppressing crime. In major cities where police have remained in their cars and simply jumped out to handle emergencies or make arrests, the public often sees them as an occupying army and distrusts them so much they provide no assistance and no information. Because intelligence data are vital to crime suppression, the police fall back on paying felons in custody (i.e., snitches) with money or reduced or dismissed charges for information or testimony about other felons. Justice is reduced to dueling attorneys, each armed with often perjured testimony from felons. I'll take the proactive, community-based approach!

As for education, and Dr. Doerner's contention we cannot afford college-educated officers, I say we cannot afford *not* to seek out, hire, and pay better-educated police. Whether it be the traditional or community-based approach, the complex people problems faced daily by police demand a well-educated, well-trained, socially and culturally aware protector of the people. A few smart, savvy officers cultivating community ties and working with community citizens to truly protect and serve them will curtail far more crime than a massive assault on the community by adrenaline pumping crimefighters.

Finally, to the charge community-policing smacks of social engineering in its worst form—allowing government representatives to set community standards and enforce them—this is clearly a possibility, but only if the entire community-oriented police movement is subverted. Indeed, community-oriented policing pushes authority down to the lower ranks and decentralizes it. The officer is encouraged and, in fact, expected to seek guidance and direction from the citizenry and to large extent adopt the agenda of the community in suppressing crime-breeding situations, but always following constitutional guidelines and respecting individual liberties. Yes, it is a tough job, but at least it offers us a chance, for the first time, for police to actually achieve their "protect and serve" mission.

PEACE IN THE 'HOOD

GENE STEPHENS

Traditional, reactive, combat law enforcement is an approach that will *never, never* lower the fear or reality of crime in America to acceptable levels. *NEVER!*

It is a system destined to fail. In fact, it is a system designed to fail.

Wars on crime and drugs are not supposed to be won! They are supposed to be waged endlessly, perpetuating The System—and dollars—they were established to maintain! Small victories—a serial killer captured, a multimillion dollar drug bust—are highly touted even as the public is warned the overall problem is endemic or even worsening.

In other words, maintenance of "fear" is essential to keeping dollars coming to law enforcement (and the rest of the criminal justice system, e.g., corrections for prison building) rather than going to education, health care, recreation, or other public services. After all, if you are likely to be assaulted on the street or killed in your home by an intruder, you have no time to worry about your other lifestyle needs.

But the fact is, the Federal Bureau of Investigation's *Uniform Crime Reports* (UCR) indicate year after year that only about 20 percent—one in five—Index crimes reported to police are *cleared* by arrest. Far fewer lead to conviction. According to National Crime Victimization Surveys (NCVS), only about one in three serious crimes is even reported to police. A fair estimate, then, would be that police make arrests in fewer than 10 percent of serious offenses (e.g., rape, robbery, burglary, larceny), and obtain convictions in fewer than 5 percent. Hardly success! If the dollars doubled for "reactive" policing and police and courts doubled their efforts, the results—20 percent arrests and 10 percent convictions if doubled efforts equaled doubled results—would still be a far cry from what is needed to truly "protect and serve" the public.

Fortunately, courageous leaders in the police profession are forging the way to refocus the nation's efforts in coping with crime and justice. It is from *within* the police and justice establishment that the community-oriented policing (COP) movement has sprung and flourished. To their credit, thousands of police and others have joined a few pioneers in a reformation that will, in the twenty-first century, change not only the police profession, but the total criminal justice and social system in the United States and beyond.

Where COP has truly been instituted, both crime and fear have decreased significantly— more than in other areas, which have also seen crime drops due to a variety of socioeconomic variables unrelated to policing style.

The task here, however, is not to examine the history and extent of COP entrenchment, but rather to clearly differentiate COP from traditional policing, probe the challenges and opportunities ahead for COP, and examine the leadership skills necessary to guide a successful COP program. My job is to convince the reader that peace in the 'hood *can* be achieved.

What Is COP?

COP is a proactive crime prevention strategy—a way of achieving community peace—under which police work with the community and social service agencies to ferret out crime-breeding problems and work together to alleviate them before crime results. Ultimately under this system, having to catch criminals is a sign of failure, and stopping crimes from occurring is a signal of success.

Primarily due to the many myths about crime and justice perpetuated by mass media, often with justice officials as accessories before and after the fact, the public has developed a "war" mentality about crime. The role of police is seen as one of doing battle with criminals, who are seen as a definable group of bad people, justifying the crimefighting image traditional law enforcement adopted and perpetuated.

In fact, the roots of policing go back to the self-help days of the Mutual Pledge System in Alfred the Great's fourth century Britain. The king, eager to collect taxes to support his court and militaristic ambitions, declared that it was the *duty* of every subject of the realm to raise the hue and cry if he had knowledge of a violation of the King's law or a breach of the peace. Subjects also had to serve on posses to hunt down and bring violators before the king's court. Failure either to sound the alarm or find the offender led to fines levied by the king. It was an ingenious system that lasted more than 1000 years and guaranteed the king his money. If a subject was rendered incapable of paying taxes because he was physically harmed or robbed, either the perpetrator was captured and made to pay or the "neighbors" who failed to capture the offender were forced to pay royal fines.

As the Middle Ages ended, the Age of Enlightenment brought industry, a population explosion, urbanization, and the beginnings of democracy. The Mutual Pledge System was replaced first by private security forces for the wealthy and then finally, in the nineteenth century, by public police. Indeed, the idea of government-controlled, tax-paid police is less than two centuries old—beginning in London in 1829 and quickly followed in Philadelphia in 1833. In the United States, as in England, early police were seen much as night watchmen and "peacekeepers." They were in fact called *peace officers.*

This peacekeeping focus—which continues in England and throughout most of the world—changed in the United States due to a unique experience—the westward movement following The War Between the States. Because of the need for peacekeeping in the West, vigilante committees were formed, and U.S. Marshals were sent West to help enforce the laws. Thus began the frontier justice model that has predominated in the United States throughout the twentieth century.

So pervasive that it became known as "traditional policing," practitioners took their cues originally from the popular news stories/fabrications of the *Wild West* of marshals/sheriffs versus gunfighters. Urban policing "back east" was just getting underway, and these largely undereducated young men were seeking guidance in determining the image a police officer should project. Wyatt Earp, Doc Holliday, and others became folk heroes and soon role models for even eastern police: quick-to-act crimefighters. It was assumed that each community was populated by good citizens threatened by bad guys, and thus the answer to protecting and serving was to declare war on the criminal element. Although the good guys always seemed to prevail in early paperback novels and motion pictures, in real life it was often much more difficult to separate good from evil or to even define the terms. Most crime, it was discovered, involved people who knew one another having problems interacting, and a lesser number involved people who had a variety of physical, emotional, psychological, and social dysfunctions that had been left unchecked.

In criminological circles, this phenomenon became known as *the dualistic fallacy*—the belief that there was a distinct difference between criminals and non-criminals. In fact, it was found that victims and perpetrators are often the same people, just swapping roles in different situations.

In the final quarter of the twentieth century, many police scholars and practitioners began to recognize the futility of the reactive law enforcement model and its war on crime, and a police community relations approach evolved into a crime prevention and finally a problem-oriented or community-oriented policing model.

Two blue ribbon panels—with sustained police practitioner presence—were appointed to seek answers to the problems that led to rioting in Los Angeles in the wake of police officers being acquitted of excessive force charges in connection with the arrest of motorist Rodney King. Both commissions came to similar conclusions. The group headed by Secretary of State Warren Christopher found excessive force was used in the riots and stemmed from police placing emphasis on "crime control over crime prevention," a policy the Commission said had distanced police from the community. The panel held that too many LAPD patrol officers viewed citizens with "resentment and hostility" and treated them rudely and disrespectfully. The other commission, led by former FBI Director William Webster and Police Foundation President Hubert Williams, cited this same hostility and distrust between police and the citizens they served and concluded: "The LAPD needs to develop a nonadversarial working partnership with the public and other government agencies" (Independent Commission on the Los Angeles Police Department, 1991). In other words, the "war" mentality of policing is detrimental to effective peacekeeping.

One of the earliest and still possibly the best definitions of this peacekeeping approach comes from scholar-practitioners Robert Trojanowicz and David Carter

(1998): "[Community policing] is a philosophy and not a specific tactic; a proactive, decentralized approach, designed to reduce crime, disorder, and fear of crime..." (p. 17). They went on to suggest one tactic was to involve the same officer(s) in the same community on a long-term basis. They acknowledged that no single program or set of programs can be established as models for community policing, because each community is different, and thus policing must be tailored to the individual community's character and needs. But, they held, community building, trust, and cooperation are cornerstones in any successful community policing endeavor, and outcomes marking success must include improved delivery of police services, improved police-community relations, and mutual resolutions to identifiable concerns.

Thus COP is, in many ways, a return to the original goals of keeping peace and maintaining order; but in some areas, peacemaking must come before peacekeeping. COP involves substituting a peace model for a war model of policing, with the outcome changing from catching criminals and fighting crime to creating and maintaining peace in the neighborhoods.

The New Jersey Criminal Justice Academy held that, like the military in time of war, traditional police agencies maintain a hierarchical top-down administration and organizational control, while COP flattens the pyramid and empowers the street officer to get directly involved with community groups and social service agencies in decision making and problem solving. Similarly, imposed authority (e.g., arrests for even minor lawbreaking) gives way to creative problem solving in many cases; relying on information from perpetrators (i.e., informants) to catch and convict other suspects is replaced by creating trust so citizens will provide information about offenses and, more important, about crime-breeding situations that need immediate attention. Establishment of trust replaces policing by intimidation. Catching suspects is seen as a Band-Aid approach that must be replaced by problem solving. The police agenda is no longer strictly a department decision, but one that must be shared with the community, based on its special character. Possibly most important, reduction of fear of crime becomes a part of the police mission, as fear debilitates and impoverishes community life.

Yet, several critical questions must be addressed if the peace keeping approach supported by COP is to become the predominant approach to the twenty-first-century policing and, indeed, prove to be the best way to accomplish the police mission of protecting and serving the citizenry.

What Is Community and Can It Be Created?

This is the first question any COP operation must face, and it *must* be resolved before any successful program can be established and maintained. Do people who live in close proximity constitute a community even if they do not know nor interact in any way with each other? Do people in the same areas necessarily have similar concerns and needs? Where are the borders of the community? Can individuals or groups be active and have concerns in more than one community? What will "peace" be for these citizens?

Success of this approach depends on defining community and often even developing community where it has not previously existed. Thus community development becomes a major new skill necessary for COP practitioners; it must include identifying distinct areas, searching for existing structure, creating forums for neighbors to meet and establish relationships, developing community leaders, mediating a consensual agenda, creating trust, sharing power, and so on. Not an easy task!

Who Is Qualified to Be a COP Practitioner?

Can an officer trained and street hardened in traditional policing assume the COP role? Can an officer move from the warrior role to that of peacekeeper? What type of new recruits should be sought for the approach? Experience indicates the answer to the first two question is both *yes* and *no*. Yes, many combat model officers have smoothly and even enthusiastically made the COP transition. They, in fact, have been pleased with the results. As one Fort Worth, Texas, officer told me: "For the first time I feel like something other than a human garbage collector. Before, I just rode around and jumped out to grab what seemed to me to be human garbage. Now I've gotten to know the people on my beat. I've begun to see they face the same problems and concerns I do, and I've found I often can help them. For the first time I really feel I am making a difference." A U.S. Department of Justice (DOJ) study of foot patrol—a critical element in many COP programs—found citizen satisfaction with police increased with addition of foot patrol, and police who patrol on foot have greater job satisfaction, less fear, and higher morale than officers who patrol in automobiles (National Institute of Justice, 1996a).

The "no" goes for traditional officers who either lack the social skills to make the transition or simply cannot accept change from the good guy/bad guy dichotomy to the COP approach. Heard often is the complaint: "I didn't become a police officer to be a social worker," or "I'm here to enforce the law and get the scum off the streets." Moving from this simplistic ideal to the complex problem-solving mode required of COP simply does not appeal to them

As for new recruits, three traits seem essential: social skills, intellectual curiosity, and creative thinking. The peacekeeper role is not mechanistic and is seldom reducible to Standard Operating Procedures (SOP). The COP practitioner must constantly be evaluating a variety of community strategies while seeking input from citizens and creating and sustaining partnerships with helping agencies. It is not a job for the undereducated thrill seeker.

Who Is Qualified to Be a COP Administrator?

With agenda and decision-making power shared by community and street-level practitioners, the administrator's role must be redefined within any COP operation. The network replaces the hierarchy, while the administrator relinquishes much of his or her management role in exchange for an enhanced leadership role.

As leader, it becomes critical that he or she create the vision of policing as a profession and service focusing on assuring peace rather than making war.

A 1993 *USA Today* Forum article suggested "the best organization is no organization," and quoted VISA founder Dee Hock as saying: "The better the organization is, the less obvious it is." Essential to this new style is provision for direct communications among all employees as well as with community social service agency partners. After all, good ideas and even problem solutions may come from any source.

Thus the primary role of the administrator is *facilitator.* An atmosphere must be established in which interactive creative problem solving is encouraged and rewarded. When the milieu becomes stagnant, the administrator must renew the vision and rouse the troops—qualities of leadership rather than management.

Can Proactive Policing Coexist with Constitutional Rights?

Some strict Constructionalists argue the Constitution prohibits any police action until there is probable cause to believe a crime has occurred and certain individuals are responsible. Traditional police advocates hold police must be reactive in nature, that is, crimefighters, to preserve civil liberties. It is an interesting argument, because the same group usually seeks to increase the exemptions to Bill of Rights requirements to unhandcuff police so they can do their jobs. Indeed, there is no constitutional prohibition to crime prevention efforts by police working in partnerships with the citizenry. When conflicts in priorities or methods do occur—as they inevitably will in our multicultural society—there is no prohibition on using mediation or arbitration to seek consensus or at least an acceptable course of action. Beyond this, ombudsmen and other watchdogs of rights are not excluded from the COP process. COP at its best seeks to be as inclusive as possible in its effort to assure peace and harmony in our communities.

But Who Handles the "Warrior" Response?

How can "peacekeepers" work with community and social service agencies to identify and alleviate crime-breeding situations and still be available at all times to respond quickly to requests for emergency assistance (e.g., robbery, rape, domestic assault)? Can COP be effective in large, multicultural, dynamic urban areas?

There is no easy answer here! To part one—who handles emergency response—the *best* (but certainly not the only or even desirable) answer seems to be rotating officers in the same neighborhood between COP activities and emergency response activities. In this way, all officers are kept up-to-date on both the short-term and long-term problems as well as the options to alleviate them and the proposals for action.

Two other alternatives worthy of note are to divide the departments into separate COP and emergency response teams or create an elite "911" response force separate from the department. In the former, a rivalry in philosophy and allegiance between the dual forces can be expected and can work against achieving a unified mission. In the latter, "911" response team members not only will see success differently from COP, but may create problems in the community via overly aggressive responses that disturb the peace rather then make or keep it.

Whether COP can work in our larger cities is another question that has provoked much thought. Possibly the best answer is: only if the city is broken down into communities and police in each community operate at the neighborhood level. Still, it would seem the officers would have to acquire knowledge of how problems of the urban area as a whole interact. Although solutions must be local, they must considered holistically within the framework of the larger community. COP truly fits the motto: Act locally, think globally.

Conclusion

Traditional policing, with its emphasis on a war on crime, has not succeeded and has no chance to succeed. It is based on myths and false premises.

Community-oriented policing, with its emphasis on community peace, is extremely difficult to initiate and sustain in practice. It takes visionary leadership, creative employees, partnerships, networks, and a constant proactive, preventive focus. But it can succeed and, done right, succeed spectacularly. Major successes have already been documented.

COP is not a tactic or even a program that can be reduced to a formula. It differs greatly from one department to another and, if successful, from one community to another. Communities share problems, but the mix of problems and opportunities is somewhat different in each community. Thus, the exact mix of COP activities should be unique to each community's needs.

Clearly the role of the COP leader and practitioner is far different from the traditional police role Possibly the most important lesson to be gained from this debate is that COP is an incredibly complex phenomenon. It is the equivalent of moving from a simplistic incremental to an all—inclusive rational planning model—a move still evolving in strategic planning operations. The COP approach, indeed, is even more holistic, as it requires collaboration, coordination, and cooperation among a wide array of community and social service organizations. Turf, ego, and competition must be set aside for COP to succeed in its mission of protecting and serving the community—a tall order indeed.

The bottom line then is that COP offers the best opportunity to date to accomplish the police mission—to maintain community peace—but it is no place for the faint of heart.

REFERENCES

Bohm, R. M. (1986). Crime, criminal, and crime control policy myths. *Justice Quarterly, 3* (2), 193–214.

Bureau of Justice Assistance, U.S. Department of Justice. (1993). *The systems approach to crime and drug prevention: A path to community policing.* Washington, DC: DOJ.

Bureau of Justice Statistics, U.S. DOJ. (Annual.) *Criminal victimization in the United States.* Washington, DC: DOJ.

BJS, DOJ. (1997). *Criminal victimization, 1973–95.* Washington, DC: DOJ.

Federal Bureau of Investigation. Annual. *Crime in the United States: Uniform crime reports.* Washington, DC: FBI.

Independent Commission on the Los Angeles Police Department (1991). *Report of the Independent Commission on the Los Angeles Police Department.* Los Angeles: Author.

Kappeler, V. E., Blumberg, M. And Potter, G. W. (1996). *The mythology of crime and criminal justice* (2nd ed). Prospect Heights, IL: Waveland Press.

A mandate for change. (1993, March 29). *USA Today,* p. 13A.

Miller, L. S., & Hess, K. M. (1994). *Community policing: Theory and practice.* St. Paul, MN: West.

National Institute of Justice. (1996a). *Law Enforcement in a Time of Community Policing.* Washington, DC: U.S. Department of Justice.

National Institute of Justice. (1996b). *Implementation challenges in community policing.* Washington, DC: DOJ.

Peak, K. J., & Glensor, R. W. (1996). *Community policing & problem solving strategies and practices.* Upper Saddle River, NJ: Prentice Hall.

Stephens, G. (1996). The future of policing: From a war model to a peace model. In Maguire, Brendan, and Rodosh, P. F. (Eds.). *The past, present, and future of criminal justice.* Dixhills, NY: General Hall, 77–93.

Trojanowicz, R., & Bucqueroux, B. (1990). *Community policing: A contemporary perspective.* Cinncinnati: Anderson.

Trojanowicz, R., & Carter, D. L. (1988). *The philosophy and role of community policing.* East Lansing, MI: National Center for Community Policing.

Wickman, D. (1993). L.A. police chief: Treat people like customers. *USA Today,* March 29, p. 13A.

Rejoinder to Dr. Stephens
WILLIAM G. DOERNER

The essay penned by Professor Stephens is quite interesting. Those comments, though, point to a deep philosophical rift between his position and the one this author takes. As a result, this rejoinder highlights some of those fundamental differences for the reader's consideration.

The most immediate point of departure concerns the basic role of the police in a democratic society. Professor Stephens envisions police officers serving as social architects. According to his formulation, the police should embrace a philosophy that involves the ideal of community-oriented policing (COP). This revised agenda includes promoting and developing a sense of community, improving the quality of life via a reduction in the fear of crime, and eliminating crime-breeding problems before they spawn criminal behavior. On the surface these goals may appear quite laudable, but each has its own dark lining when the police are involved.

Make no bones about it—the major thrust of the COP approach is social engineering! The goal is to identify, and even assemble if necessary, a series of cells or colonies in social units benignly labeled as "communities." The police would mold a collective consciousness among the inhabitants, inculcate an appropriate sense of belonging, install local leaders, and redirect energies into more socially redeeming activities. This proposal is not what we have come to expect of law enforcement in a democratic society. Instead, it contradicts the legal restraints society has placed on the police, conjures up the frightening specter of "big brother," and beckons the invasive omnipresence of government into our daily lives.

To gain the appearance of success, COP deftly directs attention away from the actual crime problem. Instead, it centers on fear of crime. This focus ignores what criminologists recognize as the "crime–fear paradox." What this term means is that the people who are most likely to become crime victims display the least amount of concern or fear over this prospect. Conversely, the least likely targets of crime exhibit the greatest amount of fear. Essentially, then, the subjective fear of crime is not consistent with the objective odds of becoming a crime victim. And, as we all know, the objective odds of victimization vary inversely with social class. Thus, crime is concentrated within the lower strata of society, and fear of crime permeates the upper levels.

Children exhibit this pattern when they encounter the ubiquitous "bogey man." The slightest noise in a dark room will send a restless child scurrying beneath the sheets. The terrified child will adopt a time-proven sure-fire technique to avoid detection. He or she will squeeze the eyes shut, take a deep breath, and remain motionless. Lo and behold, it works every time. The "bogey man" disappears, and the scared child emerges safe and sound.

The same irrational phenomenon characterizes the COP emphasis on quality of life issues. Adherents prey on the crime–fear paradox. They would mobilize neighborhood watch programs in the name of community service, a cornerstone of the COP philosophy, in areas that do not have an objective crime problem. The apparent success mesmerizes participants into thinking they are safe and that police officials are remarkably adept. What have these tax dollars paid for? Protection from the "bogey man"! Instead of concentrating on reducing the objective odds of victimization, COP wastes a considerable expenditure assuaging the frivolous and irrational fear of crime.

Supposedly, transforming police officers into community facilitators will allow the police to sniff out crime-breeding conditions and eradicate these maladies via creative solutions. Amazing! Criminologists do not agree among themselves which theory best explains the underlying causes of crime. Yet, the police somehow are going to get at the roots of crime. It is well known that theories, supposedly objective value-free statements that describe human behavior, are contaminated by domain assumptions or the basic beliefs and values to which people subscribe. Yet, almost miraculously, the transformed police will resist any dogmatic approaches, remain neutral, and ferret out the real causes of crime. Well, then, exactly which illegal behaviors will the police target? Will they emphasize pension fraud, white collar crime, sexual harassment, civil right violations, labor fraud, Medicare fraud, or computer crimes? It sounds like the mere selection of which crimes to target is dictated by some type of a broad, preconceived agenda.

COP proponents recognize that this social engineering will not revamp the world overnight. Consequently, leaders should divide police agencies into COP units and "an elite 911 response force." Whenever COP initiatives fail to produce the desired effects, these storm troopers will mobilize a more appropriate response. Which faction represents the iron hammer and which one is the velvet fist?

As the reader can see, the sentiments expressed here call for a slight revision in how I ended my original essay. I will revised that conclusion as follows: If the priority is law enforcement, then hire police officers. If the goal is to mend the social fabric, then equip social workers with the proper tools and let *them* do *their* jobs.

Community Policing: A More Efficacious Police Response or Simply Inflated Promises?

EDITOR'S NOTE: For many years, the hallmark of policing was the foot patrol officer, an officer who walked the streets of the neighborhood, knew the citizens and, more particularly, the troublemakers, and could deal with neighborhood problems as they occurred (especially in the North, the local priest was often a willing ally). But then we discovered the patrol car and the radio, and efficiency of operations took precedence over interaction with the community and real problem solving. Gradually, policing has seen a programmatic return to these roots . . . the beat officer concerned about his (and, now, her) neighborhood. Police–community relations, neighborhood-oriented policing, problem-oriented policing, and now community-oriented policing have forced policing back to its basics. As we change the programs and modify their services, a more basic dilemma become paramount: Is community policing (or any of its alternatives) *really* an answer to our prayers? Is it a more effective police response or does it merely offer inflated promises?

James S. Albritton is currently Professor and Associate Director of the Criminology and Law Studies Program at Marquette University in Milwaukee, Wisconsin. He has taught and done research in the field of criminal justice for over twenty years and has devoted considerable attention to research and writing on police matters. A former police officer, he attempts to bring that experience and perspective to bear on all aspects of his research, teaching, and writing about contemporary policing.

David L. Carter is Professor in the School of Criminal Justice and Director of the National Center for Community Policing at Michigan State University who specializes in policing issues. He received his bachelor's and master's degrees in Criminal Justice from Central Missouri, State University and a Ph.D. in Criminal Justice Administration from Sam Houston State University in Huntsville, Texas. A former Kansas City, Missouri, police officer, Dr. Carter was Chairman of the Department of Criminal Justice at the University of Texas–Pan American in Edinburg, Texas, for ten years before his appointment at Michigan State in 1985. He has presented training sessions at the FBI National Academy, the FBI Law Enforcement Executive Development Seminar (LEEDS), police "command colleges" of Texas, Florida, Ohio, and Kentucky, and the U.S. Customs Service; served as a consultant to the U.S. Drug Enforcement Administration; and served at the FBI Academy's Behavioral Science Services Unit on the first academic faculty exchange with the Bureau.

A MORE EFFICACIOUS POLICE RESPONSE

DAVID L. CARTER

Humans are dogmatic—we simply do not like to change. When faced with new ideas or responsibilities, we tend to resist them, often searching to find fault, rather than experimenting with the concept to fairly weigh its merits. This facet of humanity plays a substantial role in critics' opposition to community-oriented policing (COP) just as it is a major obstacle to implementing the philosophy.

To illustrate, all we have to do is look back to the early 1970s when the Police Foundation released its findings from the Kansas City Preventive Patrol Study (Kelling et al., 1974). Critics, relying largely on their intuition and tradition, firmly proclaimed the findings were inaccurate, despite the project's empirical nature and reliance on sound scientific methods with a rigorous research design. Criticisms of the research—many of which were published in an issue of the *Police Chief* devoted to the study—decried the impact of various scenarios: What would happen if no officers patrolled our nation's streets? How could emergency calls be answered? What would happen to citizens' feeling of safety if patrol officers were eliminated based on this research? Who would answer calls for service if there were no patrol officers?

These were emotional responses by critics who did not fully understand the research nor open their minds to the its ideas. The Kansas City study never suggested that the police should eliminate patrol officers. Rather, the study observed that assumptions about the preventive nature of marked patrol appeared to be erroneous; thus, the police should search for different ways to deploy and use uniformed officers. The gap between research findings and the emotional interpretations of the findings by critics was substantial. Such a case is common when conventional wisdom is challenged.

The parallel to community policing is significant. Critics have keyed onto certain phrases, practice, or assumptions without fully appreciating the "big pic-

ture" of COP. Indeed, critics of the concept tend to draw conclusions only on selected elements of COP, creating paradigms that were neither conceived nor
intended by advocates. Yet offering such scenarios strengthens their arguments at
an emotional level—a classic example of "going on the offensive."

An illustration will place this in perspective. Many critics focus on the word
community as the key element of COP. Community is an important variable, but
the fundamental premise of COP is much broader, focusing on changing the *philosophy* of a police organization. That is, exploring how police leaders can rethink
the way they provide police service, including the mission, role, goals, policies,
and procedures of the police organization. Similarly, many critics focus on selected operational strategies frequently employed with COP, such as bicycle patrol, foot patrol, Neighborhood Watches, or community advocacy. Although these
tactics can have an impact on crime and community concerns, they are not community policing, per se. In reality, because COP is a philosophy, it focuses on the
way the police department is *managed* and how the infrastructure can be changed
to support this management style. These are discussed in greater detail later.

Community policing emanates from both theory and empirical analysis. The
critics tend to ignore the empirical exploration of COP dating back two decades.
The ideas of Bob Trojanowicz's Neighborhood Foot Patrol were first empirically
tested in Flint, Michigan, in the late 1970s (Trojanowicz, 1978), and Herman
Goldstein's Problem-Oriented Policing (POP) was empirically tested in Newport
News, Virginia, in the mid-1980s (Spelman & Eck, 1987).

Despite assertions of critics, COP was not based on any "nostalgia for community" or participatory democracy, nor was it conceived as any form of social engineering to meet predefined social conditions. These assertions are commonly
made, but advocacy for these ideas cannot be found in the arguments of COP proponents. Indeed, just the opposite is true, which is clear from the advocates' literature. For example, most advocates go to great lengths distinguishing community
policing from past experiences of police foot patrol. Similarly, COP advocates,
while supporting the idea that the public should have input on local police priorities, nonetheless clearly reserve the ultimate decisions for police service delivery
and problem solving to the police. These are facets conveniently overlooked by the
critics who develop a substantial emotional smokescreen in their arguments. Similarly, despite the naive assertions of critics, no advocate of COP claims it is the ultimate "answer" to crime and quality of life problems. Rather, community policing
is offered as a more efficacious police response to calls for service.

The Legacy of Police Research

Community policing did not simply appear on the police landscape but evolved
from the knowledge we have gained in police patrol research. Studies of preventive
patrol, response time, differential police response, managing patrol operations,
one- versus two-officer cars, and team policing, to name a few, have all contributed

to the body of knowledge giving us insight on what works and what does not. The rich legacy of this research gave us empirical information about the effectiveness of various patrol policies and practices.

For example, because various research projects demonstrated that random preventive patrol did not prevent crime, that a fast response did not increase the probability of apprehending criminals, and that officers are both safer and more efficient in one-officer patrol units compared with two-officer cars, what are the implications? (See Radelet & Carter, 1994). The conclusions suggest that we need to explore alternate patrol deployment strategies because traditional practices are both wasteful of officer time and functionally ineffective.

With the recognition of limitations (or failures) of traditional patrol management practices, different approaches to providing police service were explored. Community policing practices slowly emerged as police leaders and researchers experimented with alternate methods of police service delivery. The consistency between new police procedures and emerging management practices made it clear that both the operational and structural character of policing was changing from traditional models. As such, a new philosophy of policing and police management was emerging under a label we have come to know as community policing.

Are the Police Just Law Enforcers?

Pundits tend to argue that community policing requires the police to step out of their "real" role of being law enforcers and pushes them into the broader role of generalist social servants. In reality, most calls for service received by the police in any American city have historically been public requests for assistance in areas that are noncriminal or only on the periphery of crime. Domestic disturbances, landlord–tenant disputes, prowlers, noise complaints, medical emergencies, and bothersome youths are examples of these types of calls. Are the police to ignore these calls from citizens because the incidents are fundamentally noncriminal? Do not citizens, who fund the police through taxes and from whom the police derive their authority, have the right to define the broad types of activities they want their police to do? If the police do not handle these incidents or refuse to be the first responder to a noncriminal crisis or emergency, who will?

The practical reality is that the police are the only real option toward which the public can turn in handling these calls in most communities. To ignore this fundamental fact is pragmatically and politically unrealistic. For a police chief to ignore this fact means that he or she will be looking for a new job.

Given that the police are obligated, de facto, to handle these calls, the responsible police manager will seek ways to do so that are most effective and expend fewest resources. That is a fundamental intent of community policing. Just as the British Constabularies are consciously changing their label from a "police force" to the "police service," we, too, must recognize the conceptual implications of noncriminal public mandates.

Analogy 1: Lessons from the Private Sector

During the 1970s and early 1980s, General Motors (GM) and Harley-Davidson Motorcycles had something in common: the quality of their products was poor, customer satisfaction was low, profits were dropping, and they were being eaten in the marketplace by Japanese imports. Both companies were making their products to meet corporate goals related to marketing, engineering, and accounting as driven by their executives' vision. The problem was that the corporate vision was not what consumers wanted.

With the emergence of quality management in the United States, both corporations took a different approach. Buying back Harley-Davidson from the parent corporation AMF, the Davidson family implemented Total Quality Management (TQM) in the design and production of motorcycles. Creating Saturn and applying TQM principles in the manufacturing of all the GM automotive lines, General Motors turned around its downward trends.

Change was difficult for both organizations. The long-standing principles of manufacturing, a rigid hierarchy and organizational culture, and various other institutional practices had to be changed. For example, assembly line workers were empowered to use more discretion to ensure quality manufacturing, even if they had to "stop the line." Similarly, engineers and designers listened to what the customers wanted. (One interesting illustration was that designers, responding to customer demands, added to the number of cup holders in vehicles as well as making them larger—the public was making final purchasing decisions based on cup holders!) The corporate culture in both organizations changed to a quality management style, which was criticized by pundits who said, "It won't work."

The analogy to policing should be clear: organizations need to evolve with society and their clientele. The willingness to explore new models becomes a necessity for the organization to survive, even when that experimentation is criticized by those who either cannot accept the need for change or are unwilling to expend the energy to move the organization forward.

Analogy 2: The Medical Model

Responses to medical emergencies initially focused on the *rapid transport* of a patient to an emergency room. Ambulance attendants were skilled transporters who responded quickly to a call and just as quickly left the scene with the patient for the emergency staff to stabilize and treat the person. This reactive approach to medical emergencies was similar to traditional police responses to calls for service.

However, new ideas began to emerge as better responses to emergency patient care. A more proactive, problem-oriented approach involved training responding personnel—Emergency Medical Technicians (EMTs)—to perform a quick diagnosis of the patient and provide life-saving interventions as well as emergency treatment to stabilize the person before transporting the patient to a trauma center. Under this model, EMTs spend more time on each call and more time at the scene, with the recognition that this investment in time provides better care for the patient.

Despite its logic, as this process evolved, there was resistance to the change. Some of the greatest resistance came from physicians who thought it was irresponsible to entrust diagnostic and medical interventions to the EMTs. Critics argued that despite diagnosis and treatment at the scene, the critical factor was rapid transport to an emergency room where physicians and sophisticated equipment were available to provide care to the patient. As the evidence of success mounted in very tangible forms—decreased mortality rates—acceptance grew.

Beyond this example, other changes in the medical model reflect a growth in quality care. For example, the importance of good physician–patient communications, attention to emotional needs of patients as well as physical needs, and the value of listening to patients' concerns and views on both diagnosis and treatment are part of the quality care movement.

Once again, the analogy to policing should be quite clear. It is more efficacious to take time "up front" to solve a problem rather than respond quickly just to "handle the call." Additionally, taking a broader, more holistic view of one's responsibility and recognizing the important role of the customer (whether he or she is a patient or a citizen) is not only the proper thing to do; it is more effective in the long term. If the medical profession can apply quality management, certainly the police can also—we simply call it community policing.

What's in a Name?

Academicians are notorious for their analysis of issues, searching for subtleties of meaning—whether intended or not. Indeed, many times critical analyses of issues and concepts blend detail and assumptions in a conspiratorial scenario that would make Oliver Stone proud. A statement of the obvious is, to many academicians, superficial and decidedly unscholarly. Although the need for detailed analytic precision has an important role, it is not always practical.

This is illustrated in the story of the hot air balloonist who crash landed in a desert for which he had no maps. On the third day after the accident, while in his shelter made from the balloon's remnants, a man drove up in a Jeep. The parched balloonist, relieved, asked the driver, "Can you tell me where I am?" "Certainly," responded the driver with confidence. "It is clear that you are in the gondola of a crashed balloon in the desert." The balloonist responded, "You must be an academic." The driver said, "Why, yes. How did you know?" The balloonist observed, "Because you gave me a precise and accurate answer that is absolutely useless!"

Such is the case in much academic analysis of the meaning of "community policing." The late Bob Trojanowicz once told the author, "the worst thing about community policing is the name." The *community policing* label evolved more out of a desire to seek a distinguishing descriptor of this approach to policing as opposed to the more traditional, reactive model. "New and improved policing" does not sound right, nor does "gen-X policing," "holistic policing," or any number of other labels. Perhaps most accurate was former Madison, Wisconsin, Chief David Couper's name of "quality policing."

Community was an adjective that emerged as researchers and practitioners tried to describe this new philosophy that used quality management principles while applying the techniques of problem solving and the broader community-based, quality-of-life approach of neighborhood foot patrol. To assign any greater meaning is largely speculation. To infer a meaning that was not intended is misleading. Once again, however, the academic literature of critics tends to offer such an overanalysis while missing the fundamental points.

So What's the Bottom Line?

Community policing is the application of modern management thought to the business of policing. Just as when August Vollmer adapted principles of Weberian bureaucracy and Taylor's scientific management to the police organization, community policing seeks to apply total quality management, continuous quality improvement, and re-engineering practices to policing. Whether a business or public service, the management goal is to direct the organization with the greatest efficiency and effectiveness. This includes:

- Responding to customer needs and demands
- Doing the job right the first time
- Solving the problem, not responding to a symptom
- Empowering line-level workers to make decisions
- Providing job enlargement to employees to make them more productive and to increase job satisfaction
- Involving customers (citizens) in setting priorities

The Proof Is in the Pudding

Beyond the empirical analysis of community policing, the conceptual forays into theoretical underpinnings, and the esoteric bantering between scholars, one needs to look at the effects of COP by street-level police officers. Pragmatic, real-world evidence from the actual practice of police officers demonstrates successes of the concept.

The author has provided community policing training and technical assistance to some one hundred police agencies over the past several years. These departments represent varying agency sizes, urban and rural settings, and virtually every geographic region of the United States, as well as several foreign countries. On balance, when implemented within the true framework of solving customer-driven problems, the concept has clearly been successful. Moreover, officer careers have been rejuvenated, and job satisfaction has increased.

Of course, neither "success" nor "community policing" is a dichotomous variable. COP implementation has occurred on a continuum just as successes have occurred on a sliding scale. Commitment by the organization, skill development of officers, organizational flexibility, and receptiveness of the community are among the critical variables. Despite the evolutionary nature and varying degrees of implementation, the author has witnessed the successes of community policing through changes in neighborhoods, resolution of endemic neighborhood problems, and enhanced quality of life as perceived by residents. Furthermore, the author has spoken with numerous officers—many of whom are nearly evangelical about the success of the concept—as well as citizens who profusely express gratitude to the police and exhort feelings of safety in their community.

Conclusion

Community policing is not a panacea and probably will not work in every community. Similarly, because of a wide range of intermixed factors such as union contracts, organizational culture, quality of personnel, and leadership style, not every police department will be suited for the concept. However, COP is clearly an experiment in public policy that has tremendous potential for success despite the cynical, unbending perspective of protagonists and pundits.

Community policing is not delusion, it is experimentation. It is not idealistic, for its successes in many police departments are evidence of its practicality. Neither is it naive, because the fundamental premises have shown successes in other institutions such as business and medicine. COP is not a deluded perspective of advocates—indeed, many strong advocates of the concept were once some of its most vocal critics. Community policing *is* reformist—police organizations have needed reform because what they were doing lacked success.

We cannot continue to plod along the tradition-bound avenue of policing for which critics would hope. Successes and development are the products of a willingness to experiment and challenge conventional wisdom. The liturgy of critics is "why change?" The answer is, "What we have been doing does not work."

REFERENCES

Kelling, G. L., Pate, T., Dieckman, D., & Brown, C. (1974). *The Kansas City preventive patrol experiment: Technical report.* Washington, DC: Police Foundation.

Radelet, L., & Carter, D. L. (1994). *The police and the community* (5th ed.). New York: Macmillan Publishing Company.

Spelman, W., & Eck, J. (1987). *Problem-oriented policing: The Newport News experiment.* Washington, DC: Police Executive Research Forum.

Trojanowicz, R. (1978). *The neighborhood foot patrol program in Flint, Michigan.* East Lansing, MI: National Neighborhood Foot Patrol Center.

Rejoinder to Dr. Carter

JAMES S. ALBRITTON

Professor Carter provides an interesting and mildly persuasive defense of the community policing "philosophy" and ideology in his discussion. His commitment to the community policing agenda is sincere, experiential, and admirable in the sense that he supports his contentions with honesty and integrity, if not modesty. Unfortunately, however, he does not do justice to the critics of community policing, and his passion for the cause of COP often obfuscates some legitimate concerns about its merits. Because I have taken a critical stance in my contribution, I offer three basic responses to Professor Carter's perspective on community policing, without modifying what I have already argued.

First, community-policing advocates initiated the debate in the 1980s about their reform proposals for a "new era" in policing in a series of well-known publications and pronouncements. Because many of their assertions about the nature, needs, and history of policing were both controversial and subject to many interpretations, a substantial debate *necessarily* ensued. Why this debate has since turned into a shouting match about evil intentions and cynical motivations is beyond my comprehension. I certainly hold no such view of the COP movement or of Professor Carter, but I would not withdraw a word from my criticism of either one. I too have experiential knowledge of the COP movement, but I do not draw the same enthusiastic conclusions or lessons about its merits. When Professor Carter asserts that "the proof is in the pudding," his flavor is vanilla and mine is chocolate, and the real-world evidence for both is in the mix.

Second, Professor Carter skips lightly over criticism of such defining assumptions as "community" in the COP/POP ideology. This is unfortunate, not because the concept of community is only an "adjective" or "one variable" in the COP/POP ideology, as Professor argues, but because the role of "community" is a *determining factor* in the ultimate success, or failure, of the COP/POP reform. Professor Carter argues that "COP advocates . . . clearly reserve the ultimate decisions for police service delivery and problem solving to the police," but this aspect is not so transparent from a careful reading of the COP/POP literature. On the contrary, much is made in the literature of "empowering" the community, of "coproduction" of police delivery of services, of the role of citizens in the problem-solving process, and of the police intervening to "create community" where none exists. Thus the terms *community* and *policing* are inextricably linked in both theory and practice, and the direct interrelationship between the two cannot be denied with impunity. Moreover, Professor Carter's notion that "detailed analytic precision has an important role" but "it is not always practical," has some merit in *general* terms, but not when we are talking about a reform movement that proposes to transform public policy toward policing. I have always found that the failure of COP theorists to provide either precise or satisfactory operational definitions of key concepts in the COP agenda to be one of the most serious and annoying flaws in the entire enterprise. To proceed by exhortation and limited experimentation alone does not make for good or lasting public policy. Nor will it silence the concerns of critics.

Finally, Professor Carter accuses the critics of missing the "big picture" of COP by focusing only on "selected elements" of the COP agenda. This is a serious charge that deserves closer scrutiny. Professor Carter defines the "bottom line" of the COP agenda in the following manner: "Community policing seeks to apply total quality management, continuous quality improvement, and reengineering practices to policing…the management goal is to direct the organization with the greatest efficiency and effectiveness." Citing the successes of quality management techniques in the private sector and medicine, Professor Carter shows how the application of these techniques has led to more efficient and effective delivery of services.

In my article *The Technique of Community-Oriented Policing,* I attempted to demonstrate that it is precisely this process of technical adaptation and transference from one field to another that defines the "big picture" in a technological society such as ours. The fact that policing must *adapt* to this process by incorporating quality management techniques into its operations is the result of technical imperatives, not "new and innovative strategies" devised exclusively by the COP/ POP movement. In reality, the search for more efficient and effective means to accomplish organizational goals is characteristic of virtually all social institutions today. Professor Carter underscores this reality when he states that "the willingness to explore new models becomes a necessity for the organization to survive." Yes, indeed, Professor Carter! The problem with the COP/POP movement, however, is that its theorists wish to make a *virtue* of necessity! And that, in my humble opinion, is the crux of the controversy.

SIMPLY INFLATED PROMISES

JAMES S. ALBRITTON

What began somewhat immodestly as the "quiet revolution" in policing in the 1980s (Kelling, 1988) has now become the "new orthodoxy" in reform policing for the 1990s. "Community-oriented policing" (COP) is the latest in a series of police reform efforts over the last thirty years, all of which have addressed and attempted to resolve the intractable problems in relations between the police and the public. Unlike previous reform movements, however, COP is primarily the product of the "research revolution" described by Walker (1992) and the brainchild of a number of prominent academic protagonists (e.g., Kelling, 1988). Moreover, "problem-oriented policing" (POP), a corollary to the COP movement, emanates from the writings of Herman Goldstein (esp. 1990; 1979), an eminent specialist in police affairs. The combination of COP and POP reform proposals now constitutes the reform agenda for the future of policing in the United States and elsewhere, as well as the "philosophical" orthodoxy on which it is supposed to be implemented (e.g., Skolnick & Bayley, 1986; Trojanowicz & Bucqueroux, 1990).

How, then, backed by such powerful credentials and specialists in the field of police studies, could anyone question the validity or viability of such an impressive enterprise? How could it not be the answer to our prayers and hopes for the future of policing? In my interpretation, the COP/POP reform agenda is nevertheless vulnerable to criticism at a number of levels, not the least of which engages its underlying assumptions and arguments about the nature of policing, community, and society. Furthermore, it is not the answer to our prayers in the sense that its catechism invokes the unholy secular trinity of ideology, ambiguity, and funding, which condition and orient its implementation. I address these and other issues both critically and successively in the following discussion.

The Ideological Catechism of Community Policing

The theorists of the COP/POP movement reflect a curious mixture of middle-class reformers and intellectuals who represent a variety ideological strains from conservative realism to liberal idealism. Beginning roughly with the Wilson and Kelling (1982) hypothesis about "broken windows," urban decay, and social disorder, to the more dogmatic formulation of the "10 Principles of Community Policing" by Trojanowicz and Bucqueroux (1990), the COP movement has progressively mobilized its adherents from the ranks of academe and policing, as well as segments of the general public and politics. The attraction of the movement lies in its proposal to resolve the problems in conventional police–public relations by devising a "new philosophy" of policing based on three essential ingredients:

- Bringing the police and the community closer together in cooperative arrangements whereby citizen fear of crime is reduced and police efficiency in crime prevention and detection is increased
- Allowing greater citizen/community input and participation in the definition and resolution of problems of disorder, decay, and crime in their communities
- Radically restructuring and reorganizing police organizations, resources, and personnel to accommodate the normative assumptions and postulates of the COP/POP philosophy

Whether the "philosophy" of COP constitutes a truly "new and revolutionary" strategy for policing is a matter of considerable debate (e.g., Greene & Mastrofski, 1988; Reichers & Roberg, 1990; Hunter & Barker, 1993), but there is little doubt about its *ideological* overtones. I use the term *ideology* in this context to emphasize the fact that the underlying assumptions of the COP movement are not founded on a disinterested, neutral, or "scientific" evaluation of the relationship between police and society or, for that matter, on the "lessons" of its history (Kelling & Moore, 1988). Rather, these assumptions are founded on predominately middle-class beliefs and values about crime, fear of crime, and social disorder, on a transparent nostalgia for "community" and "participatory democracy" among other things, and on an uncompromising insistence on the need for radical transformation of police organizations and priorities. All of these assumptions are normative, value-laden predispositions that, no matter how intelligently or persuasively presented, are nevertheless fragile and ideological by any definition (e.g., Klockars, 1988).

Trojanowicz and Bucqueroux illustrate best perhaps the ideological dimensions and assumptions of the COP movement as they set forth a virtual compendium of the central themes, principles, values, beliefs, and characteristics of COP in *Community Policing: A Contemporary Perspective* (1990). In addition to their "Ten Principles of Community Policing," Trojanowicz and Bucqueroux demonstrate persuasively, and at some length, what COP is and what it is not (1990: Ch. 1). I have critically evaluated some of these matters elsewhere (Albritton, 1995), but suffice it to say that COP is systematically presented by the authors as a totally new, revolutionary, and innovative approach, i.e., a "new philosophy of policing," a "new organizational strategy," "new Community Policing Officers (CPOs)," and a "new way of looking at the way that police departments think and act," and so forth. Their demonstration contains all of the fervor, dogmatism, and subjectivism typically associated with true believers in an ideological cause, some of which is stated explicitly:

> Community Policing rests on the belief that only by working together will people and the police be able to improve the quality of life in the community, with the police not only as enforcers, but also as advisors, facilitators, and supporters of new community-based, police-supervised initiatives. (1990, p. 3)

Others, such as Skolnick and Bayley (1986), are just as adamant in their declarations of support for this image of reform policing:

> Our recommendations about the usefulness of community-oriented policing are based...on arguments that such innovations "make sense," or on conclusions developed from field observations. But if some of the new we have praised is unproven, so too is the old. Rarely have traditional police practices been subjected to rigorous evaluation.... Because doubts about traditional strategies are so widespread, the burden of proof should be on those who seek to maintain them. (p. 226)

According to Skolnick and Bayley, then, COP is both common sensical and utilitarian, and the "burden of proof" rests not with the advocates of COP, but with those who would defend "traditional strategies" in the face of "innovation." The contrasting of the "old" and the "new" is a wonderful rhetorical technique, but it simply does not do justice to over thirty years of intense research on "traditional" policing, nor is it meant to. The propagation of a "new faith" often requires such exaggeration, but that does not make it any more acceptable, especially when it is performed by otherwise reputable scholars in the field.

Furthermore, the linking of the terms *community* and *policing* is also an interesting rhetorical device in the COP ideology. It evokes a potentially warm and congenial relationship between the police and the public, a relationship most often depicted as a "partnership" between all parties in view of improving the "quality of life" and resolving the "problems" of the community. As Seagrave (1996) points out in her excellent analysis of the deficiencies in COP/POP terminology, however,

> By repetitive use some words have symbolic values which succeed in exerting great influence on the nature and direction of an individual's thinking.... The word "community" can be seen in this light, having been described as "warmly persuasive," never used unfavorably and always intended to encourage public support. (p. 3)

Indeed, the symbolism and rhetorical ambiguities of this movement have led to some of the most scathing critiques of the COP/POP ideology since its inception (e.g., Greene & Mastrofski, 1988; Reichers & Roberg, 1990; Hunter & Barker, 1993). Yet all is not simply ideological rhetoric in the COP/POP reform commitments, and we must examine further some of the major ambiguities of the movement.

Major Ambiguities in the COP/POP Agenda

The ambiguities in the COP/POP agenda emanate directly from its ideological presuppositions about police and society. As is typical in ideological movements, there is often an attempt to rewrite the "history" of all that has preceded in terms of the "new and revolutionary" proposals being advanced. Kelling and Moore (1988) attempt to accomplish this by developing "models" of police history based on three eras: the political era, the reform era, and the emerging community era. Fraught with conceptual ambiguities, analytical weaknesses, and outright omissions to police history, the Kelling and Moore reinterpretation immediately encountered resistance from other police experts (e.g., Hartmann, 1988).

Moreover, Wilson and Kelling's (1982) "broken windows" thesis was directly challenged by Walker (1984), a well-known police historian who argues that the nostalgic return to the style of order maintenance policing advocated by Wilson, Kelling, Moore, and others, never really existed historically. The vision of history proposed by COP/POP theorists is therefore a first major source of ambiguity and controversy in their approach, especially because their immediate argument is that "traditional" modes of policing have failed dismally in controlling crime and must be replaced by community policing techniques and strategies.

A second major source of ambiguity involves the failure of COP/POP theorists to define their terminology carefully, convincingly, and comprehensively. Their constant and equivocal use of the term *community,* for example, is a central and serious flaw in the entire architecture of COP/POP reform proposals, as evoked above. Furthermore, whether there are widespread, authentic "communities" ready and willing to participate in the COP/POP project is a dubious assumption at best. Hunter and Barker (1993), for example, point realistically to "the lack of community consensus within [our] diverse and increasingly fragmented nation." More fundamentally, Seagrave (1996) and others underline the inherent vagueness and confusion in the diverse definitions of what constitutes "community," its multiple meanings and applications in social science, yet its definite and widespread political appeal—precisely because of its imprecision. The problem, however, lies in the fact that the term is virtually meaningless, especially when applied to highly diverse or transitional urban areas—or "neighborhoods," another nebulous concept—in which high crime and delinquency, social disorganization and decay, and disintegration of organic family life prevail.

Implicit in these undifferentiated social contexts is the notion that police should become the new agents of social control and order, while also rebuilding a "sense of community" where and when it does not exist naturally, and reducing the citizens' fear of crime (Reichers & Roberg, 1990). Few, if any, police organizations are willing, able, or qualified, however, to take on such an immense task, especially because the mandate for such an undertaking and the root causes of the underlying social "problems," far exceed existing definitions of police roles, responsibilities, and resources. This is nevertheless a "sink or swim" proposition for the future of COP in particular, a proposition that may well be its ultimate downfall. The *illusion of community* is indeed a poor foundation on which to erect an entire reform movement!

A third major source of ambiguity resides in the concept of policing that underpins COP/POP ideology. Declaring, with partial legitimacy, that the conventional, bureaucratic, incident-driven, motorized mode of policing is a virtual failure in achieving its goals of crime reduction and prevention, COP/POP advocates propose a complete restructuring of police organizations and priorities to fit the "strategic innovations" of the COP/POP reform agenda (Moore & Trojanowicz, 1988).

In reality, the demands for such a radical reorganization of American policing have not produced any appreciable structural changes in police organizations across the country for several reasons. First, I agree with Williams and Wagoner (1992) when they argue that "the current situation leads us to believe that nothing substantial is taking place [among police and in police organizations] except, perhaps, in idiosyncratic circumstances and isolated instances." Little of what Williams and Wagoner argue is a matter of deliberate choice or willful resistance to change within policing, as I have attempted to demonstrate previously (Albritton, 1995). Rather, it is due to the order of technical necessity that governs police organizations, just as it governs generally the "quality of life" in a technological society such as ours. In this regard, the COP agenda specifically fails to give even the slightest consideration to the broader orientations and imperatives in our society. COP theorists consistently make counterintuitive and impractical proposals, such as the complete "decentralization" of police organizations and operations, that defy the "logic" of major social and technological trends in contemporary society.

A second and related reason for the lack of substantive change in policing resides in the general confusion in the COP literature between "decentralized" police services and "deconcentrated" police operations. When Trojanowicz and Bucqueroux (1990) define community policing as a "new organizational strategy... that provides a new way for the police to provide decentralized and personalized police service that offers every law-abiding citizen an opportunity to become active in the police process," they unconsciously encourage this confusion. The "bureaucratic model" of policing continues to prevail in medium to large urban police departments, not because of a conscious, aesthetic commitment to the bureaucratic "style" of management, but because this type of highly centralized, rationalized form of organization has been required generally in society to cope with the technical imperatives associated with similarly complex organizations.

Where COP/POP has been tried and at least partially implemented through such tactics as foot patrol, mini-stations, Community Police Officers (CPOs), and community councils (among other, often ingenious, programs), many observers still remain frustrated by the often small-scale or restrictive application of the total COP agenda. That is because the majority of police organizations are only able or willing to "deconcentrate" a portion of their resources to COP experiments, while retaining the bulk of their diverse units, including "traditional" patrol, under centralized control. It is neither practical nor economical for these departments to effectively "decentralize" their operations to accommodate the desires of the COP/POP movement. Moreover, some police experts have begun to recognize, or concede, that "in most departments, community policing is not intended to completely substitute for motor patrol, but rather to supplement and complement motor patrol's reactive efforts" (Cordner & Hale, 1992:12).

Finally, the depiction of COP as an appendage to more "traditional" and "necessary" police operations is a far more realistic assessment of the present state and probable future of COP/POP proposals in American policing (Williams & Wagoner, 1992). The proposed conversion of all police resources to the COP/POP agenda has always been an expensive and often prohibitive proposition, despite the oft-mentioned "buzz words" about greater efficiency, effectiveness, and benefits in the COP literature. The funding support for community policing has always been problematic, despite President Clinton's endorsement of the concept nationally, and substantial public and private funding of academic research, pilot projects, and experimentation. "That's where the money's at," I was once told excitedly by an academic colleague; and the fact that many academic researchers are jumping on the COP/POP bandwagon for monetary reasons alone is a sure and certain sign that the movement is in deep trouble. Moreover, in his lucid analysis of the "implementation gap" in community policing, Silverman (1995) demonstrates how community policing "requires additional funding in excess of the level of the professional model" and why "the literature on community policing implementation is quite scanty, primarily anecdotal, and superficial." Silverman is also quite adept at showing how many of the claims of "success" in COP experiments are based on faulty information or analytical deficiencies. Citing Guido's presentation (1993) to John Jay College in New York, Silverman exposes the fact that "community policing is being oversold. It is widely perceived as some kind of miracle municipal antibiotic, promising to cure or alleviate the intractable problems of contemporary society" (1995, p. 37). Alas, in reality, I could not have said it better or more succinctly myself!

Conclusion

The COP/POP movement has distinguished itself by its enthusiastic and generous ideas about community, society, and policing, its often contagious idealism and reformism, and its intuitions about the need for change in certain aspects of policing. Nevertheless, none of this has overwhelmed its critics and skeptics to the point that an authentic debate about COP/POP reforms cannot continue into the future. Personally, I am convinced that the movement has missed some crucial and determining points in the analysis of the relationship between police and society. And I am further persuaded that changes in police organization, strategies, services, or programs alone cannot bring about the kinds of social transformations naively advocated in the COP/POP reform agenda. Our capacity to delude ourselves about the kind of world in which we live seems boundless, and community policing is unfortunately, just one more of these deceptions. An answer to our prayers? Hardly.

REFERENCES

Albritton, J. S. (1995). The technique of community-oriented policing: An alternative explanation. In: P. C. Kratcoski & D. Dukes (eds.). *Issues in community policing.* Cincinnati, OH: Anderson Publishing.

Cordner, G. W., & Hale, D. C. (eds.). (1992). *What works in policing?* Cincinnati, OH: Anderson Publishing.

Goldstein, H. (1990). *Problem-oriented policing.* New York: McGraw-Hill.

Goldstein, H. (1979). Improving policing: A problem-oriented approach. *Crime & Delinquency, 25,* 236–258.

Greene, J. R., & Mastrofski, S. D. (eds.). (1988). *Community policing: Rhetoric or reality.* New York: Praeger.

Hartmann, F. X. (ed.). (1988). Debating the evolution of American policing. *Perspectives on Policing,* No. 5. National Institute of Justice.

Hunter, R. D., & Barker, T. (1993). BS and buzzwords: The new police operational style. *American Journal of Police, 12* (3), 157–168.

Kelling, G. L. (1988). Police and communities: The quiet revolution. *Perspectives on Policing,* No. 1. National Institute of Justice.

Kelling, G. L., & Moore, M. H. (1988). The evolving strategy of policing. *Perspectives on Policing,* No. 4. National Institute of Justice.

Klockars, C. B. (1988). The rhetoric of community policing. In: J. R. Greene & S. D. Mastrofski (eds.). *Community policing: Rhetoric or reality.* New York: Praeger.

Moore, M. H., & Trojanowicz, R. C. (1988). Corporate strategies for policing. *Perspectives on Policing,* No. 6. National Institute of Justice.

Reichers, L. M., & Roberg, R. R. (1990). Community policing: A critical review of underlying assumptions. *Journal of Police Science and Administration, 17*(2), 105–114.

Seagrave, J. (1996). Defining community policing. *American Journal of Police, XV*(2), 1–22.

Silverman, E. B. (1995). Community policing: The implementation gap. In: P. K. Kratcoski & D. Dukes (eds.). *Issues in community policing.* Cincinnati, OH: Anderson Publishing.

Skolnick, J. H., & Bayley, D. H. (1986). *The new blue line: Police innovation in six American cities.* New York: Free Press.

Trojanowicz, R., & Bucqueroux, B. (1990). *Community policing: A contemporary perspective.* Cincinnati, OH: Anderson Publishing.

Walker, S. (1992). *The police in America: An introduction.* New York: McGraw-Hill.

Walker, S. (1984). Broken windows and fractured history: The use and misuse of history in recent police patrol analysis. *Justice Quarterly, 1* (1), 75–90.

Williams, F. P., & Wagoner, C. P. (1992). Making the police proactive: An impossible task for improbable reasons. *Police Forum, 2* (2).

Wilson, J. Q., & Kelling, G. L. (1982). Broken windows: The police and neighborhood safety. *Atlantic Monthly, 249* (March), 29–38.

Rejoinder to Dr. Albritton

DAVID L. CARTER

Professor Albritton provides an interesting analysis and food for thoughtful discussion of community policing. Such dialogue can only contribute to a better understanding of the issues. Having noted that, we must be cautious of not overstating points or assumptions. One must realize that most community policing advocates are neither blind zealots nor as evangelical as portrayed in Professor Albritton's essay. Indeed, advocates of community policing are, perhaps above all else, pragmatists. We are practical in the acceptance of certain fundamental issues: no matter how much we might hope, police do not have the luxury of dealing solely with criminal behavior. Calls for service, public attitudes and expectations, and mandates from elected officials are clearly telling the police to handle problems and issues that are either noncriminal or only quasi-criminal. Not responding to those mandates is irresponsible.

If police must respond to these type of community problems, it should be done in a manner that seeks to solve the problems (i.e., strategies of effectiveness) without wasting resources (i.e., strategies of efficiency). The value of problem solving is that it proactively seeks to accomplish this.

Policies, practices, and assumptions on which traditional police service delivery has been based have been found to be ineffective. The legacy of research on patrol, response time, deployment, and call management is its consistent demonstration that conventional wisdom has significant limitations. Consequently, it is essential to conceptualize new patrol management models that can increase the efficacy of policing. Community policing strives to accomplish this.

It is, of course, good melodrama to assert that advocates of community policing view the concept as "the answer [to] prayers." Similarly, we do not view it as a "secular trinity of ideology, ambiguity, and funding." This theme is a common mantra of critics who do not fully understand the concept.

Ideology should not be confused with philosophy (although it commonly is). Community policing advocates are not ideologues—we are not bound by an unbending belief system about how community policing should be organized and performed. Rather, we argue that there needs to be a change in the broad philosophical framework of how police responsibilities are defined and how service is provided. We simply cannot continue to be wholly reactive or have blinders that hide the relationship between disorder, crime, and quality of life that taxpayers want the police to address. The philosophy of an organization guides resource decision priorities for delivery of the primary goods or services. Without a philosophy, the organization will drift aimlessly.

Professor Albritton also asserts that community policing is *ambiguous.* This is typically heard from critics who view the concept from the traditional paradigm. Policing has been nearly obsessive in defining procedures and programs, frequently in attempts to minimize discretion and out of fear of lawsuits—the Commission on Accreditation for Law Enforcement Agencies (CALEA) accreditation movement bears witness to this. When, however, we move to a less prescriptive model and tell officers to think creatively, to identify problems and develop alternatives for solutions, this is viewed as ambiguity because rigid all-purpose processes are replaced by custom-made responses to problems. For those uncomfortable with less autocracy and more creativity in police organizations, this may be viewed as ambiguous.

On the matter of *funding,* certainly police departments have taken advantage of the hundreds of millions of dollars available from the federal government for hiring incentives, training, evaluation, and demonstration programs in community policing. Is Professor Albritton asserting that taking advantage of funding programs is irresponsible? I view it differently. To expand on the concept, however, community policing advocates argue that implementation of the philosophy does not require additional funding. If it is available from the federal government, it is certainly "icing on the cake" but not an essential ingredient. Indeed, in the long term as community policing becomes the pro forma approach to police service delivery, we will likely find it is far more cost-effective because it is a wiser use of resources.

The rationality of proactive problem solving, responding to citizen demands, and managing problems of disorder as well as crime is both responsible and good management. It requires, however, creativity, challenging conventional wisdom, and making the effort to change. The emotional response of resisting that change is much easier and certainly less risky. Is this what drives the critics?

Do Citizen Review Boards Provide a Needed Oversight of Police Practices?

EDITOR'S NOTE: The review of allegations of police misconduct has long been the province of internal police mechanisms. In major agencies, internal affairs units—"headhunters"—have conducted criminal and administrative investigations of police activity. In smaller departments, first-line supervisors, designated investigators, or outside governmental agencies, often the county law enforcement or prosecutorial authority, have been tasked with this duty. The results of either type of investigation stay within the affected agency, with discipline wholly its responsibility. In other regulated professions, however, external bodies frequently review allegations of misconduct with membership comprising both professionals and laypersons. Depending on its charge, that body might even have full authority for the discipline of professionals brought before it. With policing's current emphasis on community involvement and participation, the dilemma that now confronts us: should procedures for handling citizen complaints about police officer misconduct involve, at some point in a formalized process, citizens who are not sworn officers and not part of the police agency? More important, is the citizen review of police misconduct a needed oversight of police practices?

Alana W. Ennis began her law enforcement career in 1974 with the Dallas County Sheriff's Department in Dallas, Texas, and spent nearly seventeen years with the Durham, North Carolina, Police Department, serving in several management positions. In 1992, she became Director of Public Safety at the University of North Carolina at Chapel Hill and, in 1995, was appointed Chief of Police at Duke University, where she currently oversees a department of 140 employees.

Chief Ennis is the founder of the National Association of Internal Affairs Investigators, co-founder and first president of the National Association of Women Law Enforcement Executives, serves on the IACP Civil Rights Committee, and is an adjunct faculty member at UNC's Institute of Government. She holds a master's degree in Public Affairs from North Carolina State University.

William H. Moulder has been Chief of Police in Des Moines, Iowa, since 1984. Before that, he served for twenty-six years with the Kansas City, Missouri, Police Department. He holds a Master of Arts in Public Administration from the University of Missouri at Kansas City and is a 1986 graduate of the National Executive Institute.

YES

ALANA W. ENNIS

On the old television show, *Hill Street Blues,* one supervisor cynically advised his officers before they went out on the street for duty, "Let's do it to them before they do it to us." That attitude probably precipitated many citizen complaints against the fictional officers and would unhesitatingly do so in real life. Unlike days past, the public has less of a stomach for police misconduct—especially a blatant assault as in the Rodney King case or the case of the South Carolina state trooper who dragged an unarmed and unresisting female traffic violator from her vehicle at gunpoint. Both arrests were captured on videotape, and both aired (frequently) on national television to the horror of the viewing public. Cases such as these and others impact a frequent public perception of law enforcement as an undisciplined, overbearing, and over aggressive group.

The oversight of police activity and, more important, the review of and aggressive response to police misconduct are critical issues confronting police agencies and their communities. As Walker (1995) has noted:

> The review of citizen complaints is an important and rapidly changing aspect of police oversight. Police officer misconduct results in public dissatisfaction with police services, particularly when citizens who file formal complaints believe that their charges are not investigated thoroughly. Problems associated with the complaint process have inhibited positive relations between law enforcement agencies and the communities they serve. This issue is even more important today, as American law enforcement moves into the era of community policing with its emphasis on closer interaction between police departments and community residents.

Traditionally, police departments have reviewed citizen complaints internally. Sworn officers assigned to the internal affairs or office of professional standards unit investigate individual complaints and recommend a final disposition to the chief executive. But nationally, municipal law enforcement agencies sustain an average of only 10.1 percent of all citizen complaints reviewed internally. (Walker, 1995, p. 3)

As a result of aggressive citizen action, the external review of police conduct by citizen review boards has been used in a number of larger cities for several years. However, the practice is becoming more accepted and is increasingly seen throughout the country including, smaller jurisdictions and a few universities. Review boards were developed to reflect on and sometimes even investigate citizen complaints against the police. By 1994, there were an estimated sixty-six external complaint review bodies, a 400 percent increase over the thirteen that existed in 1980 (Walker, 1995). The number is probably even higher today.

There are several reasons for the increase in external review bodies. One is the trend toward community policing, which emphasizes a police–community partnership. Another reason, especially in larger cities, is the "political dynamics affecting police misconduct" (Walker & Wright, 1995, p. 6). In most cities, an incident involving an African American has precipitated the creation of some form of external review. Notably, citizen review bodies usually exist where there is large minority population or an effective civil rights organization. Political candidates have taken police misconduct as a platform, and review boards have been formed as a result of state statute or mayoral executive order. Even some police chiefs have created external review bodies.

The latter effort represents a reversal of opinion among police administrators. In 1965, the International Association of Chiefs of Police (IACP) adopted an official policy opposing citizen review (Walker, 1995). Both the Police Executive Research Forum (PERF) and the Commission on Accreditation for Law Enforcement Agencies (CALEA) have encouraged law enforcement agencies to develop effective means for reviewing citizen complaints. Consequently, some of the more progressive police chiefs in the country have actually embraced the concept of external review.

Former Chief Tom Koby of the Boulder, Colorado, Police Department first observed the effectiveness of citizen review boards when he was deputy chief in Houston. Then Chief Lee Brown started an external review process there and, according to Koby, "it was 100 percent successful." In light of this success, Koby initiated a review board, comprising citizens, officers, supervisors, and civilian employees, some of whom are union members, shortly after coming to Boulder. In a discussion with this writer, he expressed his feeling that this approach is better than a "stand-alone board which is always as viewed as the enemy by the police officers." Under Boulder's process, when an internal investigation is completed, it is forwarded up through the management of the police department for review and recommendation of disciplinary action. Once this internal process is completed, it is sent to the review board. The board then determines whether the investigation has been thorough, complete, and equitable and sends the report to the police chief with any further recommendations. According to Koby, the combination of group dynamics works, especially if there is an issue of integrity.

The Boulder board has three objectives: (1) to protect the citizen from abuse by police employees; (2) to protect the integrity of the department; and (3) to protect the police employee from the public. Koby feels strongly about citizen involvement: "If you don't have citizens involved in your department, politically, you're a fool." Yet, he recognizes the natural tendency of police personnel to perform their job in an acceptable fashion! "Ninety-nine percent of the officers try to do the right thing 99 percent of the time—this review board deals with the 1 percent that don't."

Robert Olson, now police chief in Minneapolis, had established a citizen review board at his previous department in Yonkers, New York, in 1991. He developed his board from various community groups and set up a board made up of four citizens and four police officers. Union members from the department are among the police officers represented. In the Yonkers approach, the chief is still responsible for discipline. Olson believes that this part is critical: "If a chief is not responsible for discipline within a police department, then he or she should resign."

On the Yonkers board, all internal affairs cases were brought to the panel and reviewed. The panel was routinely briefed on every excessive force case. After review, the panel would make a recommendation to the chief to unfound or sustain the case. The chief made the final decision and determined what discipline, if any, was to be imposed. As a further step, all citizen members of the board went through the Citizen Police Academy in Yonkers to familiarize them with police operations. Chief Olson firmly believes a citizen review is a critical element to community policing.

When Olson arrived in Minneapolis to take over the chief's position, a civilian review authority (CRA) was already established. The city of Minneapolis set this up as a separate agency to conduct investigations regarding alleged police misconduct. The agency does not investigate crimes, and citizens have the option of filing a complaint of "minor excessive force cases" and other complaints to either the CRA or the Internal Affairs Bureau of the police department. As in Yonkers, the chief has ultimate responsibility for disciplinary action.

As an interesting note, the CRA also has the authority to mediate cases. Once a case is mediated, it is considered completely confidential and cannot be placed in an officer's file within the Police Department, nor do any members of Police Administration have access to it (Minneapolis Police Department, p. 19).

Additionally, "a policy/procedure inquiry or PPI" enables citizens to explore why an officer did what he or she did without punitive action. This is only applicable for minor offenses and, if a complaint is sustained, can require retraining or counseling, the first time it occurs (Walker, 1995). This is another means of citizen involvement. Frequently, when a citizen has a question about an officer's actions, he or she expresses to the internal affairs investigator, "I don't want anything done to the officer—I just don't understand why this happened. . . ."

Chief Olson is a proponent of citizen review and believes it is an integral component of community policing. Chief Charles Moose, of the Portland, Oregon, Police Department, shares this view. Portland also has citizen oversight in the form of a committee made up of members of neighborhood associations, coalitions, and others. Approximately twelve persons sit on the committee, and they have one full-time staff person that is housed in the mayor's office. Portland police investigate their own complaints internally, but citizens have the right to appeal to the oversight committee. In addition to its appellate function, the group randomly goes through and reads complaint files for disposition. According to Chief Moose, the committee has overturned only one action during his tenure. Chief Moose holds that citizen oversight is a critical component of community policing and that the citizens and police must work together to solve problems, even if it involves problem police officers.

Deputy Chief Julia Bush of the Kansas City Police Department also commends the action of citizen oversight. The Kansas City Office of Citizen Complaints (OCC) is a separate body established by the Board of Police Commissioners "as a service agency for the community and for the [police] department." Citizen complaints are made to the OCC and, in turn, investigated by the Internal Affairs Unit of the Police Department. The investigations are reviewed by OCC and maintained in a central file. As with other review boards, disciplinary action is the exclusive function of the police chief. The OCC does classify complaints, determining whether they are sustained or unfounded. In Kansas City, the police chief has recourse if he or she disagrees with the classification. According to Deputy Chief Bush, it is important to publicize the function of the OCC so that there can be trust on both sides—the police and citizens. That being done, she believes this is an effective means of problem solving and building trust within the community. "This fits hand-in-hand with community policing and is something any progressive chief should be doing or considering doing," she stated.

The trend is toward establishing more citizen review boards in all types of jurisdictions. Citizens are either being invited to take a more active role in community policing or demanding that role because of a highly publicized incident of police misconduct, usually with racial overtones. Police chiefs have a choice: They can wait for an incident to occur with its attendant public unrest and subsequent mandate that a citizen review process be established, or they can take preemptive action. Chiefs can establish citizen review committees that represent a cross section of the community—being very careful in the planning stages to identify and deal with the critical questions: Who will select the board members? How will they be trained? To whom will they answer? What will their function be? Will the function be investigative or appellate or both? What about the confidentiality of the cases? What are the statutory considerations?

Bornstein (1993) has emphasized the considerable public disbelief, particularly in minority communities, that the police department personnel will fairly investigate complaints against their colleagues. As we enter the twenty-first century, communities in this nation will not become more homogenous; instead they will continue to become much more diverse. This diversity will be the bridge that policing must cross to prove to the community that community policing is not just "window dressing."

Historically, chiefs and sheriffs have resisted the concept of citizen review because they still have the overriding view that most citizens just do not understand the job and that others have ulterior motives and will act out their vendettas against the law enforcement agency. Sharing oversight with a citizen board or even an ombudsman is not relinquishing power or even responsibility for the maintenance of a well-run agency staffed by personnel of high integrity. All responsive law enforcement managers must address the issue of citizen review. Community policing is premised on a cooperative relationship between police and neighborhoods, and citizen oversight of police conduct and practices is a component of accountability to the community.

REFERENCES

Bornstein, J. (1993). *Police brutality: A national debate.* Hillside, NJ: Enslow Publishers.

Ennis, A. (1997). Personal interview with Deputy Chief Julia Bush, Kansas City, MO, Police Department, Feb. 25

Ennis, A. (1997). Personal interview with Chief Thomas Koby, Boulder, CO, Police Department, Feb. 20.

Ennis, A. (1997). Personal interview with Chief Charles Moose, Portland, OR, Police Department, Feb. 18.

Ennis, A. (1997). Personal interview with Chief Robert K. Olson, Minneapolis, MN, Police Department, Feb. 21.

Minneapolis Police Department Policies/Procedures Inquiries Disciplinary and Range System. (1996), p. 19.

Walker, S. (1995). *Citizen review resource manual.* Washington, DC: Police Executive Research Forum.

Walker, S., and Wright, B. (1995). "Citizen review of the police, 1994: A national survey." *Fresh Perspectives.* Washington, DC: Police Executive Research Forum.

Rejoinder to Chief Ennis   WILLIAM H. MOULDER

Citizen review boards are not inevitable, nor are they desirable. They will appear when leaders try to avoid the responsibility of being police chiefs, city managers, mayors, or council members. To be a leader means making decisions and being responsible for the decisions.

Citizen review boards constructed to reflect diversity fail because someone is always excluded. They fail because members are appointed to "fix the police department," and to do this they must find something "broken." To be fair, elaborate procedures are constructed, and form is considered over substance.

This strong opposition to citizen review boards does not mean that citizens should be excluded from decision making in the police department. Every police department that has embraced Community Policing has discovered the powerful partnerships that form between officers and the citizens served. Problems are solved and community safety improves.

In Des Moines, we take the initiative to involve citizens. We formed neighborhood associations to make sure we know what is of concern to the neighborhood and to provide a connection between the citizens and *their* officer. We have ride-along programs, citizen academies, and a frank and open relationship with the news media. We look for every opportunity to inform people of police activities. We employ citizens (who are not police officers) in management positions. We seek relationships with various advocacy groups. Trying to police a city without advice and direction from our community is not a good plan. Involvement builds trust and exclusion builds suspicion.

Complaint resolution requires a commitment to understand what is being said. Is the complaint really focused on the law? Was the loud party in the middle of the night that disturbed the neighborhood a violation or was the officer rude when the party was shut down? Was the driver arrested because of a blood alcohol level of .18 or was it because of race or sex? Complaint resolution requires a commitment to finding out all the facts available and then explaining the rationale of the decision. A matter of style that can be improved may cause the complaint. Officer performance improvement requires the involvement of the officer's supervisors, not a remote citizen review board.

Police officers have great authority and even greater responsibility to use that authority properly. The public has the expectation that the chief of police will see to it the offices meet that responsibility. Citizen review boards usurp the chief's responsibility to do his or her job.

As Chief Ennis notes, in Kansas City, Missouri, citizens are involved in reviewing complaints against police officers. The Board of Police Commissioners reviews the work of the Office of Citizen Complaints. Des Moines, Iowa, has its own citizen review process with the city manager. In both cases, the people charged with the responsibility of the operation of the department are the reviewers. They have to deal with the consequences of their decisions. Citizen review should never be cast off to a board made up of special interest agents.

Community policing has taught all of us that, to be effective, police departments must involve members of our community. They help us decide where to use police resources. In Des Moines, we have neighborhood advisory groups that help us decide how best to meet their public safety needs. They identify the objectives, such as the removal of abandoned cars or the reduction of speeders on their streets.

Community policing is meeting the needs of our community. Community policing is not abandoning the responsibility for managing the police department well.

NO

WILLIAM H. MOULDER

When I was growing up, I rode my bicycle everywhere. Because I spent a lot of time on it, I spent a lot of effort on making it run better. I put special oil on the chain, lowered the handlebars to cut wind resistance, and experimented with overinflating the tires. Finally I had this great idea that, if I put a big wheel on the back and a small one on the front, I could go faster because I would always be going down hill. The idea looked good on paper, but it did not work. It did not work because the concept is basically flawed. The same thing applies to the use of citizen boards to review police activity. The idea looks good on paper, but it does not work because it is basically flawed.

I am not saying that citizens should not be involved in reviewing police activity. We all know they are involved. Citizens (who are not police officers, because you do not have to renounce citizenship to become a police officer) serve as city managers, city council members, and mayors, and they review police activity. Citizens serve on grand juries and review police activities. In some states, a Citizen Ombudsman's Office can review any government activity, including the police department. When police arrest someone, their actions are reviewed by citizen prosecutors and citizen juries. Because police activity is the major source of daily local news, the citizen reporters provide an account for all citizens to review.

Walker's study of citizen review processes (1995) creates a typology to examine the use of citizen review processes. The typology spectrum varies from a full-time nonsworn investigator(s) that conducts initial fact finding to auditors that review complaint procedures and recommend changes. At the time of publication, Walker identified sixty-six agencies that had review processes. The current mantra is that citizen review is the wave of the future (Walker, 1995). In Iowa, there are ninety-nine county sheriffs and several times that number of police departments. Sixty-six are not half the number of law enforcement agencies in a rural state. If there is a trend, it is akin to global warming; it depends on who is measuring.

My city, Des Moines, Iowa, is not listed as having citizen review, although Dr. Walker notes that Iowa has an ombudsman's office with the power to investigate police activity (per Iowa state statutes). All complaints regarding police activity are reviewed by the Des Moines city manager, the city's legal advisor, and the human rights director, all citizens. They do not delve into the administrative action taken; instead, they look for completeness of the investigation and the validity of the conclusions. The chief of police is responsible for the administrative actions.

All involved in the reviews also have to live with the consequences of the decisions they make.

Let's look at the typical development of a citizen review process. The police officers did something. They shot someone, arrested someone, or took some official action and someone did not like it. Never mind that investigators, prosecutors, and the FBI review shooting. Never mind the prosecutor and the courts, and sometimes juries, also review the arrest. Never mind that the mayor, city council, or city manager reviews an official action. That is not good enough because they almost always say the officers were right.

Of course, they are almost always right. Police chiefs are not stupid. Police chiefs hire the best people available, train them thoroughly, supervise them with people that have proved themselves in the profession. It is their job to be right!

Why do police chiefs find that only 6 to 8 percent of the people who apply for the job are good enough? Why do police chiefs spend so much time on training? Why do police chiefs select proven people to do the job of supervision? It is because, as President Harry Truman declared, the "buck stops here." President Truman was absolutely on target. If you are the head of something, you are responsible, good or bad. No appointed group, no matter how well structured, can carry that responsibility.

Examples serve to make the point. San Francisco has a citizen review process that does not involve police officers. The Office of Citizen Complaints (OCC) handles all complaints that citizens bring. The OCC reports to the police commission. The commission, appointed by the mayor, sets policy for the department. The commission appoints the director of the OCC. There are about fifteen investigators for OCC; that number is based on the population of the city. When the OCC is investigating a complaint, the police department is shut out to the end of the complaint. At the conclusion, the OCC makes a recommendation to the chief. The police commission is the final authority.

Now, that does not sound too bad. It is pretty expensive, fifteen or so people on the payroll, but maybe the department would have to have a similar number if they conducted the investigations. Let's look at a couple of findings from the Office of Citizen Complaint:

> Case 829-91: During the arrest of a disabled woman at a demonstration in 1991, an officer confiscated a catheter in her fanny pack. While the officer did not break any known department policies, this demonstrator's allegation of unwarranted action gives notice of the need for an articulation of specific procedures. (Walker, 1995, Document 26, p. 8)

The OCC office investigated and pondered over a year on this. I do not know any more than what is given about the case, but it surely seems overblown. Even if we assume the woman needed the catheter, the officer had some responsibility to guard against the prisoner using the device to injure herself or someone else. In

Des Moines, the shoestrings and belts of people being arrested are removed. Even if the facts bring you to the conclusion that the officer's actions were improper, the "buck" would have been better handled by the chief of police telling the officer "do not do that again." I doubt the officers of San Francisco frequently rummage through the property of disabled people to confiscate their medical devices.

The OCC actions should not be characterized by a single odd finding. The second case in its annual report is offered for consideration. The disabled person was the first case in the annual report. This event occurred in January 1992. The finding is dated March 3, 1993, fourteen months after the case was filed. In Des Moines, we are concerned when it takes longer than sixty days to finish a complaint.

> Case 147-92: In the present case, the complainant was referred to with the pronoun 'sir' during a traffic stop. Although the complainant explained to the officer that she is a woman, the officer continued to address her with the masculine pronoun. (Walker, 1995, Document 26, p. 9)

I take no issue with the finding that this was improper conduct. No police chief would. It makes no sense to go out of the way to irritate someone. If the complaint had been given to the chief, I am sure he would have quickly had the officer's supervisor provide a refresher course on public relations. Failure to make a passing grade in this course usually means the employee will have some unanticipated, uncompensated leisure time to spend contemplating their future in law enforcement.

It was resolved in the investigative hearing. A representative (read "lawyer") for the involved officer observed that there are no specific department guidelines advising officers how they should refer to a person when gender identification is in question. I will bet there is no specific guideline advising officers to not pass gas or belch while handling an arrest, but I doubt whether the proper course of action is in doubt. In either event, the newest sergeant/supervisor would be able to handle the matter in short order, definitely in less than fourteen months.

The OCC recommendation is a specialized training session for new recruits and a department bulletin to be issued to all officers. This is fourteen months later! This is not an impressive product from a board that costs $500,000 a year to operate.

Citizen review commissions fail to meet expectations because of their design. They are being redesigned in Spokane, Washington, and Cincinnati, Ohio. New York City is in the third or fourth recreation of a citizen review commission. Washington, DC's review board is years behind in resolving complaints.

They fail to meet expectations because of a basic design flaw. They are political action committees. They represent special interests. They also divert the responsibility of running the city away from the city council, city manager, or mayor. It takes courage to look at a set of facts and make decisions. Police officers and police executives do it all the time. We expect to deal with the "buck" when it comes to us. We want to be accountable for our department's operation. When we make bad decisions, we deal with the consequences; sometimes that means we leave. Accountability scares city councils. A citizen review allows them to pass the "buck" to a group and avoid being responsible for a decision.

Other, less obvious forces influence the effect of citizen review. An interview with the director of the Minneapolis Civilian Police Review Authority, Patricia Hughes, helped me to understand one of them. The Minneapolis Authority, as are many citizen review processes, is limited in making public statements. The reasons are commendable. They want to guard the privacy and rights of accused officers during an investigation. I appreciate the effort at fairness.

But I have a problem with how this fairness works: An event occurs. The news media reports that an officer shot someone, made an arrest, or took some action. Someone does not like what was done and files a complaint. Now the chief of police is outside the process. The chief cannot interfere with the investigation. Maybe a parallel investigation can be performed, but the citizen review is the official investigation.

Meanwhile, back at police headquarters, the complainant and the complainant's advocacy group hold press conferences on the front steps of the police station. They are not limited to telling the truth. They can say any inflammatory thing they think will make the six o'clock news and tomorrow's headlines. The chief has no information to give the press, except that the board is investigating and when they are done they will report what they find. The officer and the department are vilified in public and can offer no information to balance the debate. In a few months or a year or so later, the review authority will most likely find in the officer's favor. If there is any news coverage, it will be minor. After all, as a veteran reporter told me, it is not news when airplanes land safely. Because we expect officers to perform properly, it is not news when they do perform properly. This is a terrible, destructive activity affecting a city, a department, and an officer.

My experience is that when the story is fresh, the citizen, the department, the community, and the officer are better served by the chief making known the findings of an investigation when there is confidence the evidence is sound. If there is error, confess it. If the San Francisco officer refused to call the woman anything but "sir," denounce it and get on with the business. If the prosecutor rules the shooting proper, put it behind you. There may be training applications the chief needs to address, but they will not be realized until the specific event is settled. This is a responsibility to the city, to the department, and to the officer.

The other influences may be only my perception. I have no evidence to support the claims. They are factors I noticed while researching this subject. I suggest they are valid because of their conformity with the theory of unintended consequences.

Citizen review, in its most noble construction, is intended to make for better policing. I agree, and I am sure the advocates agree. However, many of the citizen review processes provide for lawyers or union representatives to participate in the review process. The process becomes rigid, legalistic, and ponderous. The focus shifts from reviewing what happened to observing the review protocols. It goes from "does this make sense?" or "was it right?" to "what rules or procedures apply?"

In California, the state law contains the "Police Officer Bill of Rights." The general construction of this law limits the ability of management to conduct investigations. It limits the ability to correct behavior. It limits the ability to get rid of problem officers. Nationally we face "Police Officer Bill of Rights" in federal legislation. It is pushed by national labor organizations, the Fraternal Order of Police, and the Teamsters. I think it is a reaction to citizen review. The intention to make policing better will have the consequences of making it worse.

The examples from the San Francisco OCC offer new department procedures to be incorporated in department rules and regulations. Police officers faced with multiple rules to remember tend to avoid difficult situations. Management becomes trapped in "rule-bound" management. Innovation and judgment are inhibited. The result is that the process of evaluating policing becomes more legalistic, more bureaucratic, and less human. That is not what the advocates want. That is not what police chiefs want. That is not what I want.

Citizen review is designed to fail. Its design, to include a diversity of constituencies, does not find common ground; it amplifies differences. Its design, to be a forum of appeal, results in more second-guessing of the formal systems of police internal review, prosecutor review, court review, and manager review. It keeps issues alive and delays closure. Its design to improve policing creates elaborate boards and legalistic processes that create rules that address the minutia. Its design to be a credible source takes the authority to manage away from the chief of police, the city manager, and the council, but it does not take away the responsibility to manage the organization. The "buck" still stops with the chief of police. Citizen review belongs in the museum of failed ideas along with the Edsel, the new Coca-Cola, the perpetual motion machines, and, yes, even my anti-gravity bicycle.

REFERENCES

Personal Interview, Patricia Hughes, Director, Minneapolis Civilian Police Review Authority.

Walker, S. (1995). *Citizen Review Resource Manual.* Washington, DC: Police Executive Research Forum.

Rejoinder to Chief Moulder   ALANA W. ENNIS

This writer certainly acknowledges Chief Moulder's assertion that not all citizen review boards work well. In fact, some have been dismal failures, which is not helpful to the public or the police department. There have been cases in which citizen review panels have gotten months behind in their caseload. Admittedly, these exceptions cast a pall on the process and may even be an excuse for police management not to meet its responsibilities. Also, a lengthy review process can add legitimate difficulties to an internal affairs review and subsequent disciplinary dispositions. No solutions are perfect and all have potential pitfalls—even community policing.

The core issue is accountability to the public. Chief Moulder cites this as paramount, and I agree with him. Citizen review boards are a police department's way of practicing what we've been preaching about community involvement in the most meaningful way possible. Police departments have always viewed internal review of misconduct as a "sacred cow"—one that cannot be touched by outsiders who do not "understand how we do our jobs." Even with all those outsiders who have "hidden agendas" and "special interests," Chief Moulder fails to note that, in most of the cases reviewed, it is rare that a citizen panel rules against the police department. It certainly may be warranted in some cases. Here is a case in point:

Recently, in an eastern North Carolina county, a sheriff's deputy shot and killed an unarmed motorist. The sheriff stated the matter had been investigated internally, that the complaint of excessive force was unwarranted, and cleared the deputy publicly. Later, the State Bureau of Investigation investigated the case (as requested by the same sheriff) and sent it before a Grand Jury, where the deputy was indicted for manslaughter. The sheriff stuck by his original contention that the deputy had acted in self-defense and put him back to work. Now a deputy is actively working as a law enforcement officer while facing a charge of manslaughter. Even a further investigation of the case by the State Bureau of Investigation and indictment by the courts did not keep this officer off the streets. Chief Moulder cites these types of organizations (the FBI and the courts) as enough oversight. Granted, cases such as this are rare, but when they occur, they usually make national headlines and increase the public's perception of law enforcement as an undisciplined group.

Whenever possible the police chief should retain the exclusive power to discipline employees whom engage in misconduct. This way, the police chief retains the responsibility for the agency he or she should have. Any agency head who does not have any type of oversight or citizen involvement would do well to consider appointing a board from a cross section of the community. As long as the board has only the power to review and recommend, it will serve both the department and community well.

For all their imperfections, citizen review boards can and do contribute to an environment of openness and accountability to the public. Even if the process is not perfect, there is surely a significant value in increasing the public's perception that a law enforcement agency is not hiding anything and is willing to bring others from the community into the process of dealing with its problems.

Is the Media a Friend of Law Enforcement?

EDITOR'S NOTE: America is often characterized as a society that values its public safety and, as a result of the First Amendment, treasures the public's right to know *and* the media's ability to inform. Yet, especially in criminal investigations, the balance between effective public safety and complete public disclosure can be delicate. Acknowledging that police officers and members of the press have distinct and often conflicting roles and responsibilities, the relationship between the two becomes a major dilemma facing today's law enforcement.

Born in Nassau, Bahamas, Arnold A. Gibbs joined the Miami Police Department at age twenty-two and was promoted through the ranks, becoming Assistant Chief in 1991. He was appointed Chief of the Cape Coral, Florida Police Department, on February 22, 1994. He received his bachelor's degree from Barry University and a master's degree in Management from St. Thomas University. He is also a graduate of the FBI National Academy. He serves as an adjunct professor, teaching both criminal justice and management courses, at Barry University, Edison Community College, and Florida Gulf Coast University.

Lucy Morgan, a Pulitzer Prize winner for Investigative Reporting, serves as Florida Capital Bureau Chief and Associate Editor for the *St. Petersburg Times.* A reporter for the *Times* since 1968, she has primarily covered crime and government and has been recognized for her special projects on drug smuggling, public corruption, and organized crime. Ms. Morgan was sentenced to jail in 1973 for refusing to reveal a source for one of her stories; in 1976, the Florida Supreme Court, in *Morgan v. State* (Fla., 337 So.2d 951), overturned the sentence and granted reporters a limited right to protect their sources. Since 1991, she has served as a member of the Board of Directors of Times Publishing Company, the body governing the operations of the *Times,* and *Congressional Quarterly, Florida Trend,* and *Governing* magazines.

YES

Lucy Morgan

Okay. Right up front I will admit there are bad reporters, people that even I would not trust. But many of us can be trusted to do the right thing with your news.

We can be your best friend—or your worst enemy—all at the same time. A good law enforcement agency can count on more friendship than enmity. After all, we are citizens, too, and we do not want to be surrounded by bad cops any more than you want to be interviewed by bad reporters.

But there need not be any hostility between reporters and police—just professional respect. Each of us has a job to do. The jobs are different, but both of us provide a service to readers and taxpayers.

Our basic mission is to provide readers, most of whom are taxpayers, with the basic information that enables them to live in the communities you police and cast informed votes when they go to the polls.

Sometimes our mission clashes with the desires of police to keep things secret. Sometimes our job requires us to look at the way law enforcement agencies operate. Sometimes we have to do investigative work to get to the bottom of what is happening. Sometimes we do backgrounds on the police, backgrounds that are more thorough than those done when an officer is hired. If we find something an agency missed, it might be time for the agency to take a closer look at what it is doing before handing a badge and gun to an officer.

There are the moments we start screaming at each other.

If either side lacks a good understanding of the distinction between our jobs, real trouble begins and can last for a long time. That is why it is in all of our best interests to spend a little time talking with each other *before* a crisis occurs.

We truly can be helpful and can even keep a secret at those moments when it is in everyone's best interest!

Need help solving a crime or finding a fugitive? We are there and can immediately distribute information to thousands of people. Citizens who know a rapist is loose in the neighborhood can lock their doors and pay attention to strangers. Without a way to communicate the information, everyone loses.

Screw up and we are there then, too. When a taxpayer-supported police agency fails to uphold the law, it becomes our responsibility to tell the story.

Yes, there are bad reporters, just like there are bad cops. And just as you would like to have the best, most experienced cop investigate the crime when you are a victim, you would like the best reporter to be writing about you. Unfortunately it does not always happen.

But there are ways to keep trouble from erupting every time we communicate. First, get to know the reporters who cover you and the editors that supervise them. Find someone at the news organization you trust so that you can pick up the telephone in an emergency and explain what is going on.

If it is important to keep certain details of a crime out of the newspaper, tell them why. And be sure you have a good reason that is in the public interest. Do not try to sell us secrecy for the sake of secrecy.

Admit it when you make a mistake. I should write this in capital letters. Most of the trouble that comes to law enforcement agencies at the hands of reporters occurs because someone could not admit he or she was wrong.

The very nature of a police officer's job means that mistakes will be made. John Brannigan, an old Florida cop I have covered off and on for years, advises sheriffs to avoid letting someone "cut the dog's tail off one inch at a time."

It may be hard to admit you kicked in the wrong door, shot the wrong person, or arrested the wrong guy, but you would be surprised how quickly the bad news will pass if someone simply admits the error, apologizes, and does what can be done to make things right.

Rejoinder to Ms. Morgan Arnold A. Gibbs

It is very interesting that the theme of this writing is that the problem is centered on "bad cops" and police officials who "could not admit . . . wrong."

It is good that many reporters "can be trusted to do the right thing" with news. However, the problems between law enforcement and the media usually involve the actions of reporters (and police officials) who do not do the right thing.

In the case of a police official whose actions are deviant or unethical, official investigations and disciplinary action are rightfully demanded, and the media generally lead the charge in making such demands. However, in the case of the aberrant reporter or editorial board, the media will rarely admit that one of their own has acted unethically or take disciplinary action against the reporter. Even if they quietly acknowledge that the report was incompetent or unethical, they will not carry news stories about it. Although no one likes to air dirty linen publicly, most police chiefs recognize that it will happen and will not allow it to adversely affect their relationship with the media. But being victimized by unwarranted negative editorializing based on suspicion and a flair of sensationalism is sure to result in strained relations.

The bottom-line recommendation for improved police/media relations is for the media to make a huge paradigm shift in their view of the police; abandon the predilection that law enforcement officials are untrustworthy; report only the facts; and be as openly accountable to the public as the police are expected to be.

NO

ARNOLD A. GIBBS

The concept of police/media relations is one that elicits a multiplicity of responses from law enforcement administrators. These responses cover a spectrum of characteristics that may be abbreviated to terms such as essential, necessary, unmanageable, overranked, one-sided, and even impossible; some responses are, of course, unprintable.

As a result of many years of experience, I have come to understand and accept the fact that no opinion regarding police/media relations could be considered tenable if it is generalized. Each medium, whether it is electronic or print, must be considered on an individual basis, and then opinions about a specific medium should be carefully pronounced to ensure that the organization is not unfairly characterized by the actions of individual agents.

Having laid the groundwork, I now offer my opinion concerning police/media relations. However, in so doing, it seems appropriate to use the Code of Ethics belonging to the Society of Professional Journalists (SPJ) as a benchmark for my statements regarding police/media relations.

Media Relations and the SPJ Code of Ethics

In the preamble to its Code of Ethics, the SPJ's founders indicate that the professional journalist is one whose ultimate goal is to seek the truth and to provide a fair and comprehensive account of every newsworthy event or issue. They declare a commitment to ethical behavior and express dedication to their principles and standards of practice.

Standard I

Seek truth and report it: "Journalists should be honest, fair, and courageous in gathering, reporting and interpreting information."

Although I have dealt with a few reporters who appeared to be genuinely concerned about honesty and fairness, my experience indicates that most have not demonstrated this tendency. And, in those instances where reporters have sought to gather and report the truth, editors have cut and pasted to the extent that the truth is masked. However, one can never know for certain whether the reporter has been deceptive and fully intended to develop a more succulent and sensational story by giving it a negative slant or whether the damage was truly done by the editor. The following describes an actual case.

A reporter for a local newspaper was working on the third of several articles about an incident in which a veteran police sergeant was charged with misdemeanor battery on his girlfriend. During an interview, the reporter referred to the offense as "domestic violence" and raised a question about the arrest of the sergeant. The police chief then explained to the reporter that the incident was far from meeting the statutory requirements for classification as domestic violence and that the referenced act constituted the crime of simple battery. The police chief then informed the reporter that warrantless arrests could be made only in offenses that the state statutes classify as major crimes or felonies. He went on to indicate that, except for certain specific exemptions, the minor offenses or misdemeanors require a warrant for an arrest to be made. The next day, the newspaper story quoted the chief as saying that the incident was not major. This quote was accompanied by other verbiage that indicated that the police department did not take the incident seriously. Needless to say, a number of citizens were extremely upset by this apparent lackadaisical attitude toward a victim of a battery (which the newspaper erroneously referred to as domestic violence) by a police officer. The outcry was so loud that the chief had to appear on all of the local networks and interview with a less prominent newspaper to undo the harm done by what appeared to be a purposefully damaging article. Amazingly, one week later, that newspaper ran its fourth article on the incident, this time in the form of an editorial. This editorial was an even more brutal attack, which continued to refer to the incident as one of domestic violence and outwardly accused the chief of downplaying the incident by stating that it was "not a major crime."

I believe that the preceding incident clearly demonstrates deliberate distortion of the truth, especially when accompanied by headlines that indicated that the chief did not believe that the battery was a crime.

It has almost become standard practice for most reporters to alter or ignore the truth to preserve their preconceived negative view of law enforcement in particular and government officials in general. The following actual incident is an example of such predisposition:

A police chief was involved in a very minor traffic accident in which he struck the rear end of a vehicle. There was no damage to the vehicle he struck, and the only damage to his vehicle was a crack in the plastic grillwork in its front. Although state statutes do not require that such minor accidents even be reported, and in spite of the other driver's insistence that there was no need to report it, he called for a unit to make a report. Inexplicably, this accident drew much attention from the local press, and one reporter inquired as to whether he received a ticket. Soon a series of articles (following their "investigative" reporting) appeared in that newspaper. The series was climaxed by an editorial that lambasted the police chief for using his position to get special treatment and emphasized that he should have received a ticket like anybody else. The police chief phoned the executive editor to inform him of their egregious error, advising him of the law regarding the issuance of citations and the fact that nearly every law enforcement agency in the state has a policy of not issuing citations to *any* driver in such minor accidents. He then asked for a retraction and suggested that, in the future, the paper should contact the appropriate people to get the facts before printing unjust assaults on someone's character on the editorial page. The astonishing reply from the executive editor was that editorials are their opinions and, as a result, they would not seek such input. In other words, they did not wish to disturb the intent of the editorial by seeking the truth.

Standard II

Minimize harm: Ethical journalists treat sources, subjects, and colleagues as human beings deserving of respect. This means that they are considerate of those who might be adversely affected by their reporting, especially by unconfirmed or slanderous allegations.

As seen in the aforementioned example, not only reporters, but also many editors and executives, have developed such a lust for sensationalism that they have become almost devoid of journalistic conscience. I know, firsthand, what embarrassment family members have to endure before detrimental misinformation and wildly false and unsubstantiated allegations are disproved.

Standard III

Act independently: Journalists should be free of obligation to any interest other than the public's right to know. The one standard that dominates in regard to this principle is that reporters should not represent special interests or the agendas of political associations or personal affiliations.

I recognize the problems associated with journalists who become actively involved as members of boards or committees that deal with issues that are political or controversial in nature. I know of one individual who is on the editorial staff of a local newspaper and is actively involved in a community task force that deals with criminal justice issues. This individual consistently uses her journalistic ink to beat into submission those who oppose her in any way. And, because she does this through editorial opinion, she takes great license in her attack on her opponents.

Standard IV

Be accountable: Journalists are accountable to their readers, listeners, viewers, and each other. Members of the press are advised to admit mistakes and correct them promptly. However, some media are extremely reluctant to admit errors (including sometimes purposeful misinformation) and, when they do, it may be done long after the date of the error and the subsequent damage to the victims of their folly. Furthermore, the "retraction" is usually buried deep inside the paper, wedged between nonnews items; conversely, the initial misinformation had been headline news. The following incident demonstrates the tendency to not admit error.

Two elementary school students found a piece of aluminum foil on the playground and decided to open it. They noticed a dark-colored residue inside the crumpled foil. They sniffed it and turned it in to the DARE officer assigned to the school, indicating that they felt nauseous. An ambulance was requested, and the kids were taken to the hospital where they were determined to be in good health and returned to school. Because the DARE officer was on the scene, a call was never made directly to the police department, and therefore, no one in the police department had any information regarding the incident. A reporter from the local newspaper phoned the agency's media relations office and inquired about the incident. The media relations officer checked the computer and the dispatch center but found nothing, and advised the reporter likewise. Meanwhile, the DARE officer (who was the only department member with knowledge of the situation) completed a report, which was turned in to a patrol supervisor; her DARE supervisor and the media relations person were off-duty before she was able to complete the report. On review, the report was found to be incomplete, and the patrol sergeant placed it in the DARE officer's box. The reporter called again the following day and was told the incident was now in the system, but the report was not available. The next day, an article in the newspaper alleged that the police department and the school board were participating in the cover-up of an incident involving drugs in an elementary school. Furthermore, it alleged that the police (media relations) had two days earlier denied that the incident occurred and were, in fact, refusing to release the report. Even after the chief explained the entire situation to the reporter, she determined that the chief of police was lying and printed a similar story the following day. This "conspiracy" was picked up by all of the local media and was run for another day. To resolve this major discrepancy, the police chief and the city manager met with the executive editor and provided a chronological review of the facts. The police chief informed the executive editor that the reporter had once again acted irresponsibly and was sorely lacking in ethics. He clearly indicated that, until this reporter was disciplined and a retraction was published, he would not speak to or provide any interview for that newspaper.

It is interesting to note that the retraction was never published. It is even more interesting to note that, since the incident, neither the Chief of Police nor any other member of his department has provided the newspaper anything other than that required under state statute. Needless to say, each of the other local media is able to conduct interviews and broadcast full stories on incidents involving the police, yet that newspaper has to report bits and pieces of the facts. The paper has threatened to sue the department, but, according to legal authorities, has no legal substance to support a lawsuit.

The above-captioned incident depicts the prevailing attitude among most reporters: the attitude that public officials are not to be trusted. Many reports have espoused this attitude to a severe fault, sometimes developing sensational stories built entirely around rumors and innuendo. It is because of the tendency to ignore the facts in favor of sensationalism and misinformation that police/media relations are so impaired.

When the media decides that it is bigger than the individual rights guaranteed by our Constitution, and when any one medium clearly demonstrates a lack of regard for ethics, then it is time for police departments to take a stand. There are very few cities in which there is only one news outlet by which the citizens may be kept informed of government activities. Therefore, the best course of action would be to shut down relations altogether with that particular medium and deal only with those who abide by their own standards of ethics.

Of course, any police chief must remain ever cognizant of the fact that the medium in question has certain legal rights that must not be frustrated or compromised. As such, there must be a deliberate exercise of jurisprudence in this strategy. To be effective in responding to—and hopefully curtailing—unethical media conduct, a law enforcement executive should answer the following questions:

- Is the practice of unethical abuse of journalistic privilege ongoing?
- Has the police chief or the department been hindered in its effectiveness as a result of the ongoing misrepresentation of facts?
- Is the executive able to prove the above facts?
- Has the management of this media entity been alerted to the conflicts but failed to take action to correct the problem?

If the answers to these questions are "yes," then the police chief's decision to terminate relations with that particular media outlet would be wise. As stated before, certain guidelines must be followed to avoid litigation:

- Avoid press conferences and deal with other media individually.
- If a press conference is announced, notify the problem media as well.
- Avoid press releases that are unsolicited. All reputable media seeking information should be offered interviews, as, in many states, any written releases are subject to public records requests. Members of the disreputable press should be directed to the media relations office, where a prepared statement may be made or is available in writing.
- Honor all requests for information from the disreputable press and do so as quickly as is practicable. Although a sense of reluctance is understandable, their legitimate public records requests must be honored as all others.
- Provide as much information as is possible to all other media to protect against a claim that there is an attempt to withhold information from the

public. In fact, along with the provision of current and relevant updated information to the public through the more ethical and trustworthy media, I have implemented a program whereby I provide the general public with current information on all issues of controversy. Our internal community publication (called *The Police Report*) is available at one hundred local business, making 3000 copies accessible to the general public monthly. Not only do we offer the "straight scoop" to counter the sensationalized fiction offered by a disreputable medium on controversial incidents and issues, we also provide informative insights into the internal workings of our police force.

Conclusion

Any police CEO who does not recognize the importance of good police/media relations will experience difficulty in protecting his or her department against unfair criticism and organizational (as well as individual) character assassination. However, this does not mean that the CEO should stoke the furnace of any disreputable medium by whom he or she is consistently burned. What it does mean is that the CEO must be open and honest at all times when dealing with *all* media, ensuring that every member of the agency authorized to discuss departmental issues does likewise.

The bottom line is that most reporters are ethical and moral and that every effort should be made to maintain open lines of communication with the media. Even when your organization is criticized and portrayed in a bad light, this, too, must be endured as long as the truth is told. However, when the infamous "spin" is applied to purposefully mislead the public, and when this misinformation results in damage to the CEO and the department's image and ability to effectively carry out its responsibility, a chief must act in the greater interest of the citizens and the government. His or her greatest impact lies in his or her ability to shut down all relations with the offending media.

Any offer or attempt by that medium to discuss the problems should be honored. But the CEO (as well as the city manager, mayor, and city attorney) must stand firm on his or her commitment to bring that medium around to the fact that they are expected to abide by the "rules of engagement" when pursuing news stories. Once an offending media organization acknowledges a problem of a lack of journalistic ethics and expresses its genuine commitment to hold reporters accountable, then communications with that media organization should be reopened; in which case, everybody wins.

Rejoinder to Chief Gibbs   Lucy Morgan

Every citizen, especially police officers, should understand the basic difference between what appears on the editorial pages of a newspaper and news stories about events. While I agree that editorial writers and reporters should both get their facts straight, I have to emphasize that they are performing different tasks. The beat reporter is trying to factually describe what happened. The editorial writer is stating the paper's official *opinion* on what happened. At most newspapers these are strictly separated functions. At the *St. Petersburg Times,* for instance, reporters work for editors—not editorial writers—in an entirely different department. Even we in journalism believe that editorial writers are a different breed of cat and, contrary to what some would have you believe, one does not direct the other. To ask an editorial writer who has stated an opinion to retract the opinion reflects a lack of understanding of what the writer is doing. It would be incredibly rare for an *editorial* writer to change his mind about an event.

Although each situation is different, I suggest that it is a matter of semantics to quibble over whether it is "domestic violence" when an officer hits his girlfriend. I do not know the reporter or officer involved in the chief's complaint, but I suggest that a common understanding of violence in an interpersonal relationship could easily be called domestic whether or not it is a legal definition. Remember, we are not writing a legal journal, but trying to communicate with the average reader, who knows little about the criminal justice system.

Yet Chief Gibbs must recognize that many police departments have not viewed domestic violence as a serious problem. Police officials should be aware of this and be very cautious about the language they use to describe such incidents. There is a national hue and cry over this very subject that should make police officers as well as reporters sensitive to this issue. To tell a reporter that a battery was not serious enough to prompt an immediate arrest is an invitation to trouble. Perhaps the chief should learn to phrase statements such as this with more delicacy. Put the blame where it belongs: tell the reporter that the legislature, in its wisdom, has passed a law that allows arrests only under certain circumstances.

I acknowledge that police beats often draw the newest and greenest reporter in any organization, just as traffic duty befalls the greenest police officer, but both need someone to help them learn. An officer who takes the time to explain the details of a crime will generally get better news stories.

There is no excuse for failing to report the truth, but I suggest that any police officer involved in a traffic accident might want to act out of an abundance of caution and report the incident to another agency. That would help avoid any question about what happened and would save an officer—or a chief—a lot of grief in the long run.

When mistakes get into print or on the nightly news, call the reporter and complain. But pick your shots. Do not get labeled as a constant whiner over minor details. If you do not get a response from the reporter, call the boss. News organizations cannot afford to keep reporters who make frequent mistakes.

Newspaper editors respond better to reasonable complaints that are not filled with scatological insults. You will also be more likely to get results if you do not develop a reputation for whining about everything. Think of the citizen who telephones the police with every little complaint and has trouble getting attention when something is really wrong, and act accordingly.

A good journalist does not become involved in the boards and organizations that are covered by his or her news organization. Anyone who does this is violating the most basic ethical requirement for journalists. It is too much like investigating your own behavior—a huge conflict of interest. Any editorial writer who takes a position based on his or her own involvement on a community task force should be dismissed.

The chief's problem with the DARE officer's missing report could have been avoided if his public information officer had taken the time to contact the officer at the school and question whether the incident occurred. Information should be dispensed on a timely basis. Delays are always troubling and unfair to citizens, who should know of such problems as soon as possible.

When reporters covering a police department make serious mistakes, complain in writing, but do not be so quick to assume there is some sinister motive for the mistakes. Most mistakes are made in the rush of getting information, trying to write coherent news stories, and making deadlines. Most reporters do not have time to dream up ways to attack a police officer; we are too busy chasing information.

The bottom line: the easiest way to avoid unfair criticism from the news media is to run a good department, acknowledge your mistakes, and be open and honest. Agencies that muzzle officers, work hard to keep everything secret, and do not adequately deal with wrongdoing by their own officers will always attract unfavorable attention. If you do get in an ongoing confrontation with your local news media, deliver your news in writing and remember that you have a duty, not to the press but to the taxpayers who support you, to communicate what is happening.

The Controversial Issues in Criminal Justice Series
Steven A. Egger, Series Editor

Complete your set of books in the Controversial Issues in Criminal Justice Series with these additional titles—only $24.00 each!

Available Now!

Controversial Issues in Corrections
by Charles B. Fields
Order No. 0-205-27491-9

Controversial Issues in Criminology
by John R. Fuller and Eric W. Hickey
Order No. 0-205-27210-X

Controversial Issues in Policing
by James D. Sewell
Order No. 0-205-27209-6

Available Fall 1999*

Controversial Issues in Criminal Justice
by Frank Horvath
Order No. 0-205-29214-3

Controversial Issues in Gender
by Donna Hale
Order No. 0-205-29215-1

*Prices and Titles are subject to change

To Place an Order:

MAIL:
Allyn & Bacon Publishers
111 10th Street
Des Moines, IA 50309

CALL:
Toll-Free: 1-800-278-3525
Fax: 1-515-284-2607
WEBSITE: www.abacon.com

Name: _____

Address:_____

City: _____ State: _____ Zip Code: _____

Phone: _____ E-Mail:_____

Charge my: _____Amex _____Visa _____Mastercard _____Discover

Card # _____ Exp. Date _____

Enclosed find my: _____Check _____Money Order

*Shipping and handling charges will be added unless order is prepaid by check or money order.